Teen Titans

FAMILY LOST

Geoff Johns Writer

Mike McKone Ivan Reis Tom Grummett Pencillers

Marlo Alquiza Kevin Conrad Marc Campos Norm Rapmund Inkers

Jeromy Cox Sno Cone Colorists

Comicraft Letterer

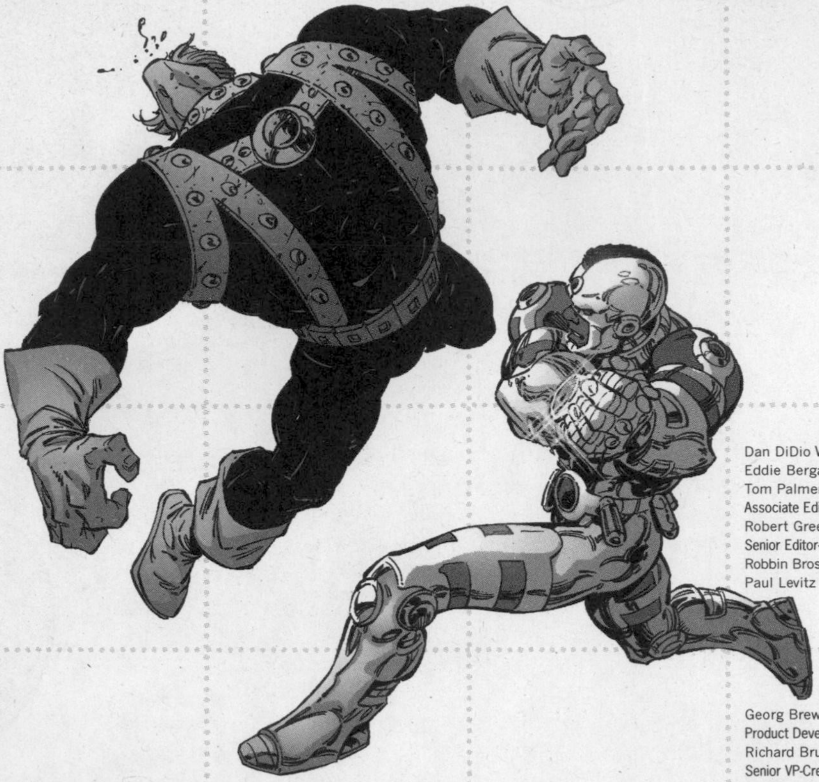

Dan DiDio VP-Editorial
Eddie Berganza Editor-original series
Tom Palmer, Jr.
Associate Editor-original series
Robert Greenberger
Senior Editor-collected edition
Robbin Brosterman Senior Art Director
Paul Levitz President & Publisher

Georg Brewer VP-Design & Retail
Product Development
Richard Bruning
Senior VP-Creative Director
Patrick Caldon
Senior VP-Finance & Operations
Chris Caramalis VP-Finance
Terri Cunningham VP-Managing Editor
Alison Gill VP-Manufacturing
Rich Johnson VP-Book Trade Sales
Hank Kanalz VP-General Manager,
WildStorm
Lillian Laserson Senior VP &
General Counsel
Jim Lee VP-Editorial Director-WildStorm
David McKillips
VP-Advertising & Custom Publishing
John Nee VP-Business Development
Gregory Noveck
Senior VP-Creative Affairs
Cheryl Rubin
Senior VP-Brand Management
Bob Wayne VP-Sales & Marketing

TEEN TITANS: FAMILY LOST
Published by DC Comics.

DC Comics, 1700 Broadway, New York, NY 10019. A Warner Bros. Entertainment Company.
Printed in Canada. First Printing.
ISBN: 1-4012-0238-1.
Cover illustration by Mike McKone & Marlo Alquiza.

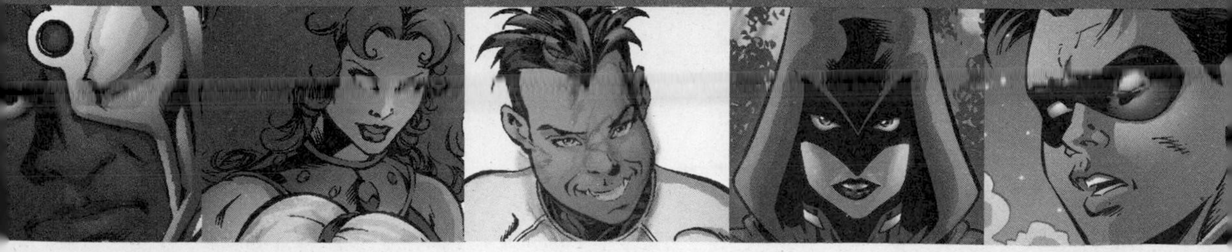

W H O ' S   W H O

THE TEEN TITANS
There has always been a next generation of hero to be trained. As much can be learned from fellow novices as from a mentor, so were born the Teen Titans. Over the years the lineup has changed, but the need for guidance remains as does the spirit of comradery and friendship.

CYBORG
Victor Stone's parents were research scientists for S.T.A.R. Labs, and during an experiment his mother accidentally unleashed a destructive force, killing her and destroying most of Vic's body. His father saved the youth's life with cybernetic components, making Vic feel like an outsider. He only came to accept his fate when he joined the Titans. Through many changes, Vic remains committed to the team. Currently, Cyborg has taken it upon himself to re-form the Titans and usher in today's teenaged superheroes at the new Titans Tower in San Francisco.

STARFIRE
Princess Koriand'r of Tamaran was sacrificed by her father to save their world. Subjected to horrendous experiments, she gained the ability to generate energy bolts in addition to her natural gift of flight. Escaping her tormentors, she made her way to Earth and found a new life as Starfire. Her world is now gone, a victim of Imperiex. Starfire tends to be impatient, and that, combined with her disinterest in being anyone's teacher, has made her uncomfortable about her role on the new team.

BEAST BOY
Garfield Logan was poisoned with Sakutia, a rare African toxin. His geneticist parents used an experimental treatment to save his life, and in so doing imbued him with green skin and the ability to transform himself into any animal life form. When his parents died in an accident, he was adopted by Rita Farr and Steve Dayton of the Doom Patrol. Gar desperately wants to be an actor but is most comfortable serving with the various incarnations of the Titans. At age 19, Beast Boy finds himself acting as the mediator between the older and younger Titans, a role he readily accepts.

RAVEN
The daughter of a human and the demon Trigon, she has spent much of her life trying to escape her father's influence. Raven was warned to always keep her anger and frustrations in check, else she might give in to her father's demonic influence. When Trigon wanted to invade Earth, she preceded him, helping form one version of the Titans to stop him. Since then, she has opposed Trigon frequently, losing her mortal body in the process. Without a body to inhabit, Raven's soul-self wandered the world aimlessly until recently.

ROBIN
Perhaps the best prepared of the younger heroes, Tim Drake has been trained by the best – Batman and the first Robin, Dick Grayson. Tim wants to fight crime, but not forever, and uses his quick mind and strong body in addition to a veritable arsenal to stop crime. He has hated lying to his father about his costumed exploits and recently suffered the crushing dissolution of Young Justice, a team he led. Robin remains a mystery to those around him. Even when the Titans began to believe they could predict his next move, they found out they were mistaken.

SUPERBOY

In the wake of Superman's death, a clone was formed using DNA drawn from not only Superman, but from Lex Luthor. Being a hybrid human/Kryptonian, Superboy has a different set of abilities including flight, strength, speed, limited invulnerability and something he calls tactile telekinesis. Impulsive, the clone strives to do the right thing but acts without thinking. Superman recently asked his adoptive parents, the Kents, to help raise the teen. He also entrusted the youth, now called Conner, with Krypto's safekeeping.

KID FLASH

Bart Allen has quite a legacy to live up to. His grandfather was Barry Allen, the second Flash. Born in the 30th century, Bart was brought to the 21st century by his grandmother to be properly schooled in the use of his natural super-speed. For a time, he operated as Impulse, under the tutelage of Max Mercury, Zen master of speed. After recent events, Bart decided it was time to grow up, and toward that goal he has speed-read and memorized the contents of the San Francisco Public Library. He has the wisdom but now needs the experience to be worthy of the Flash mantle. Changing his name to Kid Flash was the first step in the process.

WONDER GIRL

Cassie Sandsmark was thrilled to befriend Diana, the Themysciran princess known as Wonder Woman, so much so that during a crisis, she borrowed the Sandals of Hermes and the Gauntlet of Atlas to aid Diana. She then boldly asked Zeus for additional powers. Amused, he granted her strength and flight and she adventured as Wonder Girl. She began training under Artemis until the death of Donna Troy, the first Wonder Girl. Cassie's secret identity was exposed, and she now attends a private school. Cassie continues to grow into her heroic role, discovering new limits to her powers and finding new allies and enemies lurking among Ancient Myth, such as the war god Ares who recently gave her a golden lasso.

DEATHSTROKE

Slade Wilson underwent a series of treatments while in the Army that enhanced his strength, speed, agility, stamina and mind (and granted him immortality). Once he mustered out, Slade became a mercenary, rapidly earning a reputation as one of the world's deadliest assassins. He and his wife Adeline had two sons, Grant and Joe, the eldest following in his father's footsteps. Joe, as the first Ravager, died trying fulfill a contract to kill one version of the Titans. Slade, as Deathstroke, began a series of encounters with the team. Joe, with his body-possessing abilities, joined the Titans as Jericho to stop his father. Jericho seemingly died, but it was recently learned that his spirit inhabited Slade's body.

RAVAGER

On a contract, Deathstroke met Lillian "Sweet Lili" Worth and they became lovers, resulting in the birth of Rose. Lili moved to New York City, hiring private tutors to teach and train Rose, keeping her existence secret from Deathstroke. Slade's half-brother Wade DeFarge, the second Ravager, discovered Rose's existence and kidnapped her. Lili seemingly died in rescuing her daughter, who was then placed in Slade Wilson's custody. He, in turn, arranged for her to be looked after by the Titans, who trained her but were concerned about her aggressive style. She developed extensive precognitive vision, the limits of which are still being explored. Briefly, she was Arsenal's nanny for Lian but left that post to return to her father's side as the latest Ravager. Dangerous and unpredictable, her destiny remains to be explored.

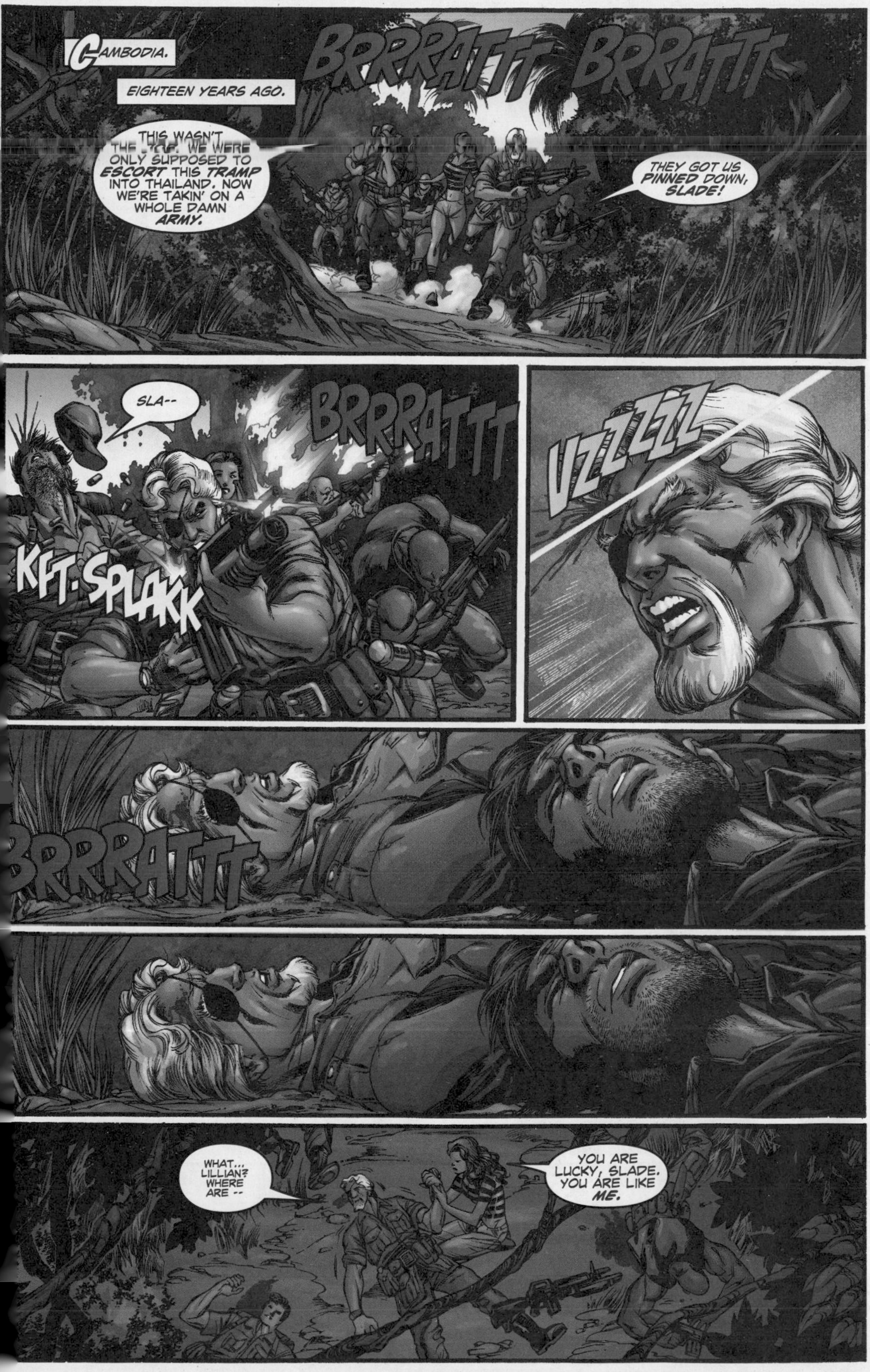
CAMBODIA.
EIGHTEEN YEARS AGO.
BRRRATTT BRRATTT
THIS WASN'T THE . WE WERE ONLY SUPPOSED TO ESCORT THIS TRAMP INTO THAILAND. NOW WE'RE TAKIN' ON A WHOLE DAMN ARMY.
THEY GOT US PINNED DOWN, SLADE!
SLA--
BRRRATTT
KFT. SPLAKK
VZZZZZ
BRRRATTT
WHAT... LILLIAN? WHERE ARE --
YOU ARE LUCKY, SLADE. YOU ARE LIKE ME.

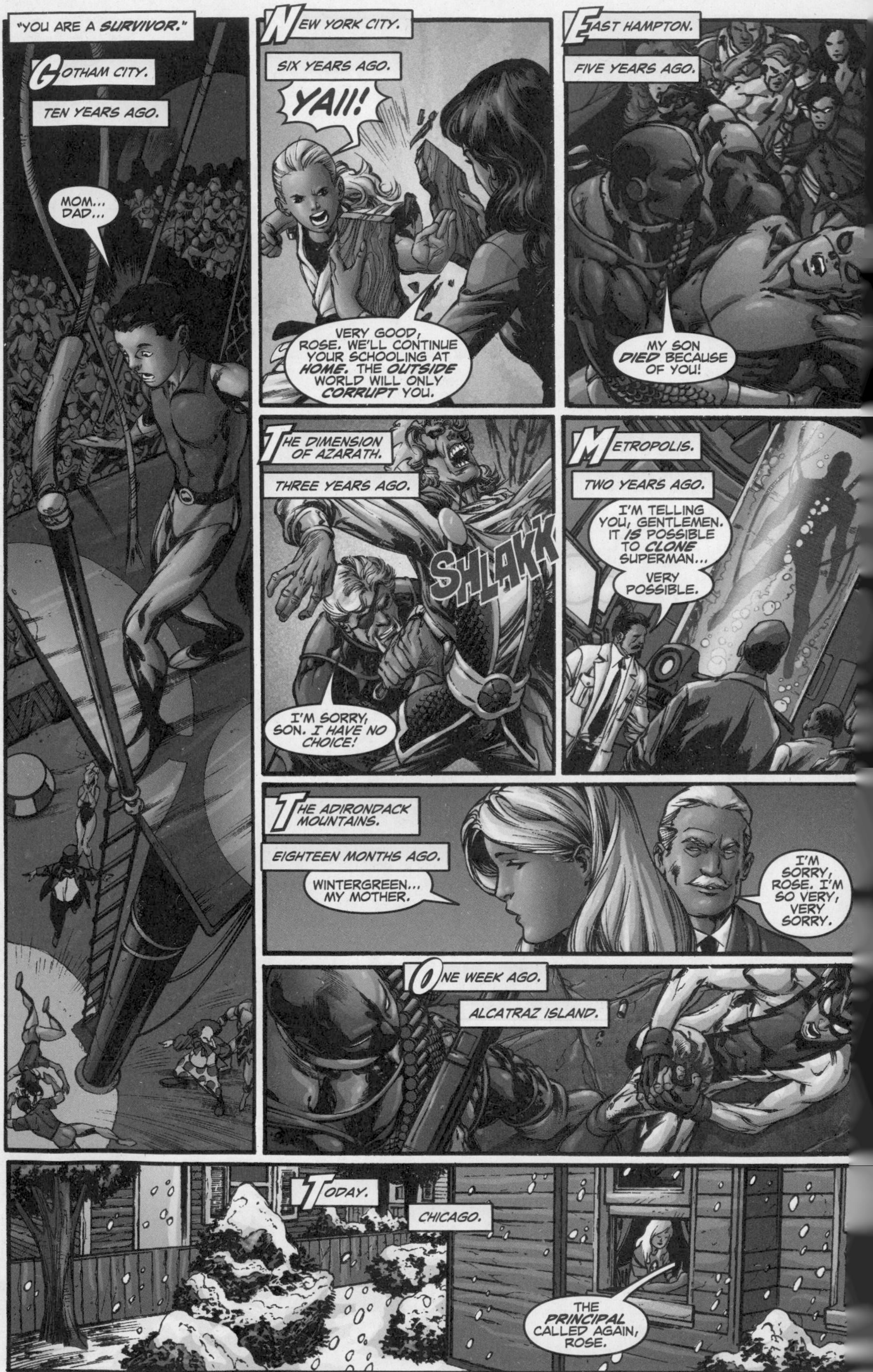

"YOU ARE A SURVIVOR."
GOTHAM CITY.
TEN YEARS AGO.
MOM... DAD...
NEW YORK CITY.
SIX YEARS AGO.
YAII!
VERY GOOD, ROSE. WE'LL CONTINUE YOUR SCHOOLING AT HOME. THE OUTSIDE WORLD WILL ONLY CORRUPT YOU.
EAST HAMPTON.
FIVE YEARS AGO.
MY SON DIED BECAUSE OF YOU!
THE DIMENSION OF AZARATH.
THREE YEARS AGO.
SHLAKK
I'M SORRY, SON. I HAVE NO CHOICE!
METROPOLIS.
TWO YEARS AGO.
I'M TELLING YOU, GENTLEMEN. IT IS POSSIBLE TO CLONE SUPERMAN...
VERY POSSIBLE.
THE ADIRONDACK MOUNTAINS.
EIGHTEEN MONTHS AGO.
WINTERGREEN... MY MOTHER.
I'M SORRY, ROSE. I'M SO VERY, VERY SORRY.
ONE WEEK AGO.
ALCATRAZ ISLAND.
TODAY.
CHICAGO.
THE PRINCIPAL CALLED AGAIN, ROSE.

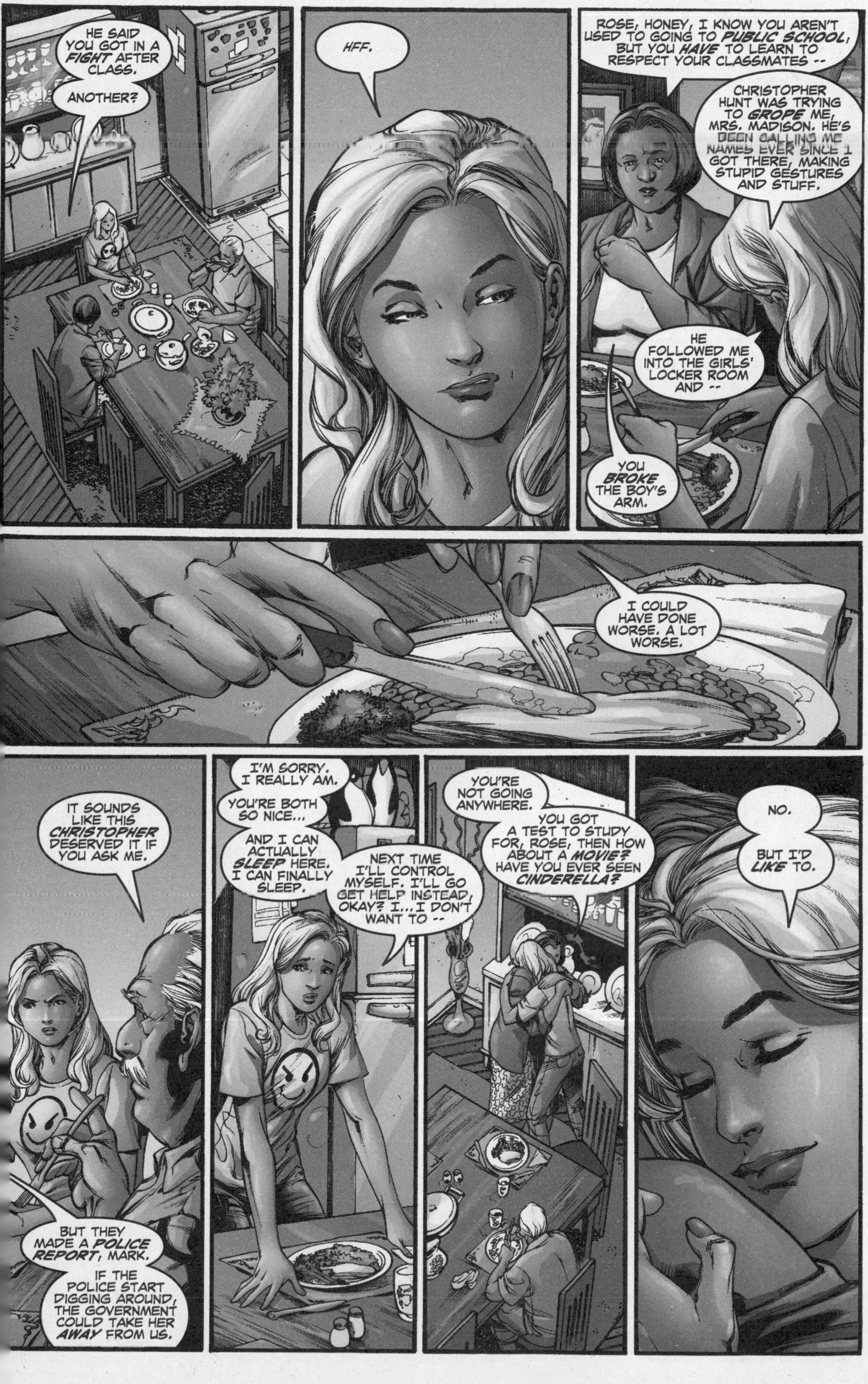
HE SAID YOU GOT IN A FIGHT AFTER CLASS.
ANOTHER?
HFF.
ROSE, HONEY, I KNOW YOU AREN'T USED TO GOING TO PUBLIC SCHOOL, BUT YOU HAVE TO LEARN TO RESPECT YOUR CLASSMATES --
CHRISTOPHER HUNT WAS TRYING TO GROPE ME, MRS. MADISON. HE'S BEEN CALLING ME NAMES EVER SINCE I GOT THERE, MAKING STUPID GESTURES AND STUFF.
HE FOLLOWED ME INTO THE GIRLS' LOCKER ROOM AND --
YOU BROKE THE BOY'S ARM.
I COULD HAVE DONE WORSE. A LOT WORSE.
IT SOUNDS LIKE THIS CHRISTOPHER DESERVED IT IF YOU ASK ME.
BUT THEY MADE A POLICE REPORT, MARK.
IF THE POLICE START DIGGING AROUND, THE GOVERNMENT COULD TAKE HER AWAY FROM US.
I'M SORRY. I REALLY AM.
YOU'RE BOTH SO NICE...
AND I CAN ACTUALLY SLEEP HERE. I CAN FINALLY SLEEP.
NEXT TIME I'LL CONTROL MYSELF. I'LL GO GET HELP INSTEAD, OKAY? I... I DON'T WANT TO --
YOU'RE NOT GOING ANYWHERE.
YOU GOT A TEST TO STUDY FOR, ROSE, THEN HOW ABOUT A MOVIE? HAVE YOU EVER SEEN CINDERELLA?
NO.
BUT I'D LIKE TO.

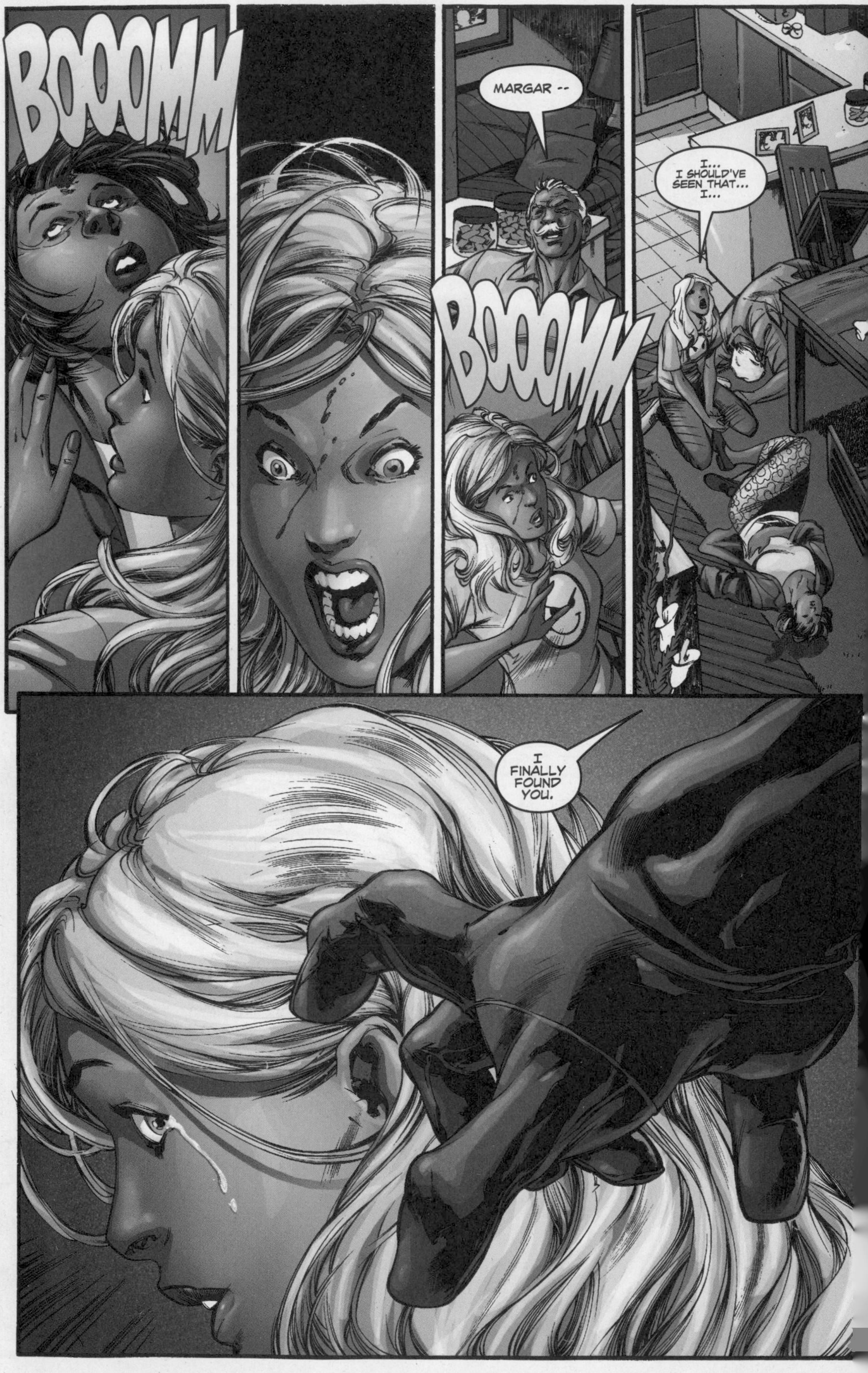
BOOOMM
MARGAR --
BOOOMM
I... I SHOULD'VE SEEN THAT... I...
I FINALLY FOUND YOU.

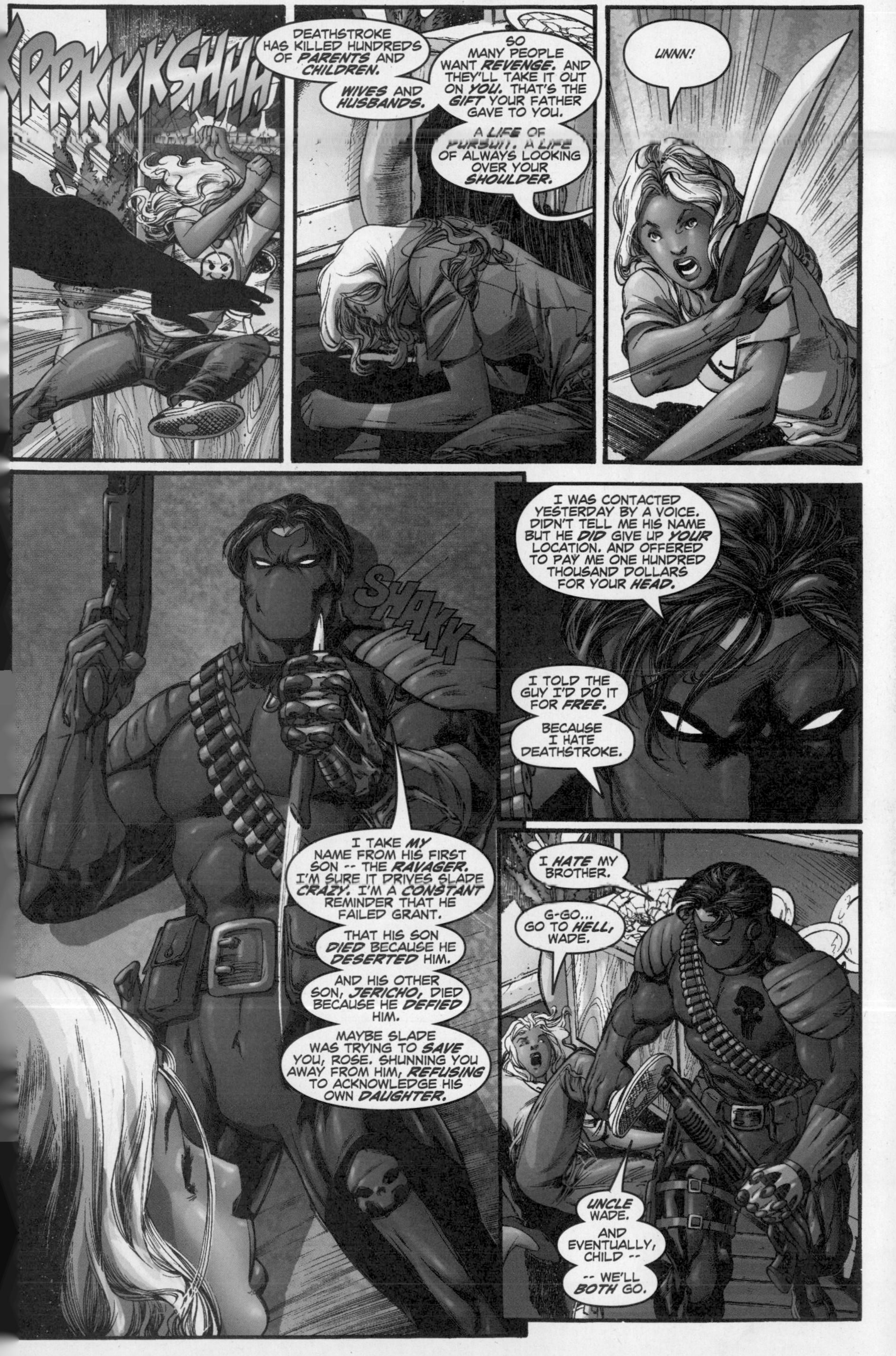
KRRKKKSHHH
DEATHSTROKE HAS KILLED HUNDREDS OF PARENTS AND CHILDREN.
WIVES AND HUSBANDS.
SO MANY PEOPLE WANT REVENGE. AND THEY'LL TAKE IT OUT ON YOU. THAT'S THE GIFT YOUR FATHER GAVE TO YOU.
A LIFE OF PURSUIT. A LIFE OF ALWAYS LOOKING OVER YOUR SHOULDER.
UNNN!
SHAKK
I TAKE MY NAME FROM HIS FIRST SON -- THE RAVAGER. I'M SURE IT DRIVES SLADE CRAZY. I'M A CONSTANT REMINDER THAT HE FAILED GRANT.
THAT HIS SON DIED BECAUSE HE DESERTED HIM.
AND HIS OTHER SON, JERICHO, DIED BECAUSE HE DEFIED HIM.
MAYBE SLADE WAS TRYING TO SAVE YOU, ROSE. SHUNNING YOU AWAY FROM HIM, REFUSING TO ACKNOWLEDGE HIS OWN DAUGHTER.
I WAS CONTACTED YESTERDAY BY A VOICE. DIDN'T TELL ME HIS NAME BUT HE DID GIVE UP YOUR LOCATION. AND OFFERED TO PAY ME ONE HUNDRED THOUSAND DOLLARS FOR YOUR HEAD.
I TOLD THE GUY I'D DO IT FOR FREE.
BECAUSE I HATE DEATHSTROKE.
I HATE MY BROTHER.
G-GO... GO TO HELL, WADE.
UNCLE WADE.
AND EVENTUALLY, CHILD --
-- WE'LL BOTH GO.

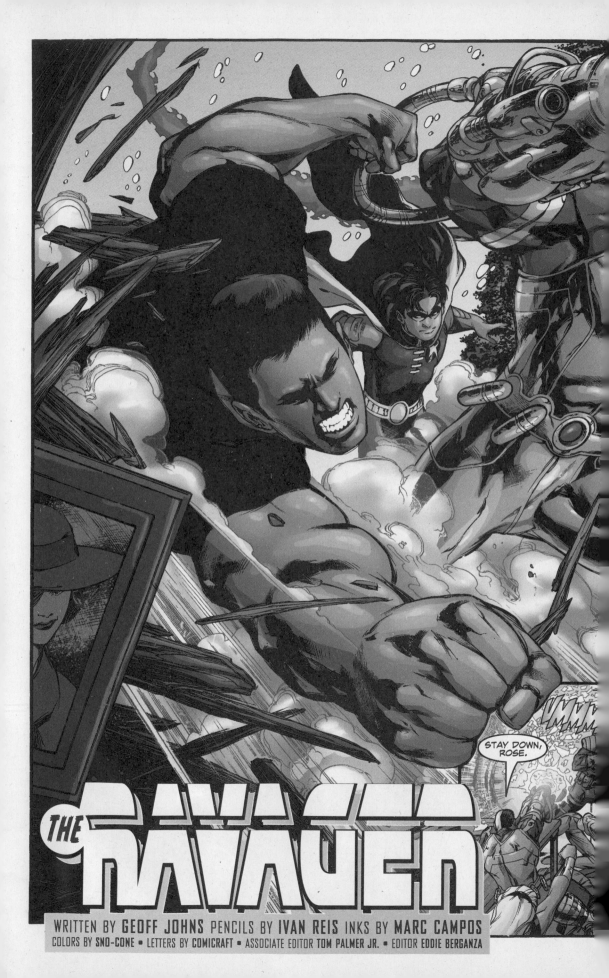

STAY DOWN, ROSE.

THE RAVAGER

WRITTEN BY GEOFF JOHNS PENCILS BY IVAN REIS INKS BY MARC CAMPOS
COLORS BY SNO-CONE • LETTERS BY COMICRAFT • ASSOCIATE EDITOR TOM PALMER JR. • EDITOR EDDIE BERGANZA

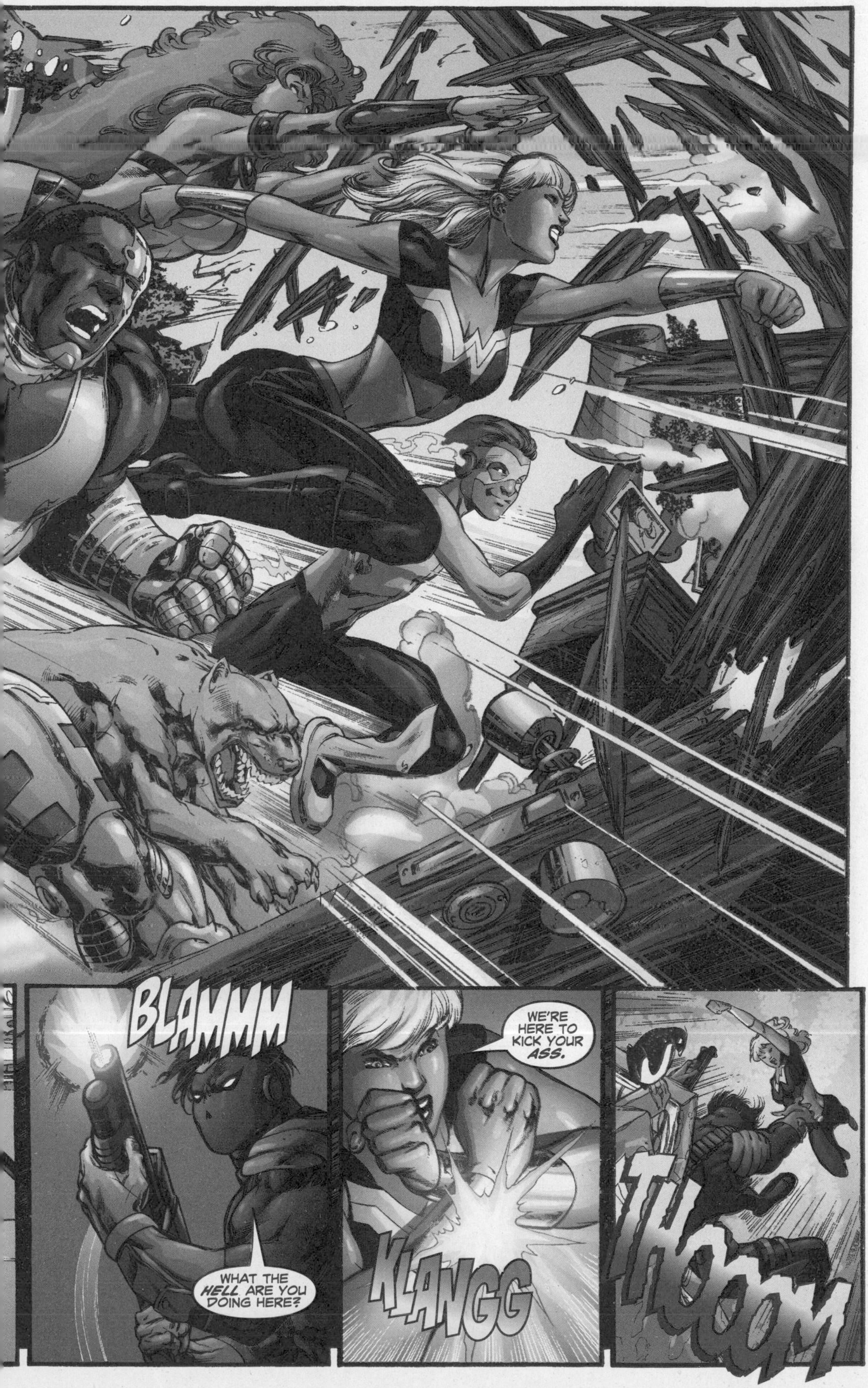
BLAMMM
WHAT THE HELL ARE YOU DOING HERE?
WE'RE HERE TO KICK YOUR ASS.
KLANGG
THOOOM

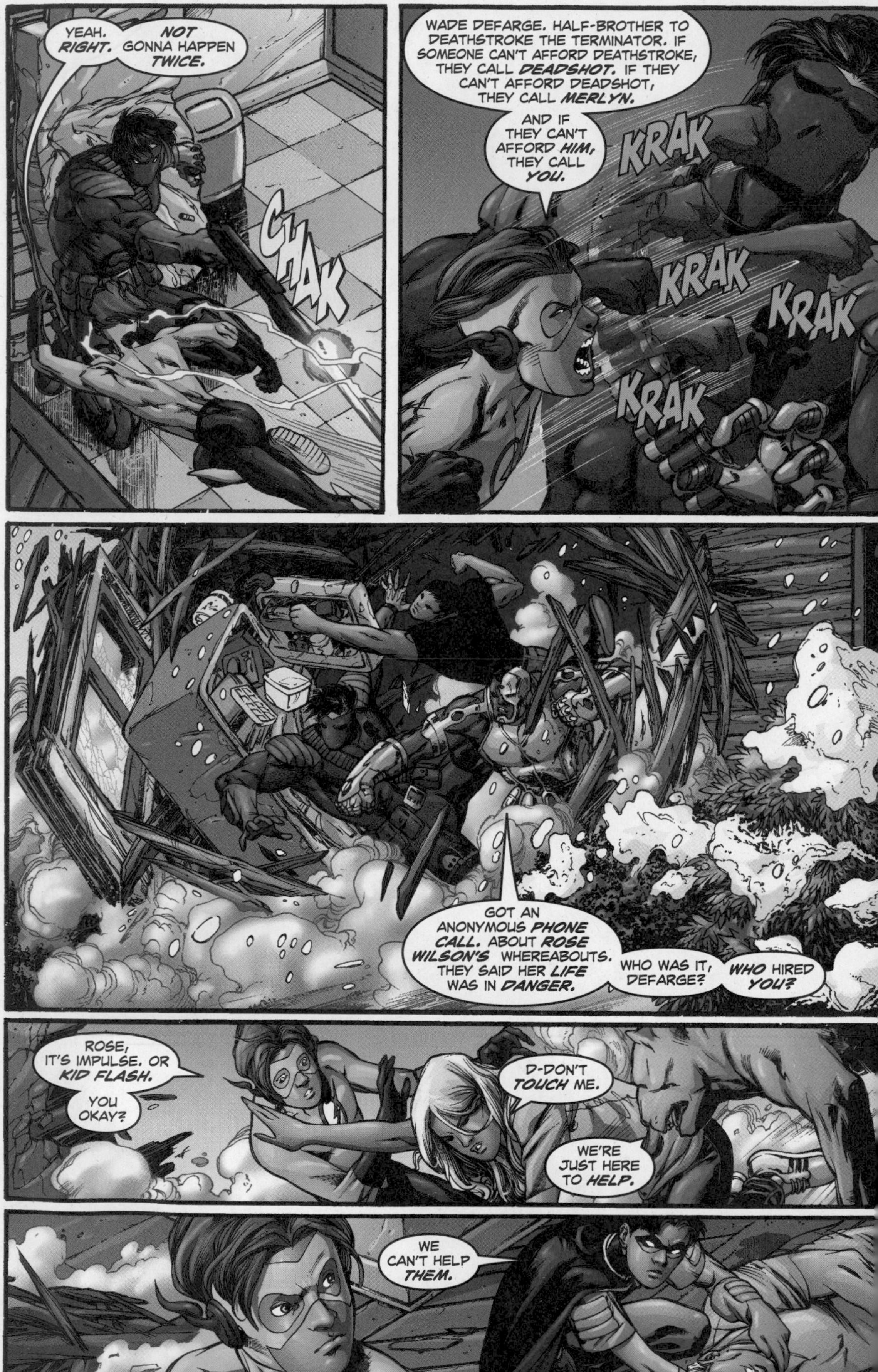

YEAH. RIGHT.
NOT GONNA HAPPEN TWICE.
CHAK
WADE DEFARGE. HALF-BROTHER TO DEATHSTROKE THE TERMINATOR. IF SOMEONE CAN'T AFFORD DEATHSTROKE, THEY CALL DEADSHOT. IF THEY CAN'T AFFORD DEADSHOT, THEY CALL MERLYN.
AND IF THEY CAN'T AFFORD HIM, THEY CALL YOU.
KRAK
KRAK
KRAK
KRAK
GOT AN ANONYMOUS PHONE CALL. ABOUT ROSE WILSON'S WHEREABOUTS. THEY SAID HER LIFE WAS IN DANGER.
WHO WAS IT, DEFARGE?
WHO HIRED YOU?
ROSE, IT'S IMPULSE. OR KID FLASH.
YOU OKAY?
D-DON'T TOUCH ME.
WE'RE JUST HERE TO HELP.
WE CAN'T HELP THEM.

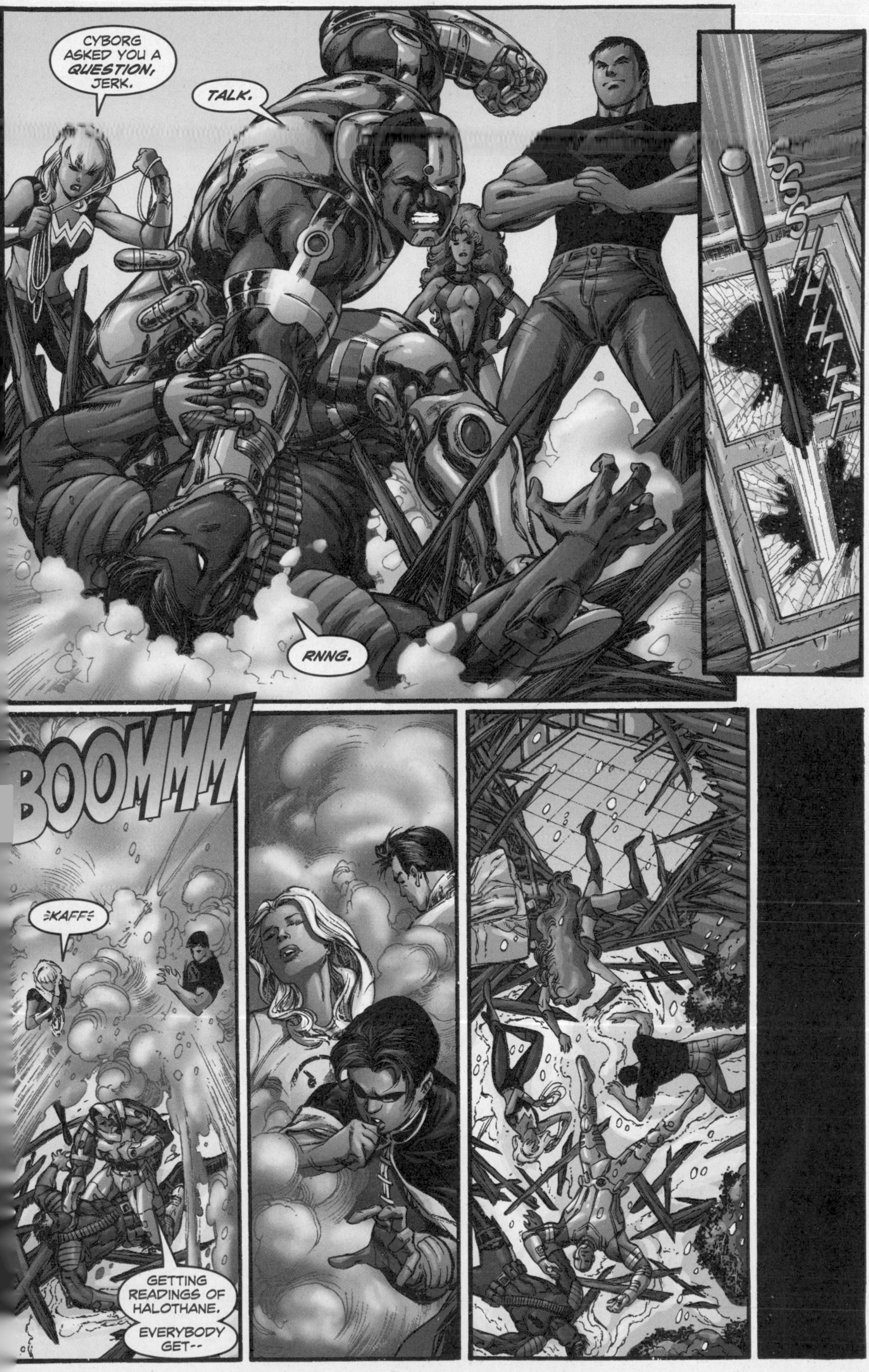
CYBORG ASKED YOU A QUESTION, JERK.
TALK.
RNNG.
SSSHHHHH
BOOMMM
KAFF
GETTING READINGS OF HALOTHANE.
EVERYBODY GET--

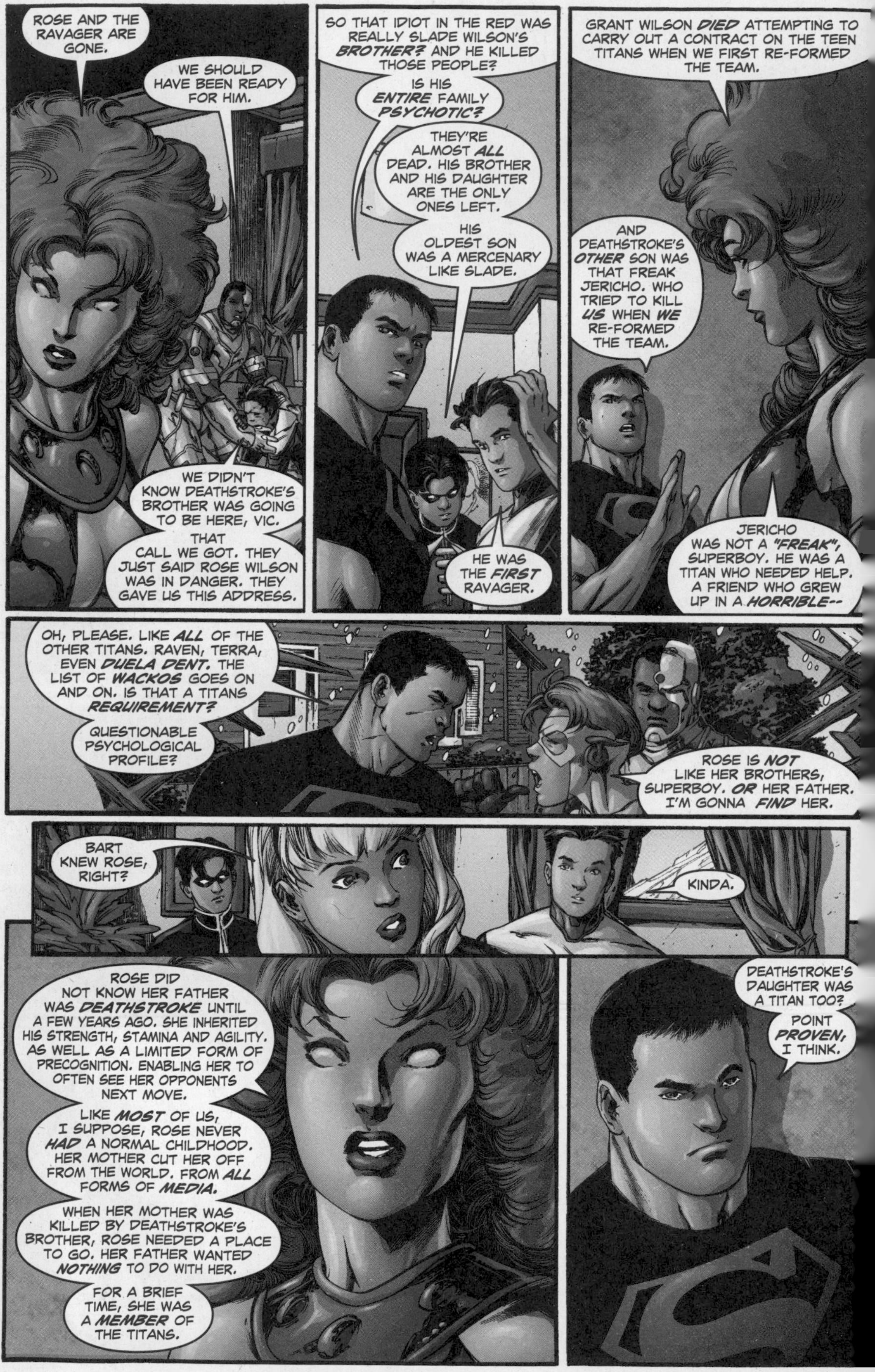
ROSE AND THE RAVAGER ARE GONE.
WE SHOULD HAVE BEEN READY FOR HIM.
WE DIDN'T KNOW DEATHSTROKE'S BROTHER WAS GOING TO BE HERE, VIC.
THAT CALL WE GOT. THEY JUST SAID ROSE WILSON WAS IN DANGER. THEY GAVE US THIS ADDRESS.
SO THAT IDIOT IN THE RED WAS REALLY SLADE WILSON'S BROTHER? AND HE KILLED THOSE PEOPLE?
IS HIS ENTIRE FAMILY PSYCHOTIC?
THEY'RE ALMOST ALL DEAD. HIS BROTHER AND HIS DAUGHTER ARE THE ONLY ONES LEFT.
HIS OLDEST SON WAS A MERCENARY LIKE SLADE.
HE WAS THE FIRST RAVAGER.
GRANT WILSON DIED ATTEMPTING TO CARRY OUT A CONTRACT ON THE TEEN TITANS WHEN WE FIRST RE-FORMED THE TEAM.
AND DEATHSTROKE'S OTHER SON WAS THAT FREAK JERICHO. WHO TRIED TO KILL US WHEN WE RE-FORMED THE TEAM.
JERICHO WAS NOT A "FREAK", SUPERBOY. HE WAS A TITAN WHO NEEDED HELP. A FRIEND WHO GREW UP IN A HORRIBLE--
OH, PLEASE. LIKE ALL OF THE OTHER TITANS. RAVEN, TERRA, EVEN DUELA DENT. THE LIST OF WACKOS GOES ON AND ON. IS THAT A TITANS REQUIREMENT?
QUESTIONABLE PSYCHOLOGICAL PROFILE?
ROSE IS NOT LIKE HER BROTHERS, SUPERBOY. OR HER FATHER. I'M GONNA FIND HER.
BART KNEW ROSE, RIGHT?
KINDA.
ROSE DID NOT KNOW HER FATHER WAS DEATHSTROKE UNTIL A FEW YEARS AGO. SHE INHERITED HIS STRENGTH, STAMINA AND AGILITY. AS WELL AS A LIMITED FORM OF PRECOGNITION. ENABLING HER TO OFTEN SEE HER OPPONENTS NEXT MOVE.
LIKE MOST OF US, I SUPPOSE, ROSE NEVER HAD A NORMAL CHILDHOOD. HER MOTHER CUT HER OFF FROM THE WORLD. FROM ALL FORMS OF MEDIA.
WHEN HER MOTHER WAS KILLED BY DEATHSTROKE'S BROTHER, ROSE NEEDED A PLACE TO GO. HER FATHER WANTED NOTHING TO DO WITH HER.
FOR A BRIEF TIME, SHE WAS A MEMBER OF THE TITANS.
DEATHSTROKE'S DAUGHTER WAS A TITAN TOO?
POINT PROVEN, I THINK.

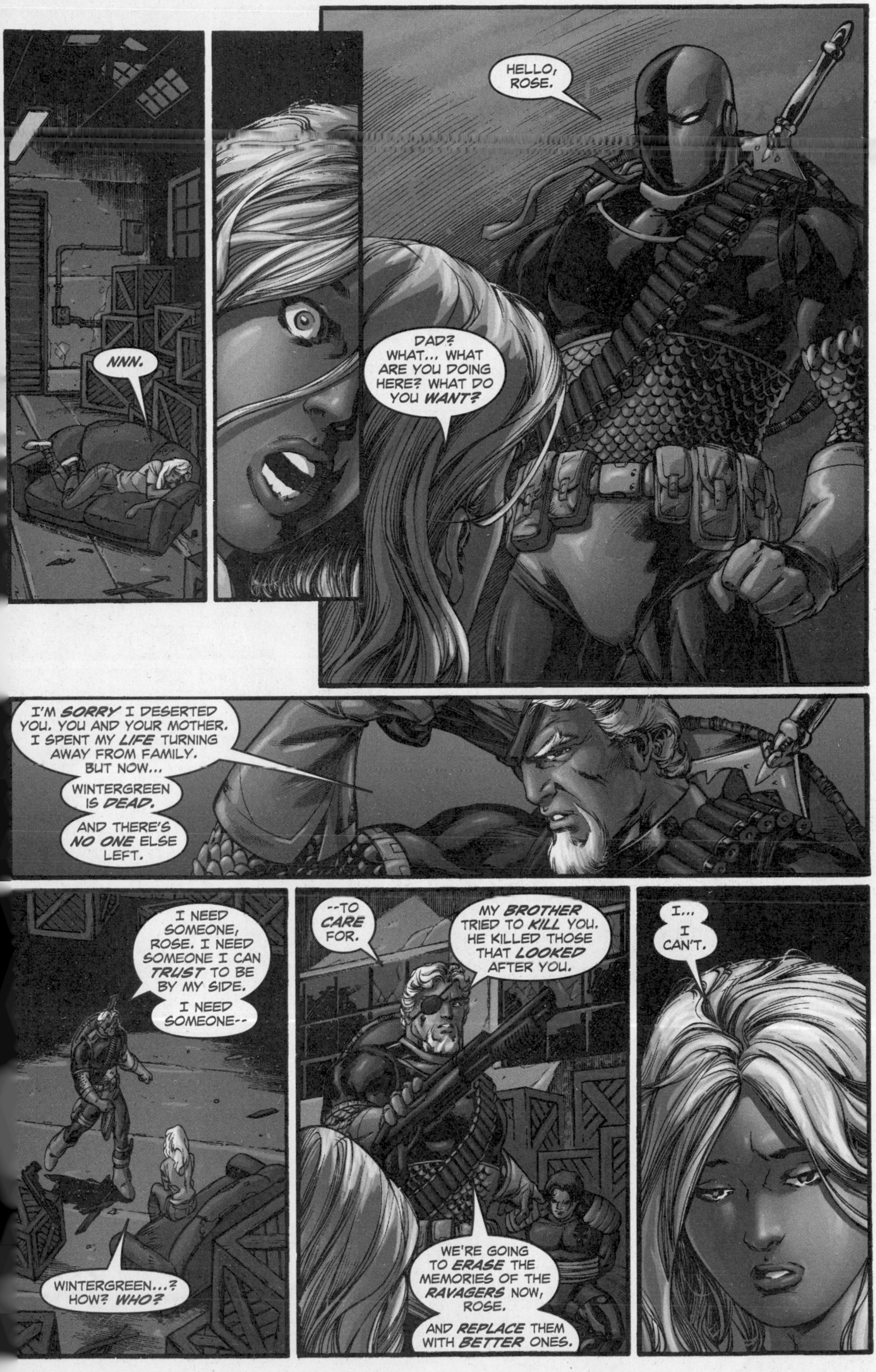
NNN.
HELLO, ROSE.
DAD? WHAT... WHAT ARE YOU DOING HERE? WHAT DO YOU WANT?
I'M SORRY I DESERTED YOU. YOU AND YOUR MOTHER. I SPENT MY LIFE TURNING AWAY FROM FAMILY. BUT NOW...
WINTERGREEN IS DEAD.
AND THERE'S NO ONE ELSE LEFT.
I NEED SOMEONE, ROSE. I NEED SOMEONE I CAN TRUST TO BE BY MY SIDE.
I NEED SOMEONE--
WINTERGREEN...? HOW? WHO?
--TO CARE FOR.
MY BROTHER TRIED TO KILL YOU. HE KILLED THOSE THAT LOOKED AFTER YOU.
WE'RE GOING TO ERASE THE MEMORIES OF THE RAVAGERS NOW, ROSE.
AND REPLACE THEM WITH BETTER ONES.
I... I CAN'T.

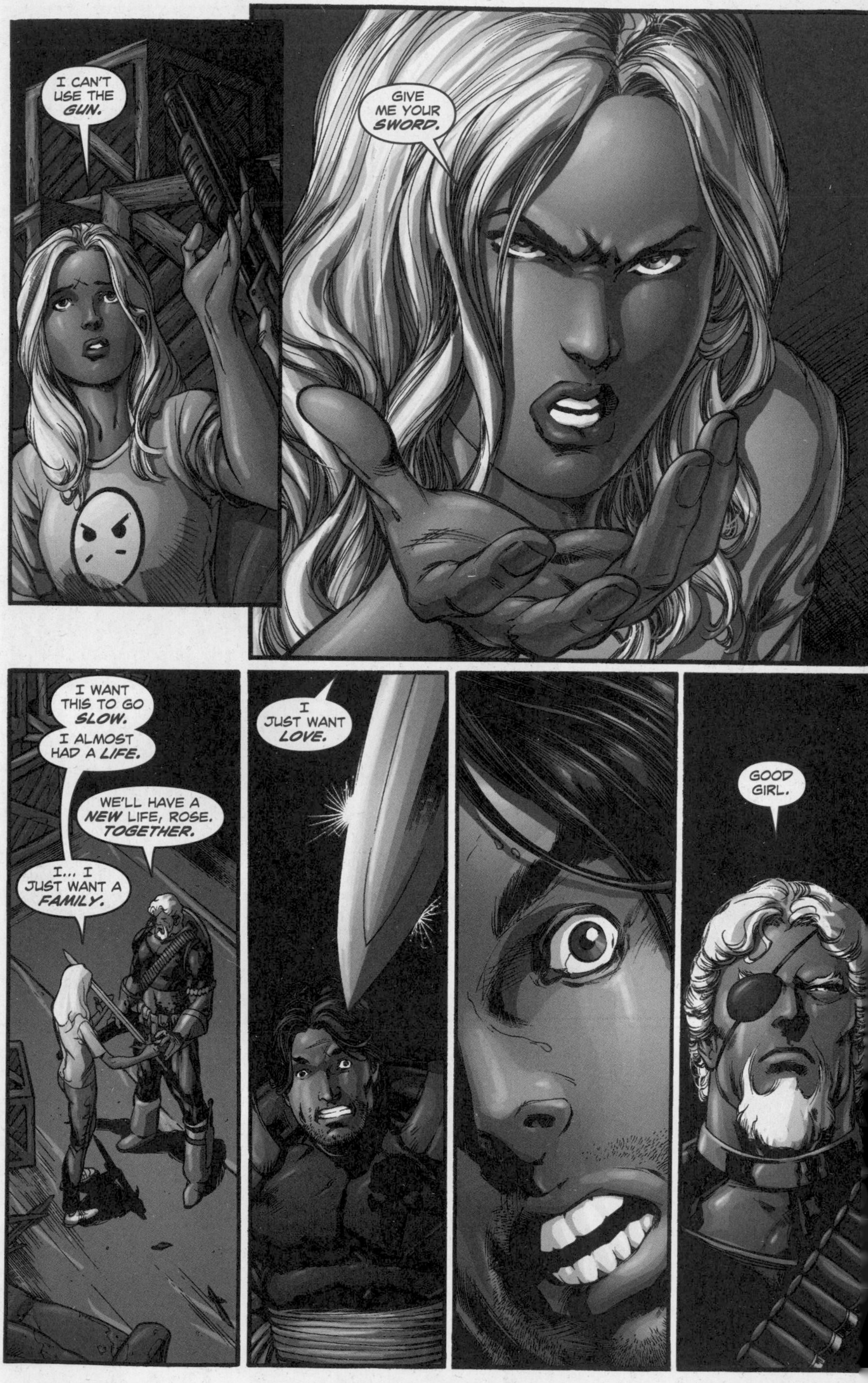
I CAN'T USE THE GUN.
GIVE ME YOUR SWORD.
I WANT THIS TO GO SLOW.
I ALMOST HAD A LIFE.
WE'LL HAVE A NEW LIFE, ROSE. TOGETHER.
I... I JUST WANT A FAMILY.
I JUST WANT LOVE.
GOOD GIRL.

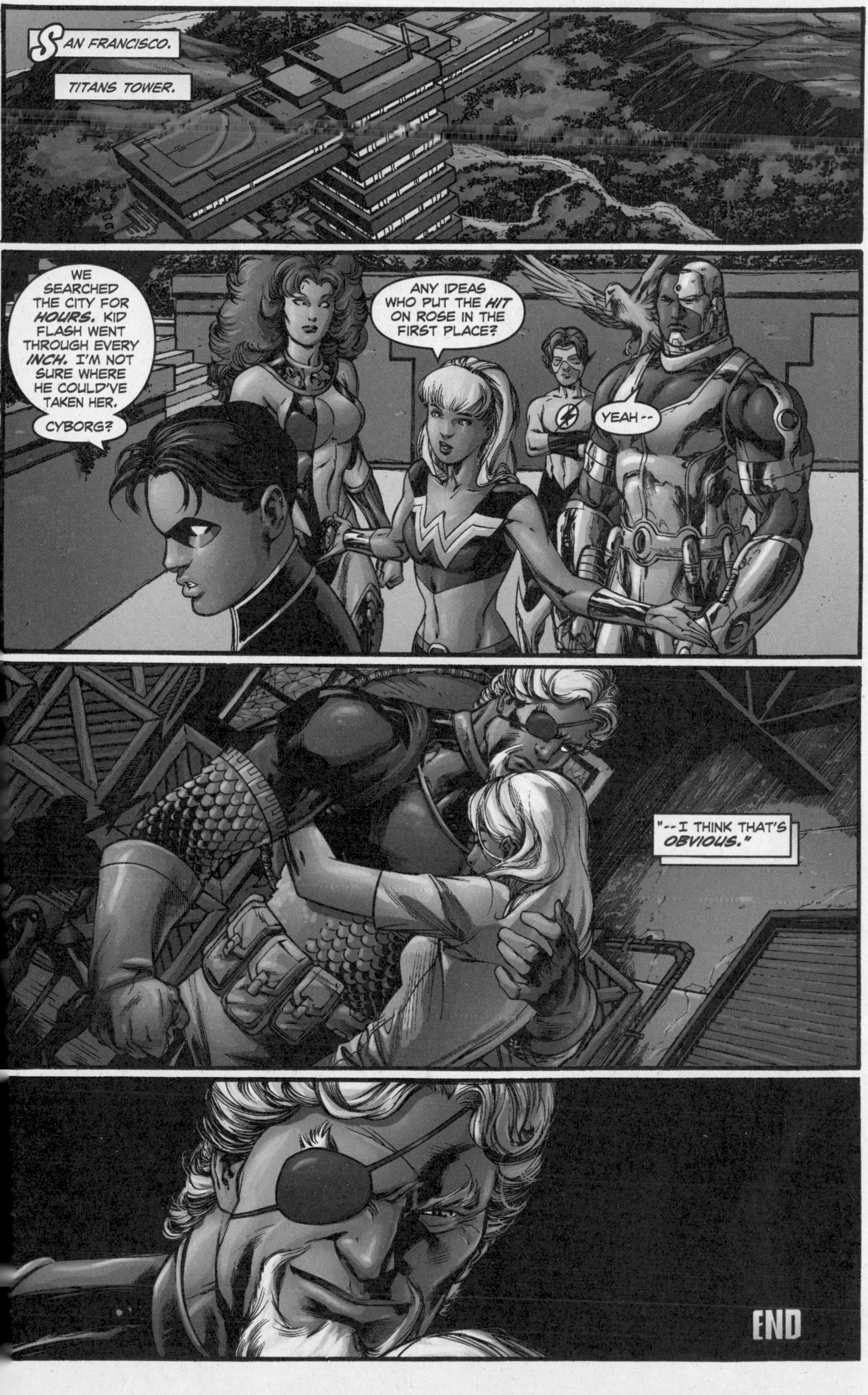
SAN FRANCISCO.
TITANS TOWER.
WE SEARCHED THE CITY FOR HOURS. KID FLASH WENT THROUGH EVERY INCH. I'M NOT SURE WHERE HE COULD'VE TAKEN HER.
CYBORG?
ANY IDEAS WHO PUT THE HIT ON ROSE IN THE FIRST PLACE?
YEAH --
"-- I THINK THAT'S OBVIOUS."
END

Teen Titans

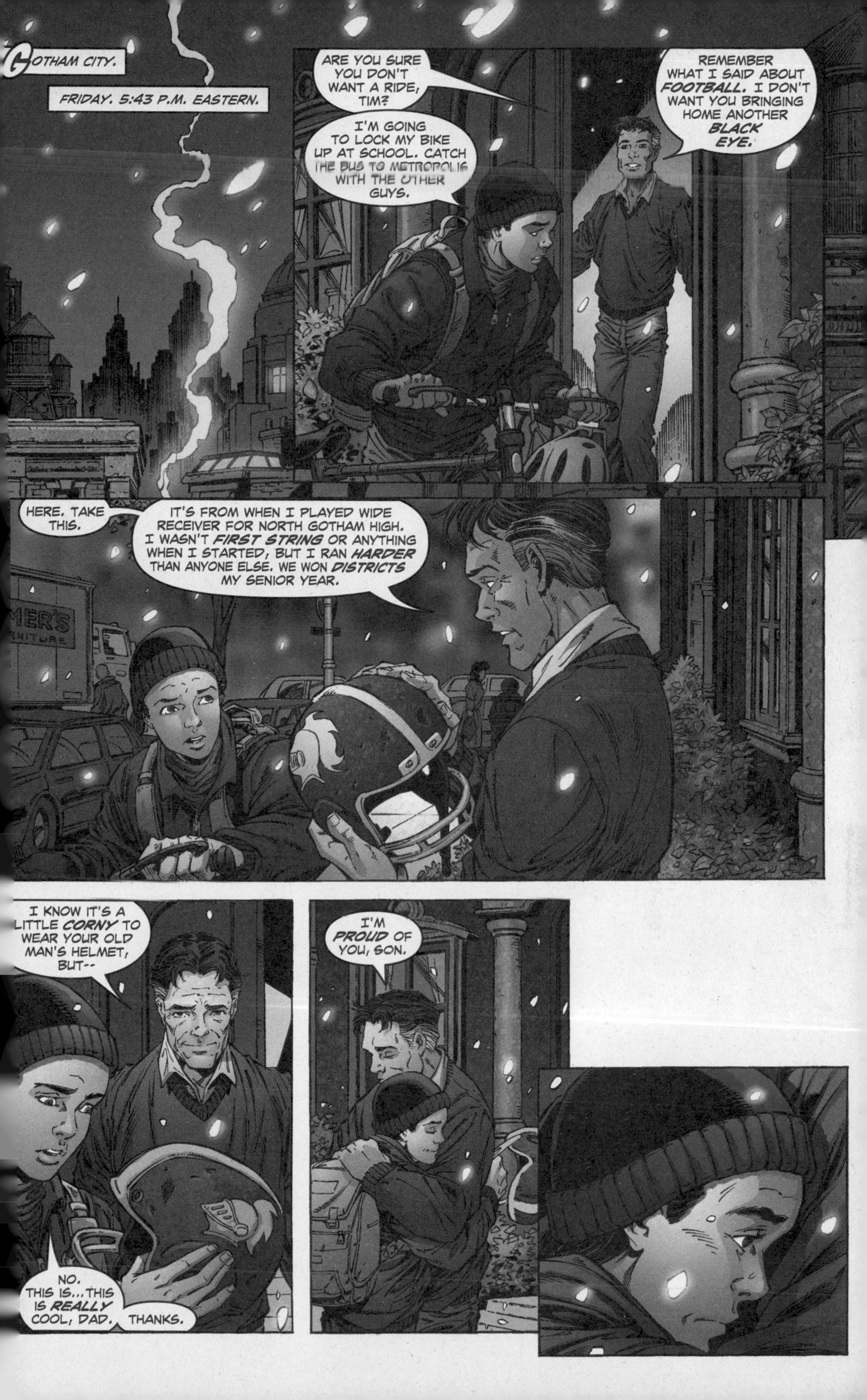
GOTHAM CITY.
FRIDAY. 5:43 P.M. EASTERN.
ARE YOU SURE YOU DON'T WANT A RIDE, TIM?
I'M GOING TO LOCK MY BIKE UP AT SCHOOL. CATCH THE BUS TO METROPOLIS WITH THE OTHER GUYS.
REMEMBER WHAT I SAID ABOUT FOOTBALL. I DON'T WANT YOU BRINGING HOME ANOTHER BLACK EYE.
HERE. TAKE THIS.
IT'S FROM WHEN I PLAYED WIDE RECEIVER FOR NORTH GOTHAM HIGH. I WASN'T FIRST STRING OR ANYTHING WHEN I STARTED, BUT I RAN HARDER THAN ANYONE ELSE. WE WON DISTRICTS MY SENIOR YEAR.
I KNOW IT'S A LITTLE CORNY TO WEAR YOUR OLD MAN'S HELMET, BUT--
NO. THIS IS...THIS IS REALLY COOL, DAD.
THANKS.
I'M PROUD OF YOU, SON.

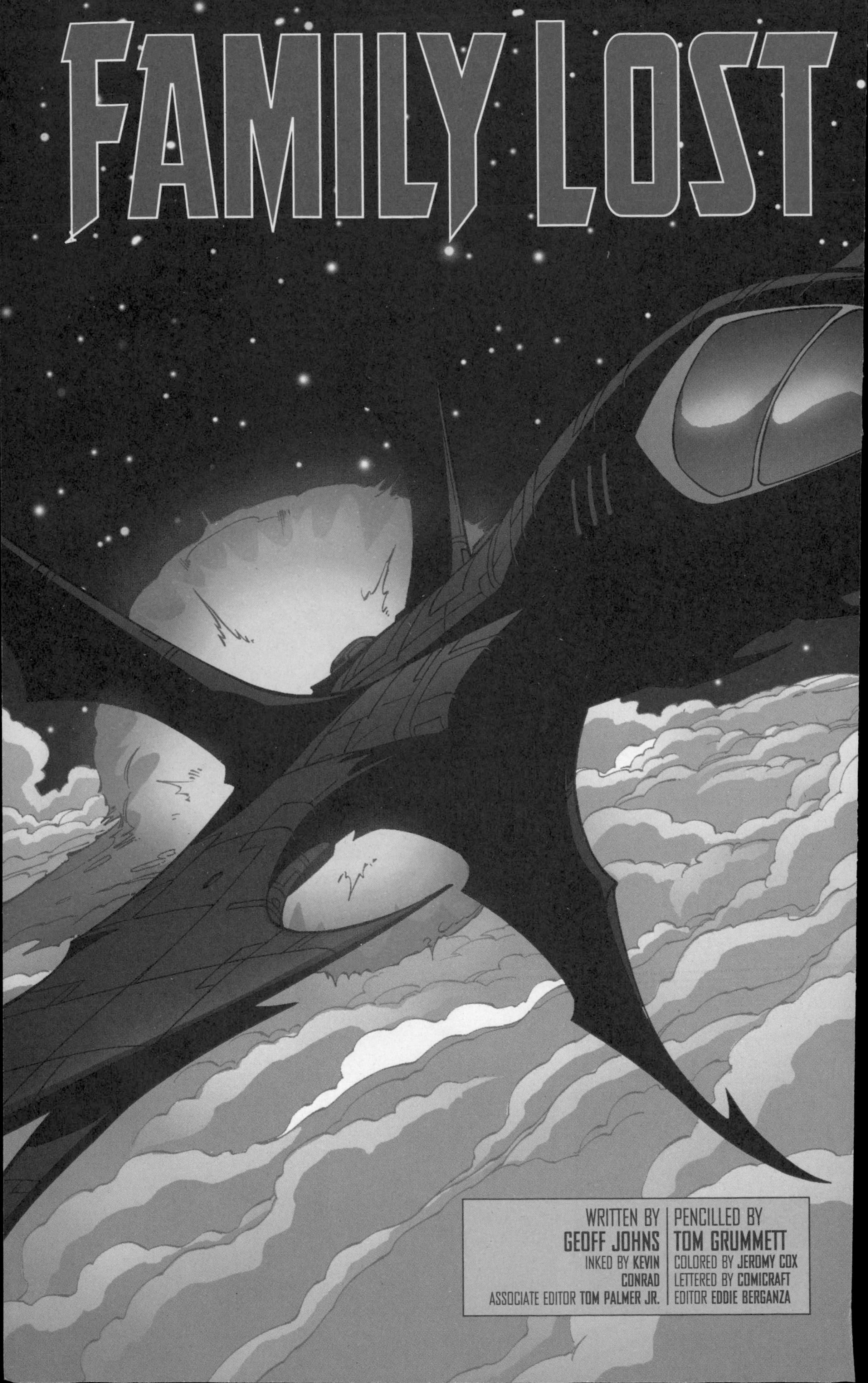
FAMILY LOST
WRITTEN BY GEOFF JOHNS
PENCILLED BY TOM GRUMMETT
INKED BY KEVIN CONRAD
COLORED BY JEROMY COX
LETTERED BY COMICRAFT
ASSOCIATE EDITOR TOM PALMER JR.
EDITOR EDDIE BERGANZA

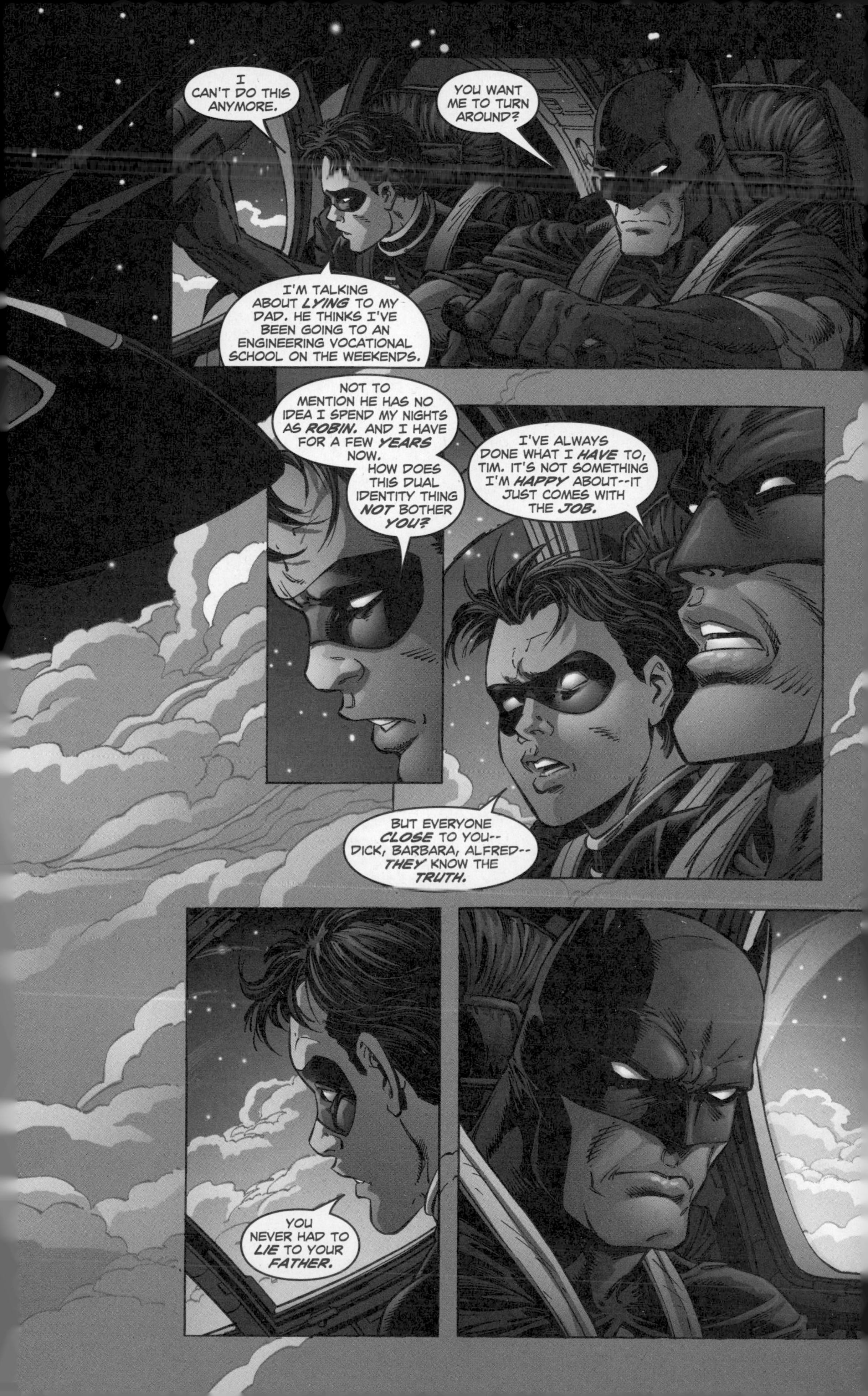
I CAN'T DO THIS ANYMORE.
YOU WANT ME TO TURN AROUND?
I'M TALKING ABOUT LYING TO MY DAD. HE THINKS I'VE BEEN GOING TO AN ENGINEERING VOCATIONAL SCHOOL ON THE WEEKENDS.
NOT TO MENTION HE HAS NO IDEA I SPEND MY NIGHTS AS ROBIN. AND I HAVE FOR A FEW YEARS NOW.
HOW DOES THIS DUAL IDENTITY THING NOT BOTHER YOU?
I'VE ALWAYS DONE WHAT I HAVE TO, TIM. IT'S NOT SOMETHING I'M HAPPY ABOUT--IT JUST COMES WITH THE JOB.
BUT EVERYONE CLOSE TO YOU--DICK, BARBARA, ALFRED--THEY KNOW THE TRUTH.
YOU NEVER HAD TO LIE TO YOUR FATHER.

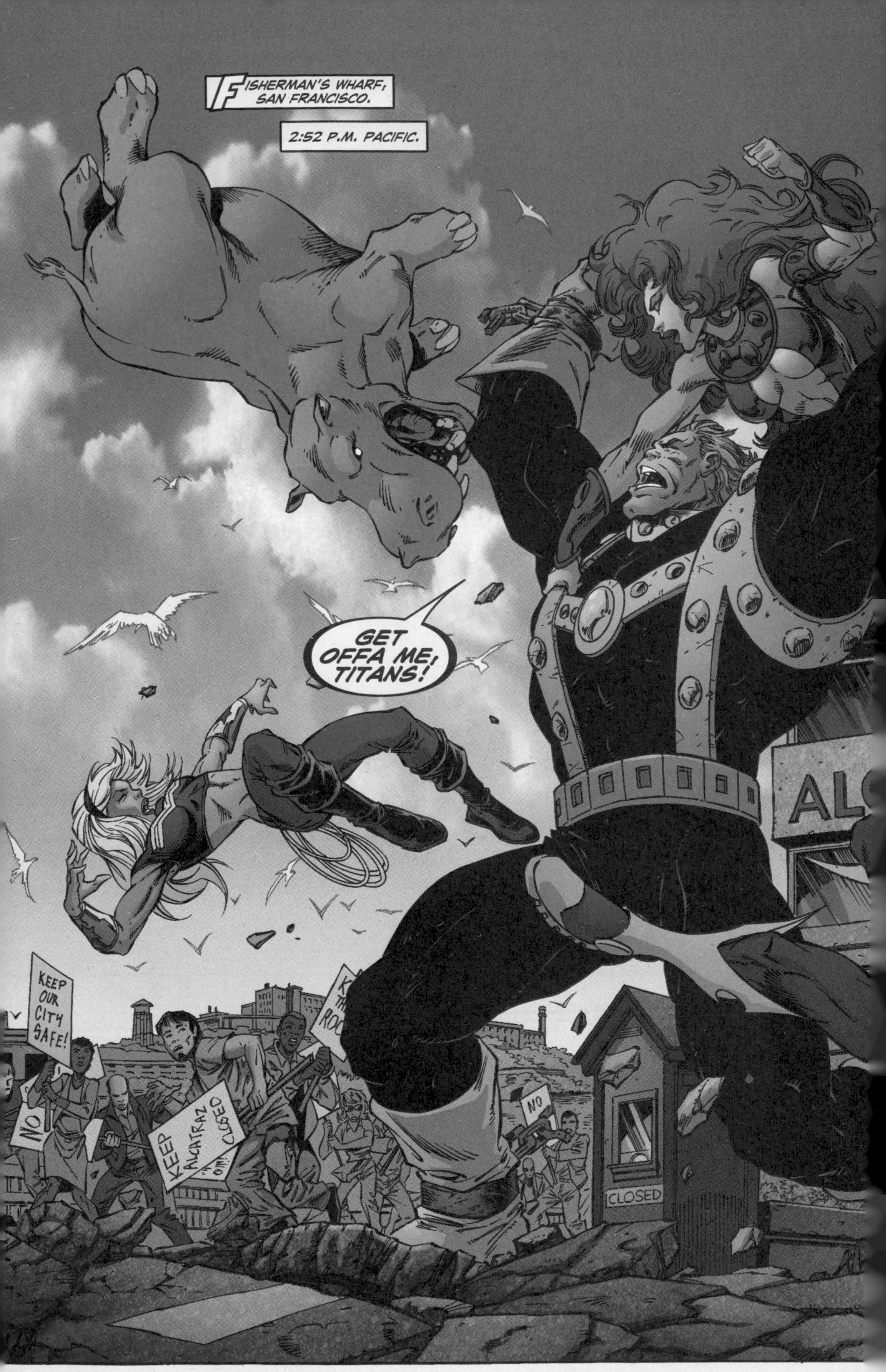
FISHERMAN'S WHARF, SAN FRANCISCO.
2:52 P.M. PACIFIC.
GET OFFA ME, TITANS!
KEEP OUR CITY SAFE!
NO
KEEP ALCATRAZ CLOSED
NO
CLOSED

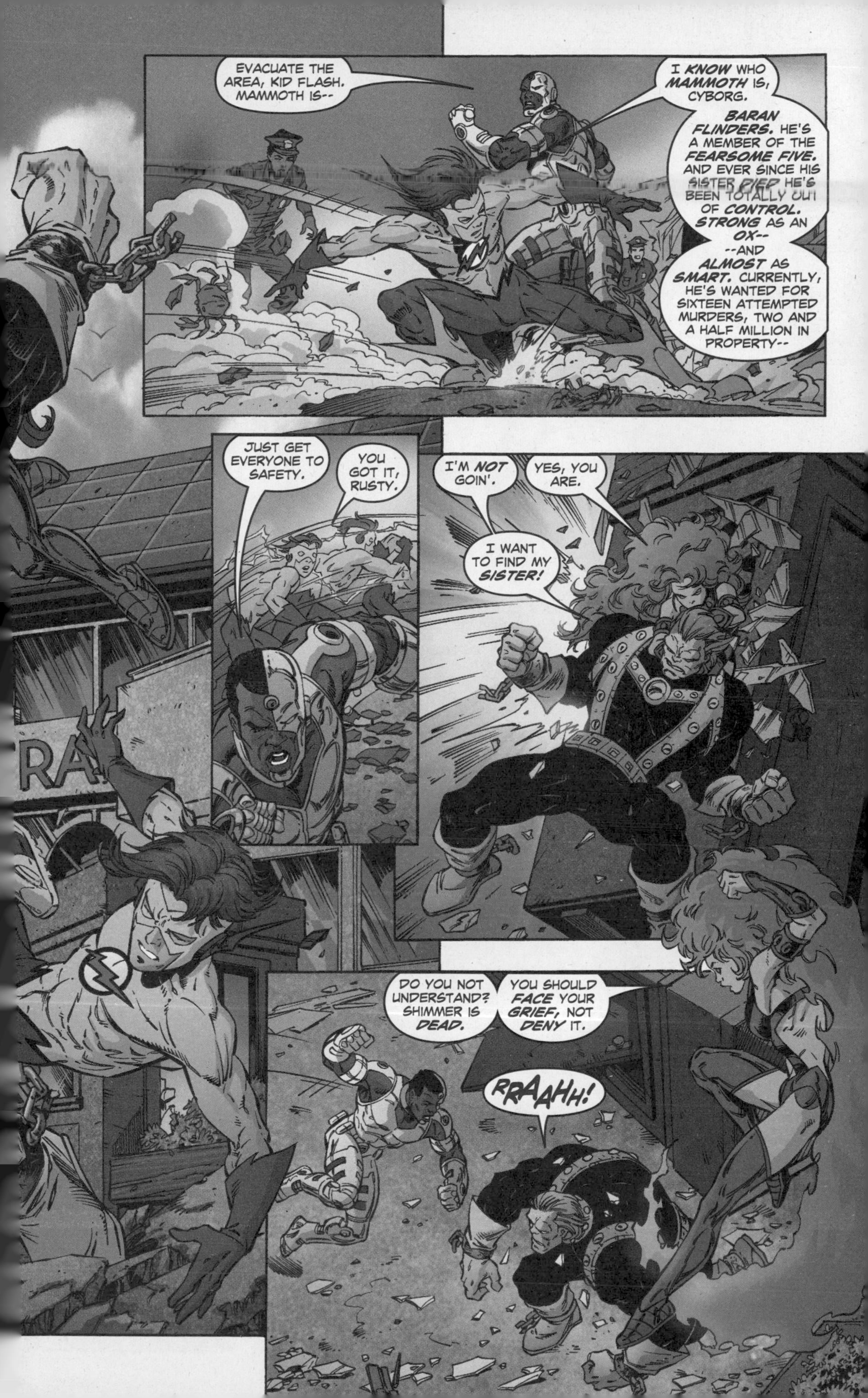
EVACUATE THE AREA, KID FLASH. MAMMOTH IS--
I KNOW WHO MAMMOTH IS, CYBORG.
BARAN FLINDERS. HE'S A MEMBER OF THE FEARSOME FIVE. AND EVER SINCE HIS SISTER DIED HE'S BEEN TOTALLY OUT OF CONTROL. STRONG AS AN OX--
--AND ALMOST AS SMART. CURRENTLY, HE'S WANTED FOR SIXTEEN ATTEMPTED MURDERS, TWO AND A HALF MILLION IN PROPERTY--
JUST GET EVERYONE TO SAFETY.
YOU GOT IT, RUSTY.
I'M NOT GOIN'.
YES, YOU ARE.
I WANT TO FIND MY SISTER!
DO YOU NOT UNDERSTAND? SHIMMER IS DEAD.
YOU SHOULD FACE YOUR GRIEF, NOT DENY IT.
RRAAHH!

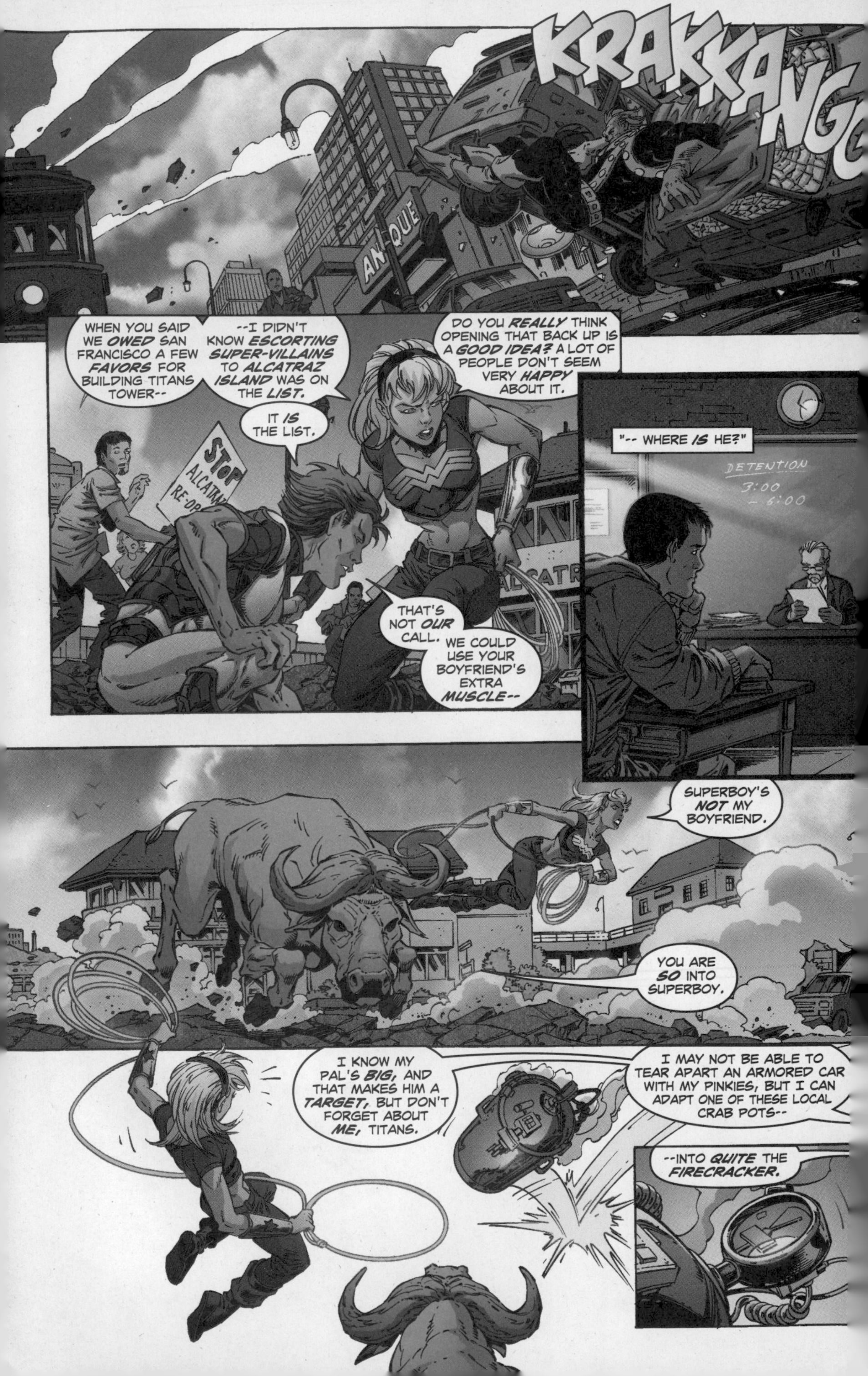
KRAKKANG
AN QUE
WHEN YOU SAID WE OWED SAN FRANCISCO A FEW FAVORS FOR BUILDING TITANS TOWER--
--I DIDN'T KNOW ESCORTING SUPER-VILLAINS TO ALCATRAZ ISLAND WAS ON THE LIST.
IT IS THE LIST.
DO YOU REALLY THINK OPENING THAT BACK UP IS A GOOD IDEA? A LOT OF PEOPLE DON'T SEEM VERY HAPPY ABOUT IT.
STOP ALCATRAZ RE-OP
THAT'S NOT OUR CALL.
WE COULD USE YOUR BOYFRIEND'S EXTRA MUSCLE--
"-- WHERE IS HE?"
DETENTION 3:00 - 6:00
SUPERBOY'S NOT MY BOYFRIEND.
YOU ARE SO INTO SUPERBOY.
I KNOW MY PAL'S BIG, AND THAT MAKES HIM A TARGET, BUT DON'T FORGET ABOUT ME, TITANS.
I MAY NOT BE ABLE TO TEAR APART AN ARMORED CAR WITH MY PINKIES, BUT I CAN ADAPT ONE OF THESE LOCAL CRAB POTS--
--INTO QUITE THE FIRECRACKER.

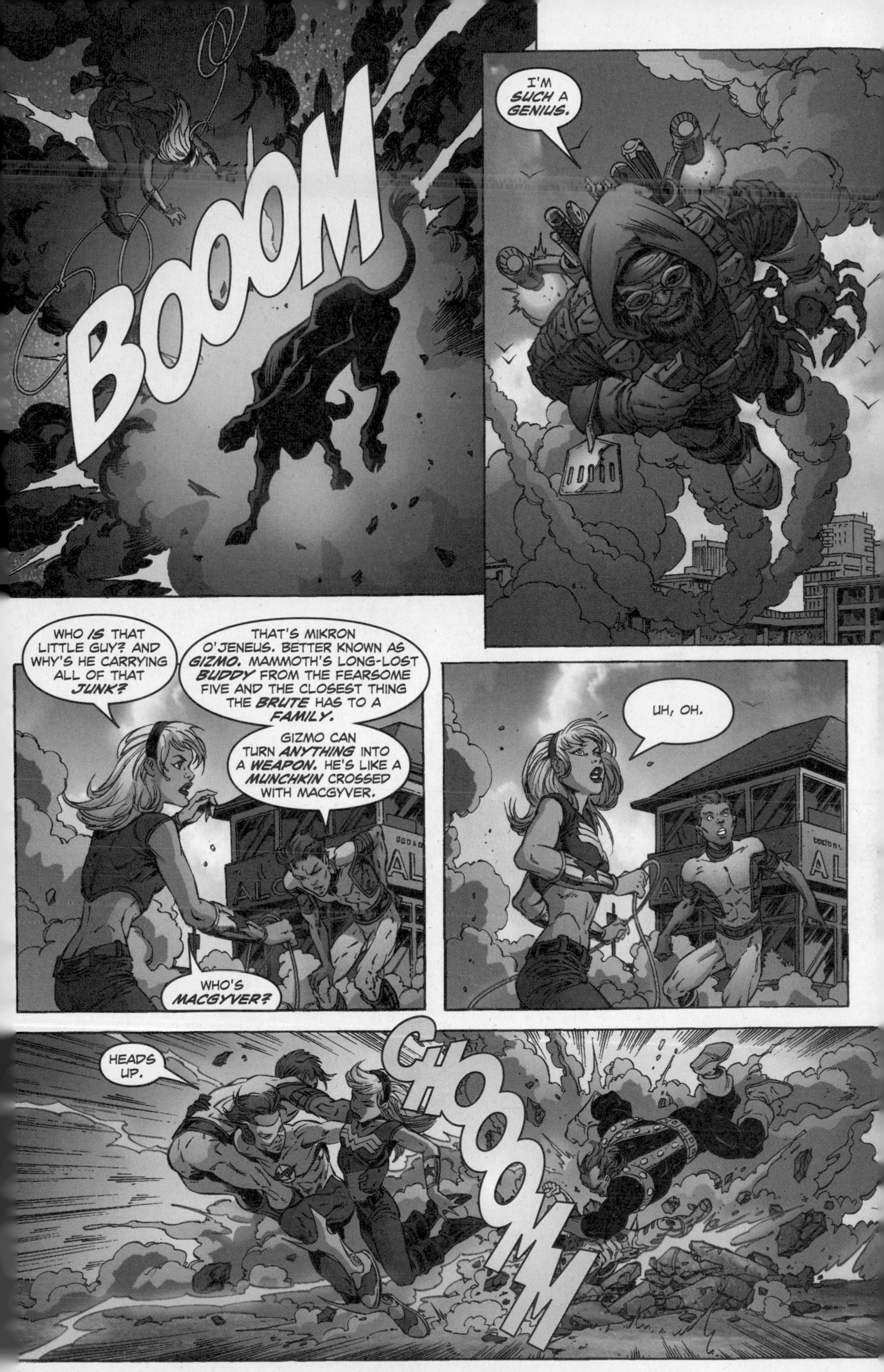
BOOOM
I'M SUCH A GENIUS.
WHO IS THAT LITTLE GUY? AND WHY'S HE CARRYING ALL OF THAT JUNK?
THAT'S MIKRON O'JENEUS. BETTER KNOWN AS GIZMO. MAMMOTH'S LONG-LOST BUDDY FROM THE FEARSOME FIVE AND THE CLOSEST THING THE BRUTE HAS TO A FAMILY.
GIZMO CAN TURN ANYTHING INTO A WEAPON. HE'S LIKE A MUNCHKIN CROSSED WITH MACGYVER.
WHO'S MACGYVER?
UH, OH.
HEADS UP.
CHOOOMM

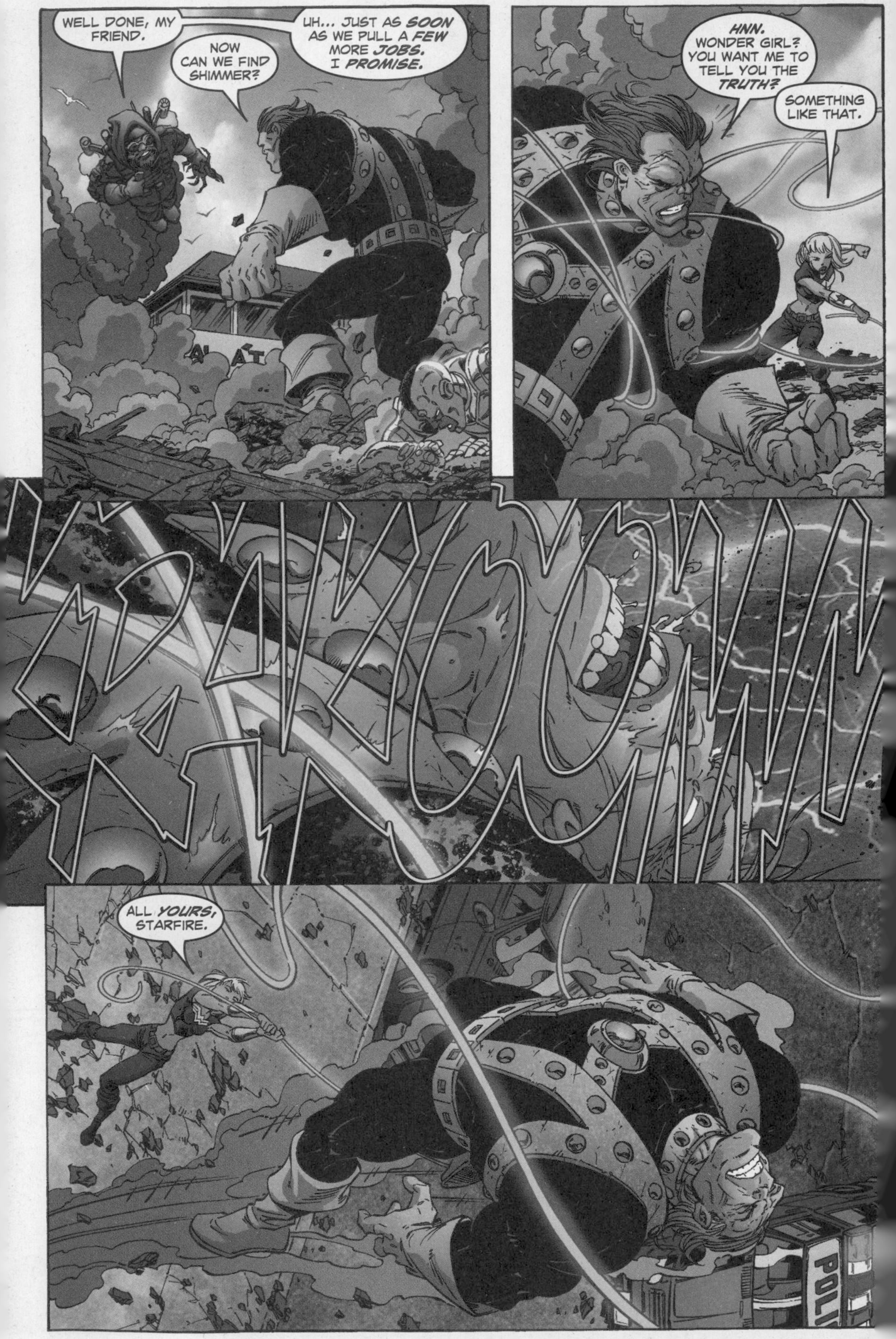
WELL DONE, MY FRIEND.
NOW CAN WE FIND SHIMMER?
UH... JUST AS SOON AS WE PULL A FEW MORE JOBS. I PROMISE.
HNN. WONDER GIRL? YOU WANT ME TO TELL YOU THE TRUTH?
SOMETHING LIKE THAT.
ALL YOURS, STARFIRE.
POLI

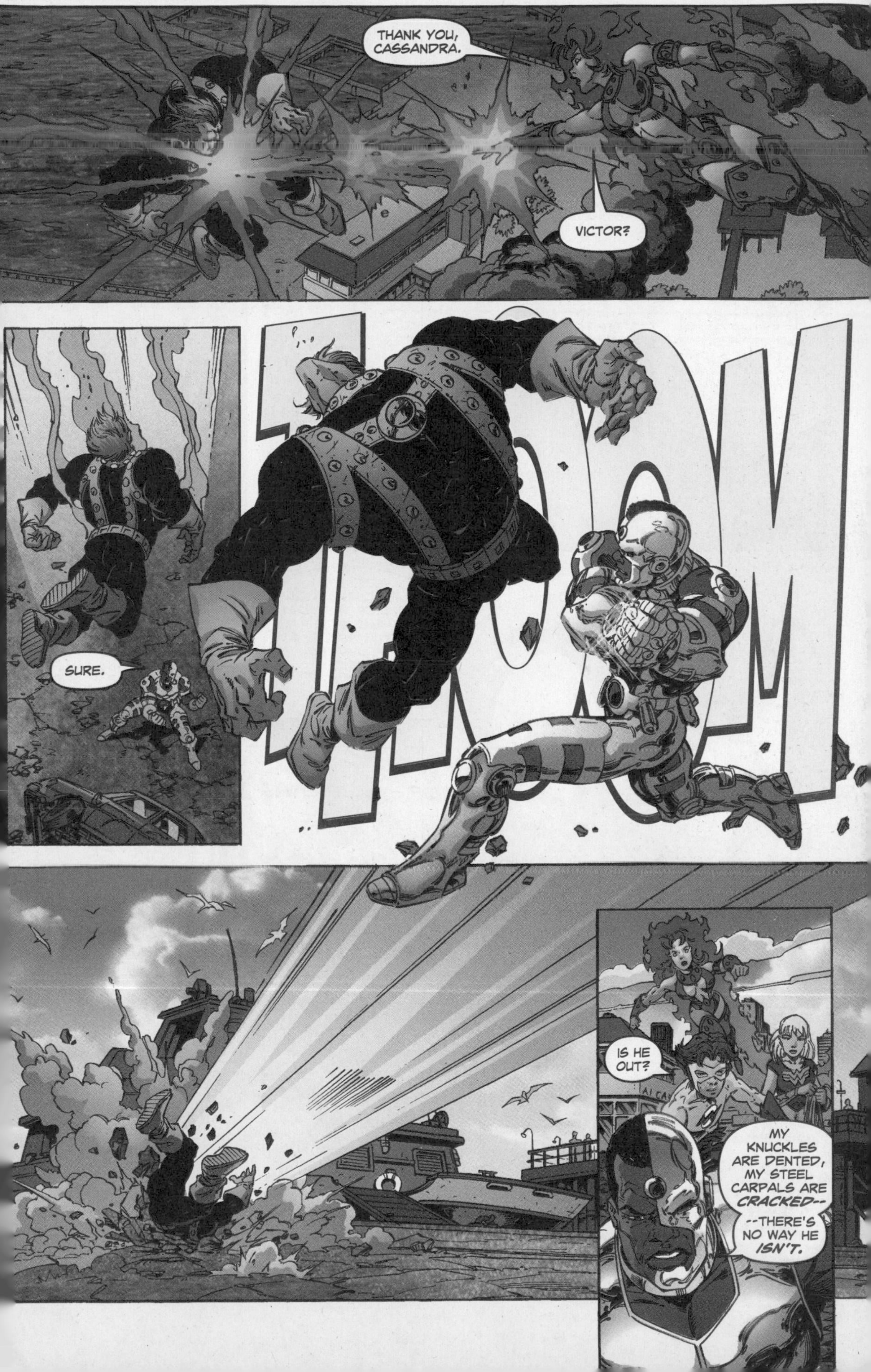
THANK YOU, CASSANDRA.
VICTOR?
SURE.
THROOM
IS HE OUT?
MY KNUCKLES ARE DENTED, MY STEEL CARPALS ARE CRACKED--
--THERE'S NO WAY HE ISN'T.

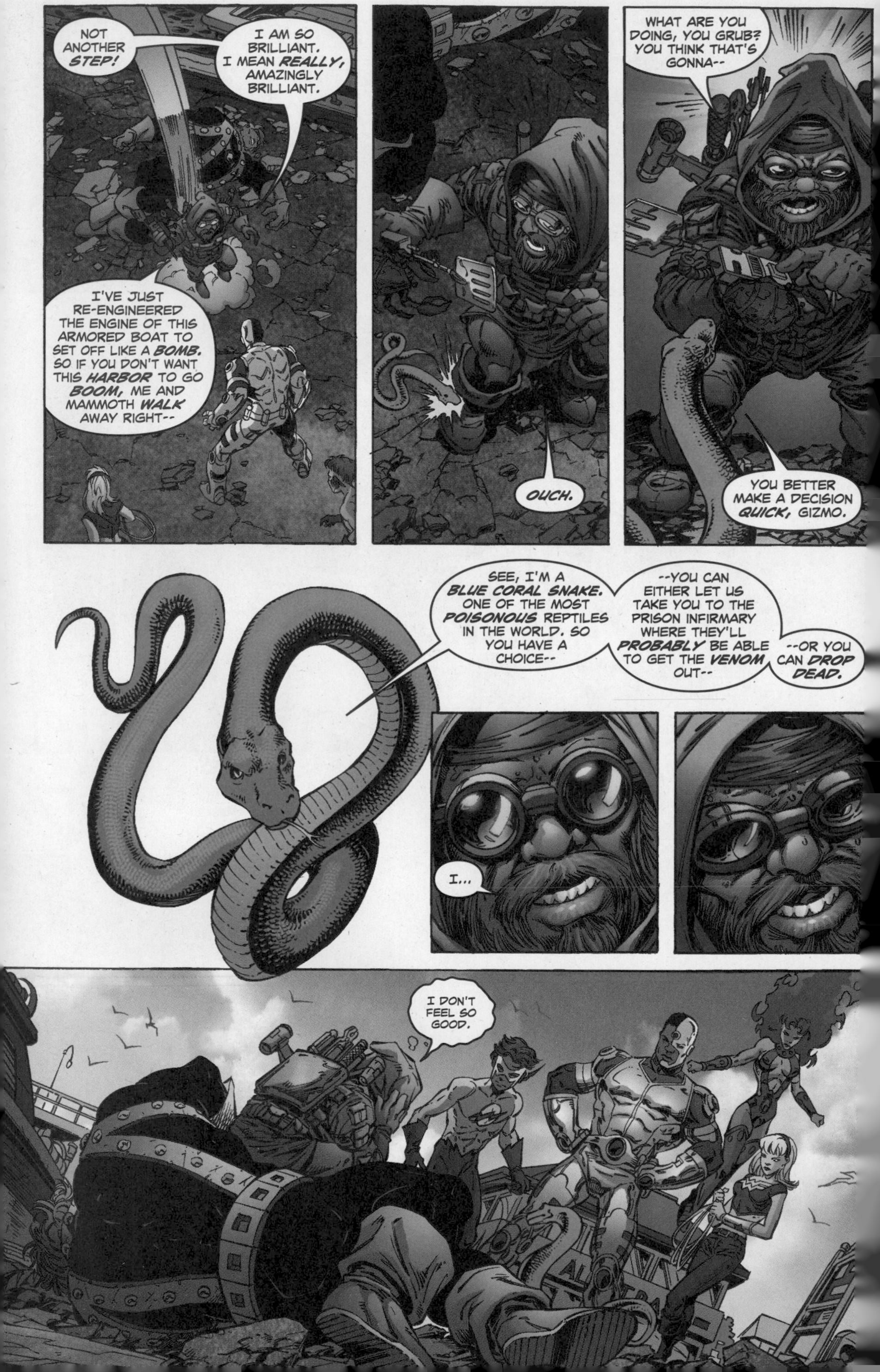
NOT ANOTHER STEP!
I AM SO BRILLIANT. I MEAN REALLY, AMAZINGLY BRILLIANT.
I'VE JUST RE-ENGINEERED THE ENGINE OF THIS ARMORED BOAT TO SET OFF LIKE A BOMB. SO IF YOU DON'T WANT THIS HARBOR TO GO BOOM, ME AND MAMMOTH WALK AWAY RIGHT--
OUCH.
WHAT ARE YOU DOING, YOU GRUB? YOU THINK THAT'S GONNA--
YOU BETTER MAKE A DECISION QUICK, GIZMO.
SEE, I'M A BLUE CORAL SNAKE. ONE OF THE MOST POISONOUS REPTILES IN THE WORLD. SO YOU HAVE A CHOICE--
--YOU CAN EITHER LET US TAKE YOU TO THE PRISON INFIRMARY WHERE THEY'LL PROBABLY BE ABLE TO GET THE VENOM OUT--
--OR YOU CAN DROP DEAD.
I...
I DON'T FEEL SO GOOD.

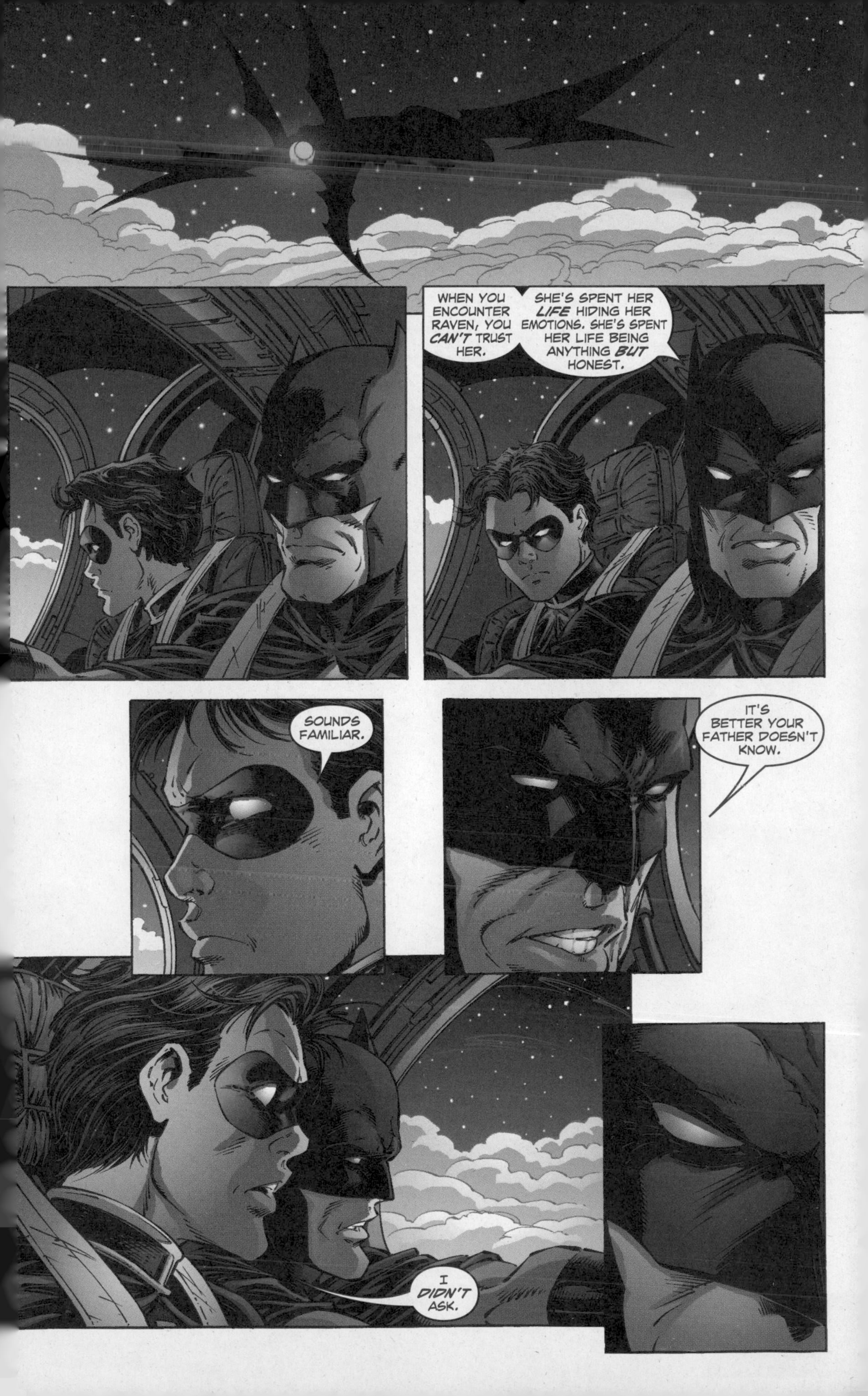
WHEN YOU ENCOUNTER RAVEN, YOU CAN'T TRUST HER.
SHE'S SPENT HER LIFE HIDING HER EMOTIONS. SHE'S SPENT HER LIFE BEING ANYTHING BUT HONEST.
SOUNDS FAMILIAR.
IT'S BETTER YOUR FATHER DOESN'T KNOW.
I DIDN'T ASK.

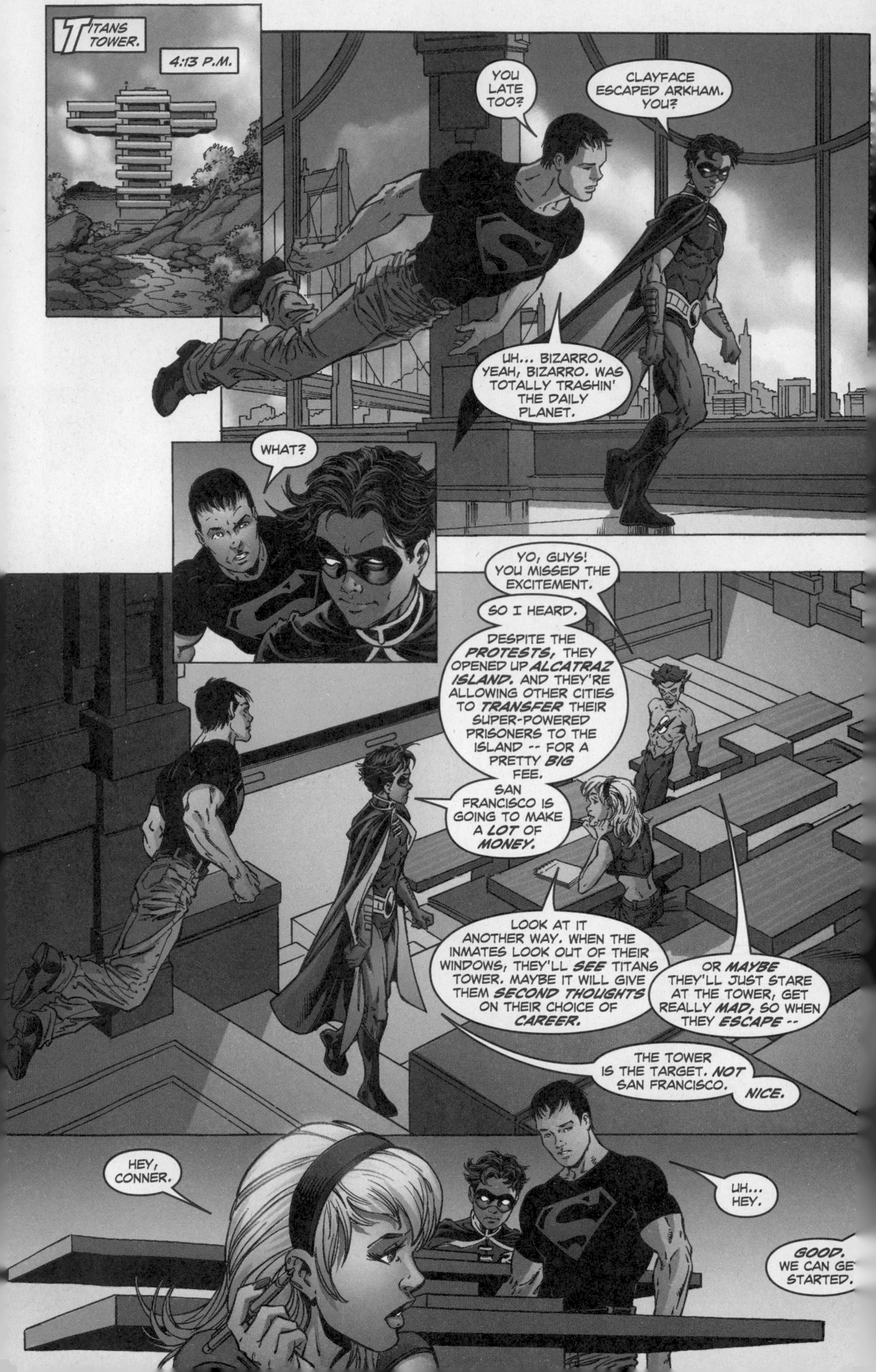
TITANS TOWER.
4:13 P.M.
YOU LATE TOO?
CLAYFACE ESCAPED ARKHAM. YOU?
UH... BIZARRO. YEAH, BIZARRO. WAS TOTALLY TRASHIN' THE DAILY PLANET.
WHAT?
YO, GUYS! YOU MISSED THE EXCITEMENT.
SO I HEARD.
DESPITE THE PROTESTS, THEY OPENED UP ALCATRAZ ISLAND. AND THEY'RE ALLOWING OTHER CITIES TO TRANSFER THEIR SUPER-POWERED PRISONERS TO THE ISLAND -- FOR A PRETTY BIG FEE.
SAN FRANCISCO IS GOING TO MAKE A LOT OF MONEY.
LOOK AT IT ANOTHER WAY. WHEN THE INMATES LOOK OUT OF THEIR WINDOWS, THEY'LL SEE TITANS TOWER. MAYBE IT WILL GIVE THEM SECOND THOUGHTS ON THEIR CHOICE OF CAREER.
OR MAYBE THEY'LL JUST STARE AT THE TOWER, GET REALLY MAD, SO WHEN THEY ESCAPE --
THE TOWER IS THE TARGET. NOT SAN FRANCISCO.
NICE.
HEY, CONNER.
UH... HEY.
GOOD. WE CAN GET STARTED.

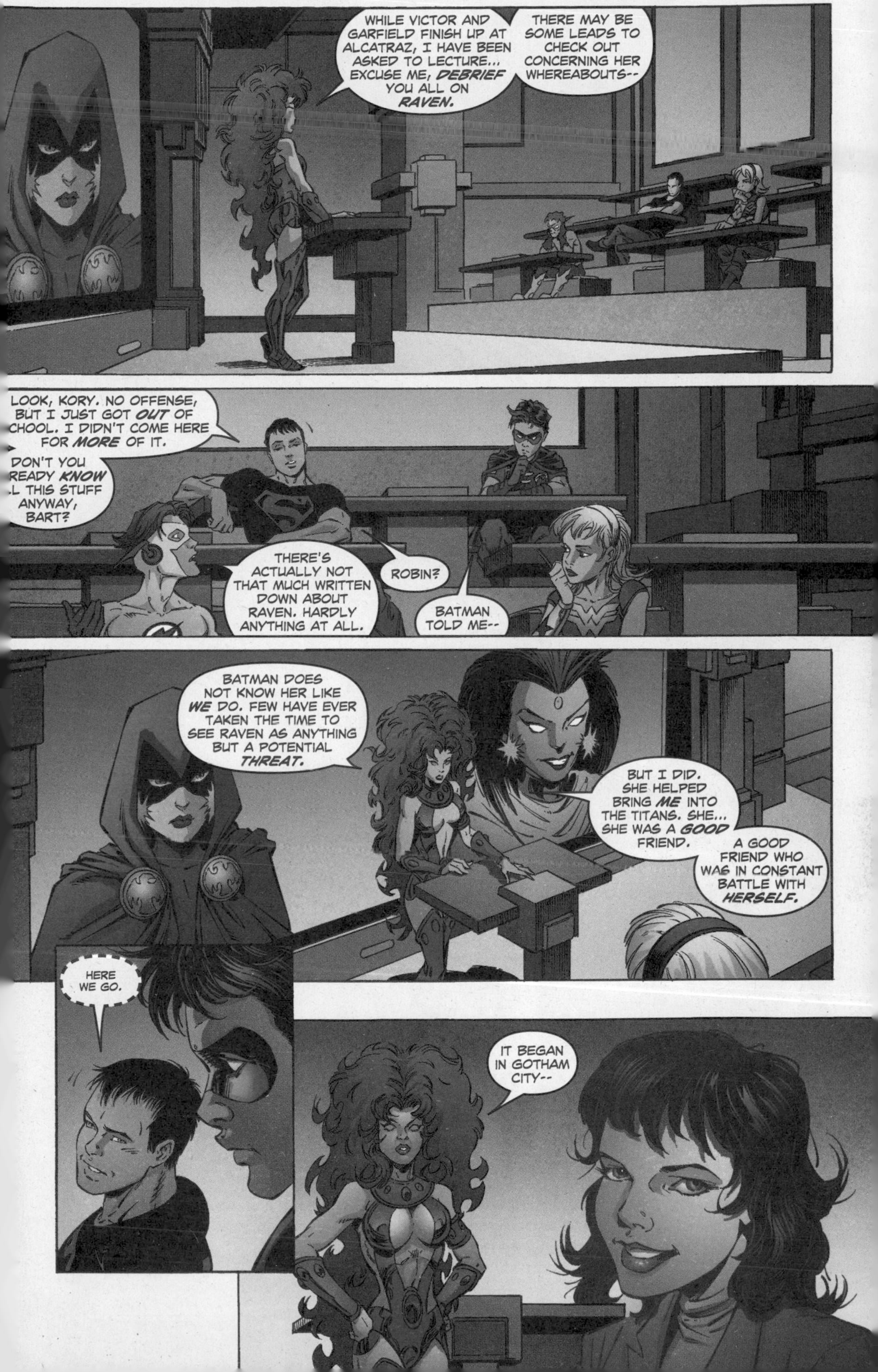
WHILE VICTOR AND GARFIELD FINISH UP AT ALCATRAZ, I HAVE BEEN ASKED TO LECTURE... EXCUSE ME, DEBRIEF YOU ALL ON RAVEN.
THERE MAY BE SOME LEADS TO CHECK OUT CONCERNING HER WHEREABOUTS--
LOOK, KORY. NO OFFENSE, BUT I JUST GOT OUT OF CHOOL. I DIDN'T COME HERE FOR MORE OF IT.
DON'T YOU READY KNOW L THIS STUFF ANYWAY, BART?
THERE'S ACTUALLY NOT THAT MUCH WRITTEN DOWN ABOUT RAVEN. HARDLY ANYTHING AT ALL.
ROBIN?
BATMAN TOLD ME--
BATMAN DOES NOT KNOW HER LIKE WE DO. FEW HAVE EVER TAKEN THE TIME TO SEE RAVEN AS ANYTHING BUT A POTENTIAL THREAT.
BUT I DID. SHE HELPED BRING ME INTO THE TITANS. SHE... SHE WAS A GOOD FRIEND.
A GOOD FRIEND WHO WAS IN CONSTANT BATTLE WITH HERSELF.
HERE WE GO.
IT BEGAN IN GOTHAM CITY--

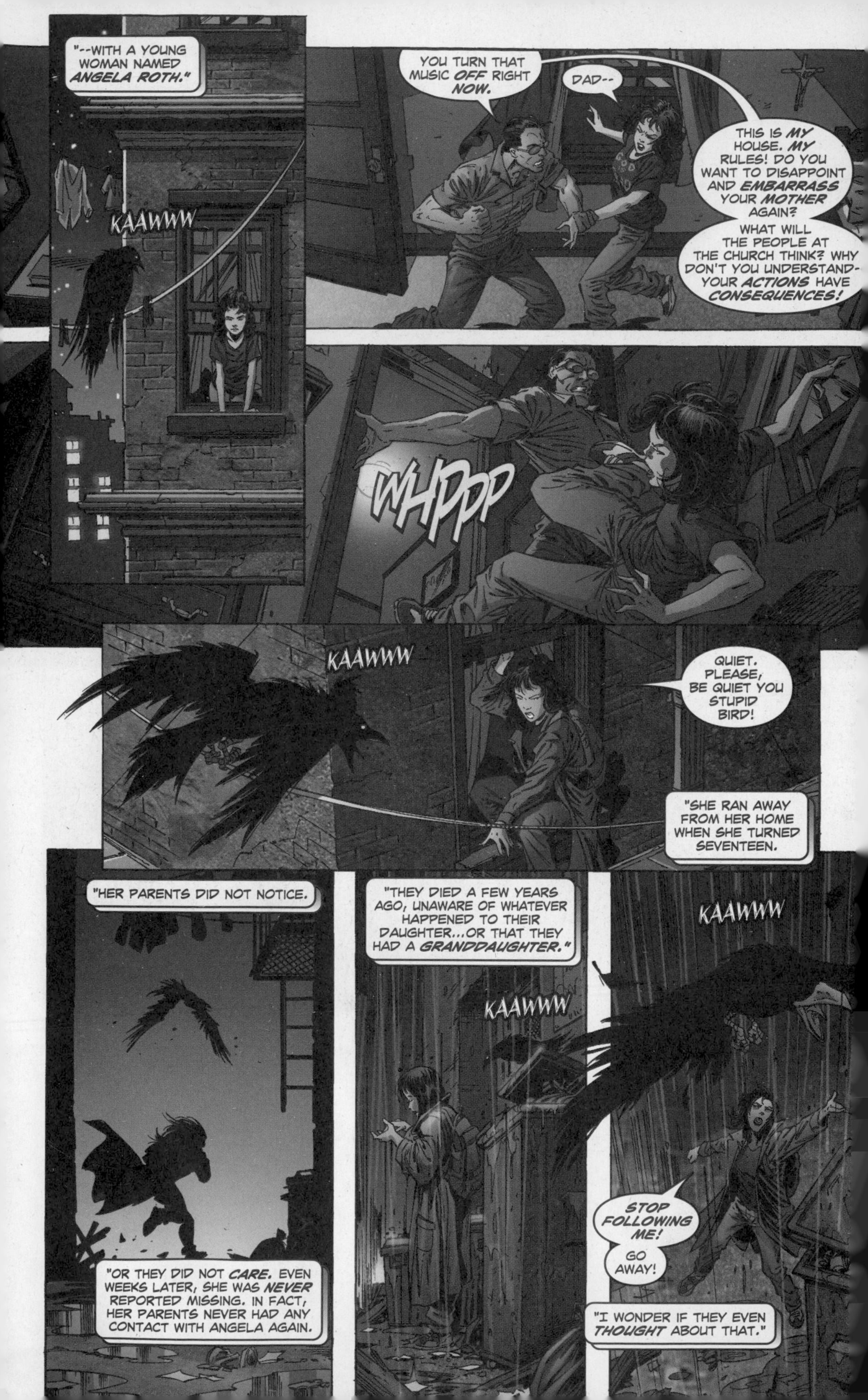
"--WITH A YOUNG WOMAN NAMED *ANGELA ROTH.*"
KAAWWW
YOU TURN THAT MUSIC *OFF* RIGHT *NOW.*
DAD--
THIS IS *MY* HOUSE. *MY* RULES! DO YOU WANT TO DISAPPOINT AND *EMBARRASS* YOUR *MOTHER* AGAIN?
WHAT WILL THE PEOPLE AT THE CHURCH THINK? WHY DON'T YOU UNDERSTAND-- YOUR *ACTIONS* HAVE *CONSEQUENCES!*
WHPPP
KAAWWW
QUIET. PLEASE, BE QUIET YOU STUPID BIRD!
"SHE RAN AWAY FROM HER HOME WHEN SHE TURNED SEVENTEEN.
"HER PARENTS DID NOT NOTICE.
"OR THEY DID NOT *CARE.* EVEN WEEKS LATER, SHE WAS *NEVER* REPORTED MISSING. IN FACT, HER PARENTS NEVER HAD ANY CONTACT WITH ANGELA AGAIN.
"THEY DIED A FEW YEARS AGO, UNAWARE OF WHATEVER HAPPENED TO THEIR DAUGHTER...OR THAT THEY HAD A *GRANDDAUGHTER.*"
KAAWWW
KAAWWW
STOP FOLLOWING ME!
GO AWAY!
"I WONDER IF THEY EVEN *THOUGHT* ABOUT THAT."

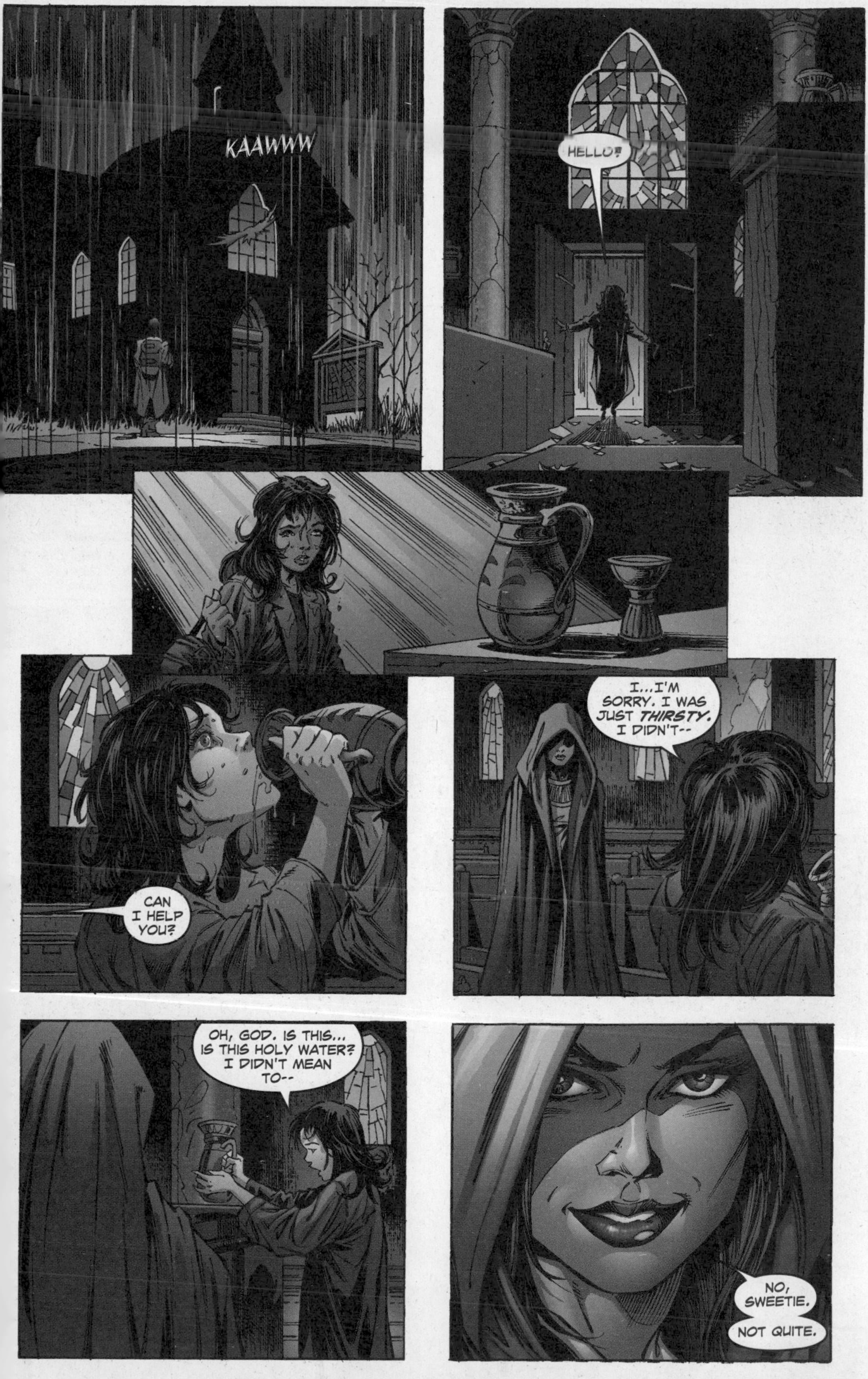
KAAWWW
HELLO?
CAN I HELP YOU?
I...I'M SORRY. I WAS JUST THIRSTY. I DIDN'T--
OH, GOD. IS THIS... IS THIS HOLY WATER? I DIDN'T MEAN TO--
NO, SWEETIE.
NOT QUITE.

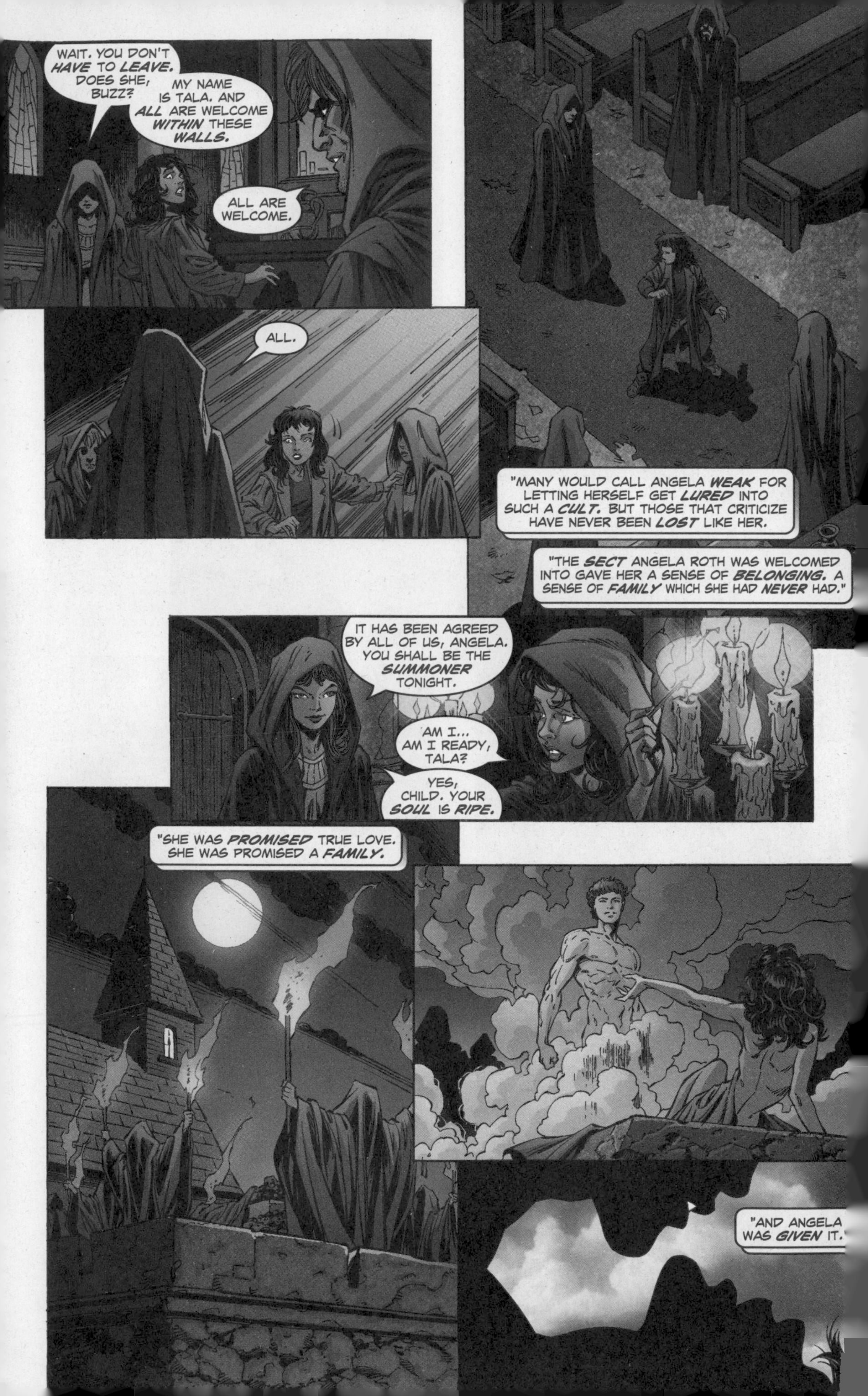
WAIT. YOU DON'T HAVE TO LEAVE. DOES SHE, BUZZ?
MY NAME IS TALA. AND ALL ARE WELCOME WITHIN THESE WALLS.
ALL ARE WELCOME.
ALL.
"MANY WOULD CALL ANGELA WEAK FOR LETTING HERSELF GET LURED INTO SUCH A CULT. BUT THOSE THAT CRITICIZE HAVE NEVER BEEN LOST LIKE HER.
"THE SECT ANGELA ROTH WAS WELCOMED INTO GAVE HER A SENSE OF BELONGING. A SENSE OF FAMILY WHICH SHE HAD NEVER HAD."
IT HAS BEEN AGREED BY ALL OF US, ANGELA. YOU SHALL BE THE SUMMONER TONIGHT.
AM I... AM I READY, TALA?
YES, CHILD. YOUR SOUL IS RIPE.
"SHE WAS PROMISED TRUE LOVE. SHE WAS PROMISED A FAMILY.
"AND ANGELA WAS GIVEN IT.

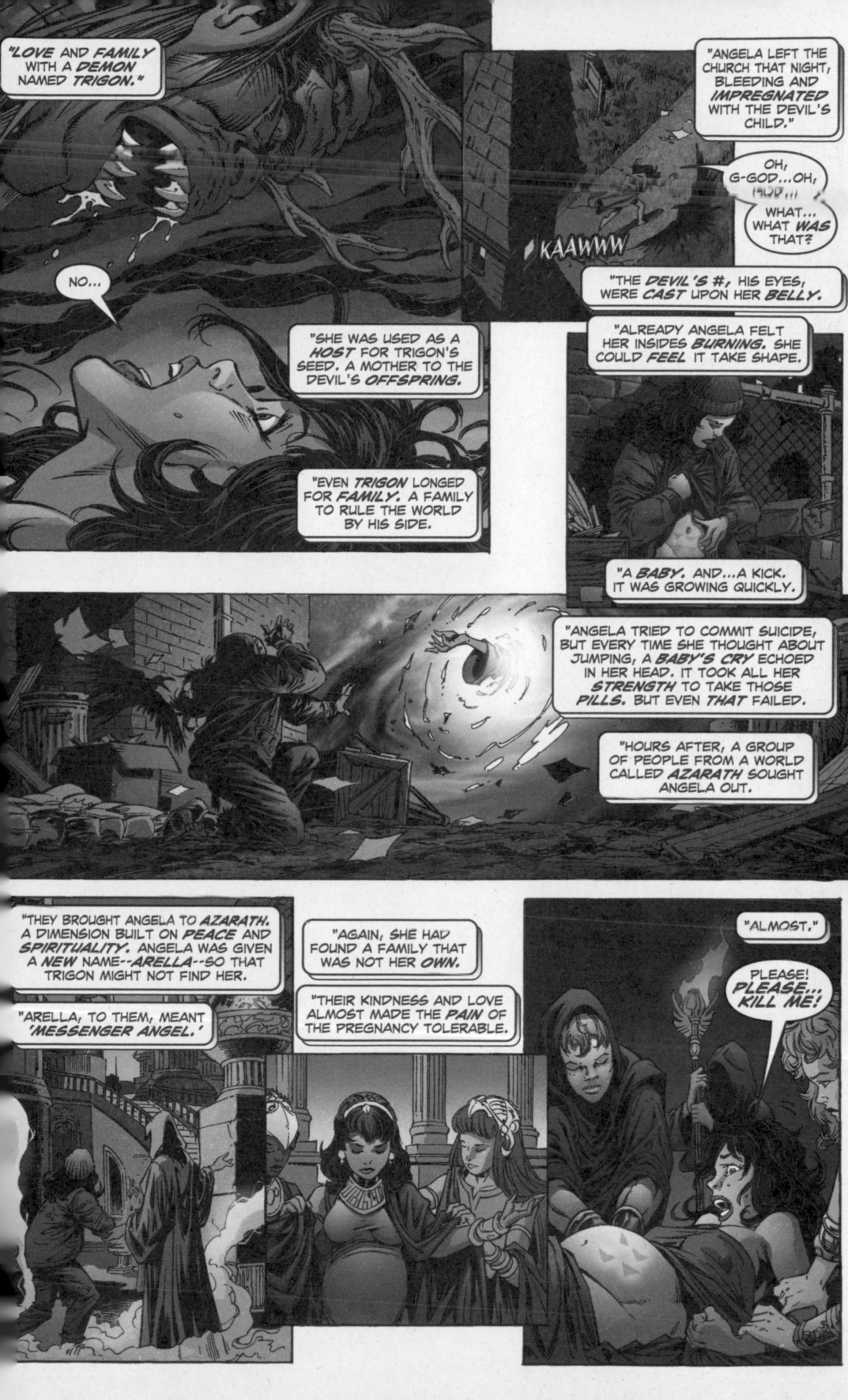

"LOVE AND FAMILY WITH A DEMON NAMED TRIGON."
"ANGELA LEFT THE CHURCH THAT NIGHT, BLEEDING AND IMPREGNATED WITH THE DEVIL'S CHILD."
OH, G-GOD...OH,
WHAT... WHAT WAS THAT?
KAAWWW
NO...
"THE DEVIL'S #, HIS EYES, WERE CAST UPON HER BELLY.
"SHE WAS USED AS A HOST FOR TRIGON'S SEED. A MOTHER TO THE DEVIL'S OFFSPRING.
"ALREADY ANGELA FELT HER INSIDES BURNING. SHE COULD FEEL IT TAKE SHAPE.
"EVEN TRIGON LONGED FOR FAMILY. A FAMILY TO RULE THE WORLD BY HIS SIDE.
"A BABY. AND...A KICK. IT WAS GROWING QUICKLY.
"ANGELA TRIED TO COMMIT SUICIDE, BUT EVERY TIME SHE THOUGHT ABOUT JUMPING, A BABY'S CRY ECHOED IN HER HEAD. IT TOOK ALL HER STRENGTH TO TAKE THOSE PILLS. BUT EVEN THAT FAILED.
"HOURS AFTER, A GROUP OF PEOPLE FROM A WORLD CALLED AZARATH SOUGHT ANGELA OUT.
"THEY BROUGHT ANGELA TO AZARATH. A DIMENSION BUILT ON PEACE AND SPIRITUALITY. ANGELA WAS GIVEN A NEW NAME--ARELLA--SO THAT TRIGON MIGHT NOT FIND HER.
"ARELLA, TO THEM, MEANT 'MESSENGER ANGEL.'
"AGAIN, SHE HAD FOUND A FAMILY THAT WAS NOT HER OWN.
"THEIR KINDNESS AND LOVE ALMOST MADE THE PAIN OF THE PREGNANCY TOLERABLE.
"ALMOST."
PLEASE! PLEASE... KILL ME!

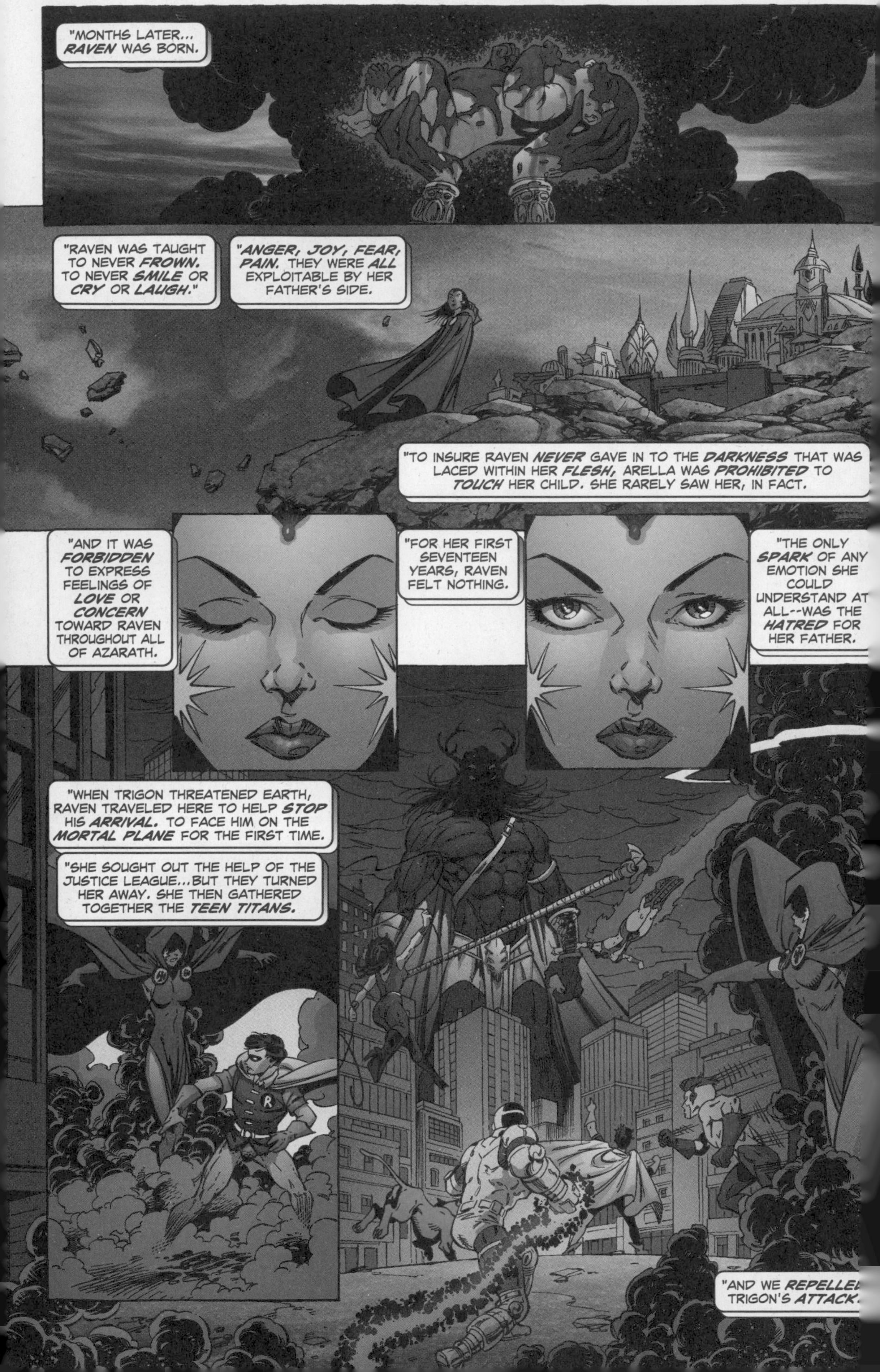
"MONTHS LATER... RAVEN WAS BORN.
"RAVEN WAS TAUGHT TO NEVER FROWN. TO NEVER SMILE OR CRY OR LAUGH."
"ANGER, JOY, FEAR, PAIN. THEY WERE ALL EXPLOITABLE BY HER FATHER'S SIDE.
"TO INSURE RAVEN NEVER GAVE IN TO THE DARKNESS THAT WAS LACED WITHIN HER FLESH, ARELLA WAS PROHIBITED TO TOUCH HER CHILD. SHE RARELY SAW HER, IN FACT.
"AND IT WAS FORBIDDEN TO EXPRESS FEELINGS OF LOVE OR CONCERN TOWARD RAVEN THROUGHOUT ALL OF AZARATH.
"FOR HER FIRST SEVENTEEN YEARS, RAVEN FELT NOTHING.
"THE ONLY SPARK OF ANY EMOTION SHE COULD UNDERSTAND AT ALL--WAS THE HATRED FOR HER FATHER.
"WHEN TRIGON THREATENED EARTH, RAVEN TRAVELED HERE TO HELP STOP HIS ARRIVAL. TO FACE HIM ON THE MORTAL PLANE FOR THE FIRST TIME.
"SHE SOUGHT OUT THE HELP OF THE JUSTICE LEAGUE...BUT THEY TURNED HER AWAY. SHE THEN GATHERED TOGETHER THE TEEN TITANS.
"AND WE REPELLED TRIGON'S ATTACK.

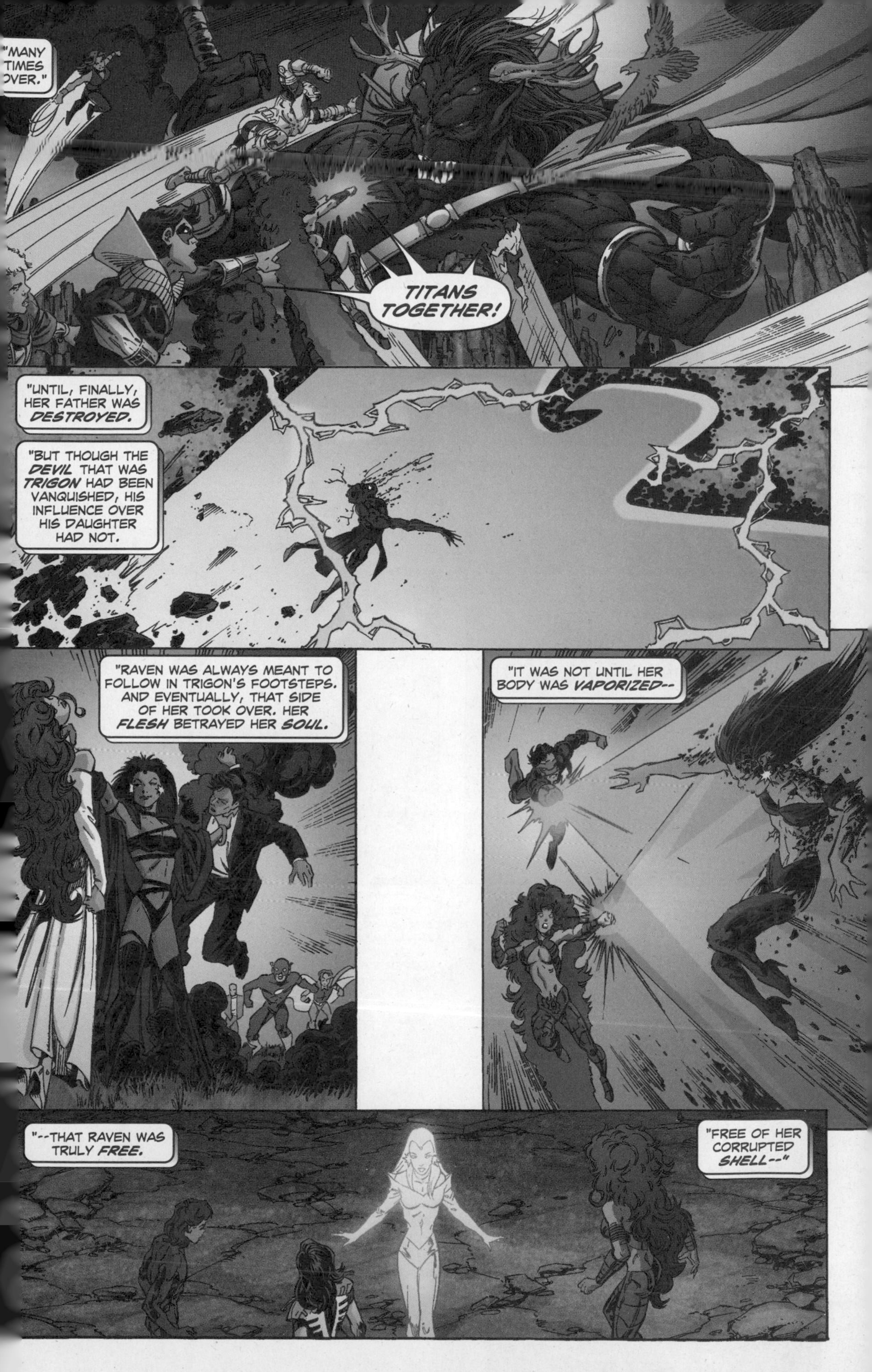

"MANY TIMES OVER."
TITANS TOGETHER!
"UNTIL, FINALLY, HER FATHER WAS DESTROYED.
"BUT THOUGH THE DEVIL THAT WAS TRIGON HAD BEEN VANQUISHED, HIS INFLUENCE OVER HIS DAUGHTER HAD NOT.
"RAVEN WAS ALWAYS MEANT TO FOLLOW IN TRIGON'S FOOTSTEPS. AND EVENTUALLY, THAT SIDE OF HER TOOK OVER. HER FLESH BETRAYED HER SOUL.
"IT WAS NOT UNTIL HER BODY WAS VAPORIZED--
"--THAT RAVEN WAS TRULY FREE.
"FREE OF HER CORRUPTED SHELL--"

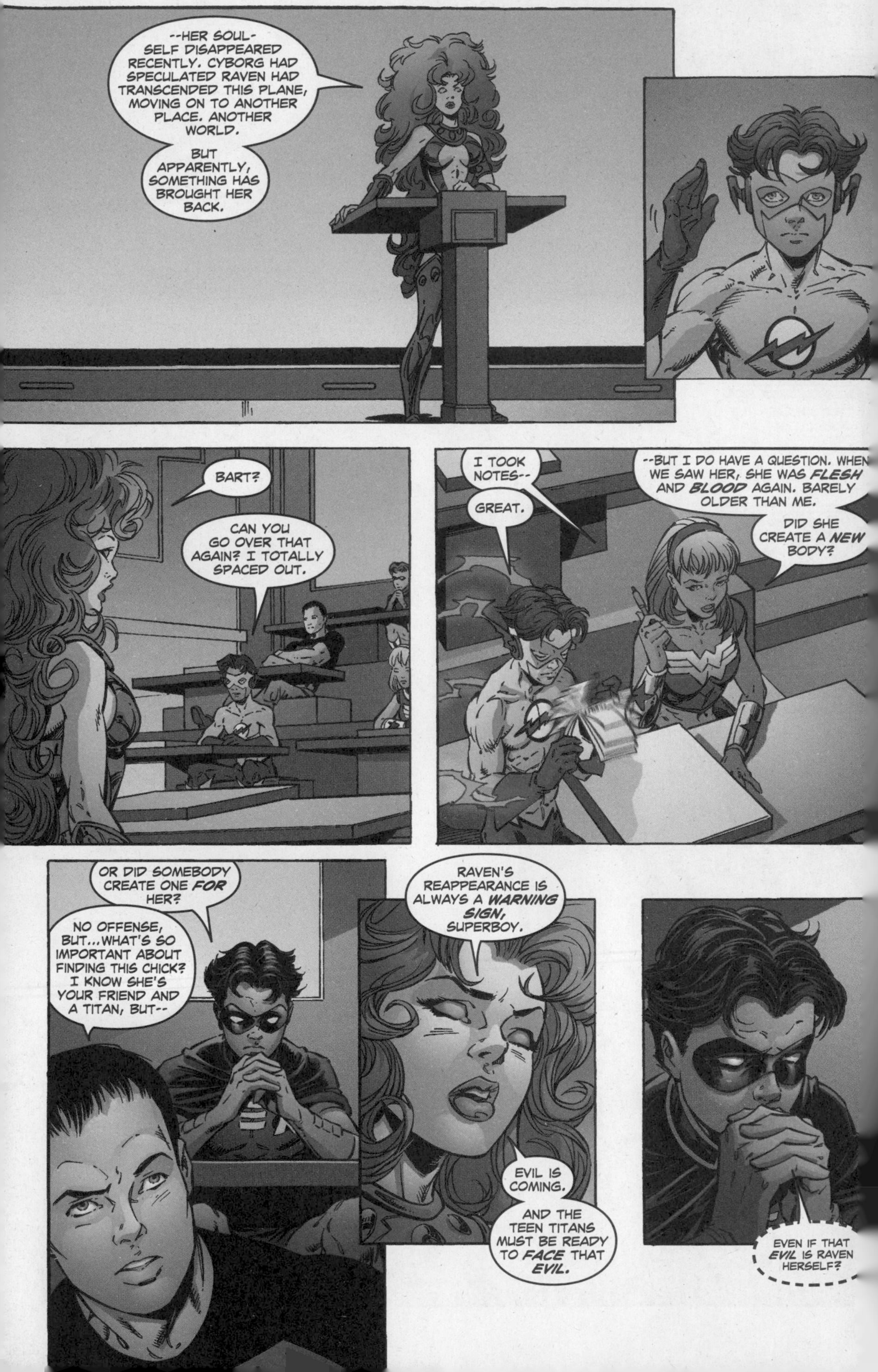
--HER SOUL-SELF DISAPPEARED RECENTLY. CYBORG HAD SPECULATED RAVEN HAD TRANSCENDED THIS PLANE, MOVING ON TO ANOTHER PLACE. ANOTHER WORLD.
BUT APPARENTLY, SOMETHING HAS BROUGHT HER BACK.
BART?
CAN YOU GO OVER THAT AGAIN? I TOTALLY SPACED OUT.
I TOOK NOTES--
GREAT.
--BUT I DO HAVE A QUESTION. WHEN WE SAW HER, SHE WAS FLESH AND BLOOD AGAIN. BARELY OLDER THAN ME.
DID SHE CREATE A NEW BODY?
OR DID SOMEBODY CREATE ONE FOR HER?
NO OFFENSE, BUT...WHAT'S SO IMPORTANT ABOUT FINDING THIS CHICK? I KNOW SHE'S YOUR FRIEND AND A TITAN, BUT--
RAVEN'S REAPPEARANCE IS ALWAYS A WARNING SIGN, SUPERBOY.
EVIL IS COMING.
AND THE TEEN TITANS MUST BE READY TO FACE THAT EVIL.
EVEN IF THAT EVIL IS RAVEN HERSELF?

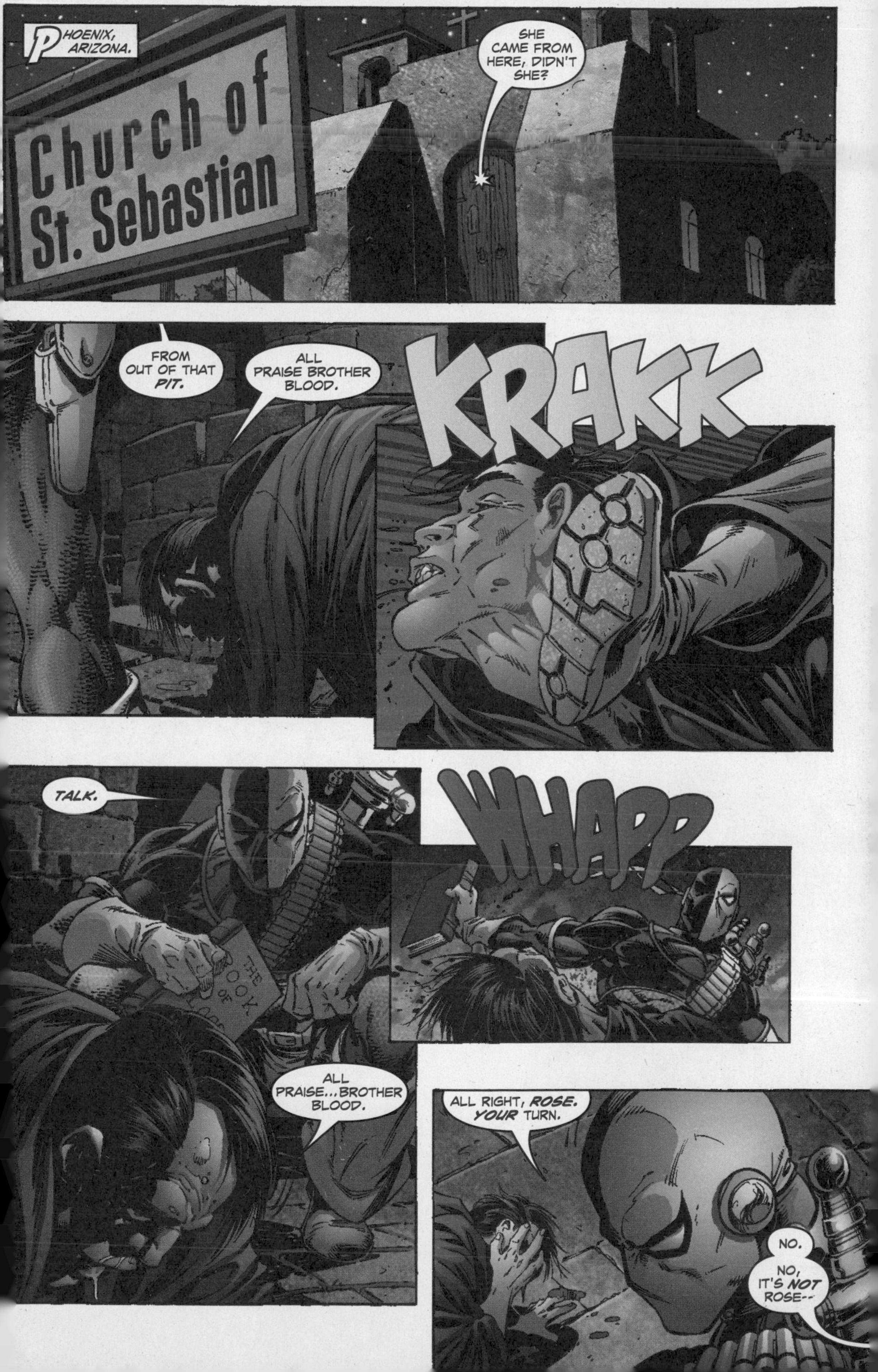
PHOENIX, ARIZONA.
Church of St. Sebastian
SHE CAME FROM HERE, DIDN'T SHE?
FROM OUT OF THAT PIT.
ALL PRAISE BROTHER BLOOD.
KRAKK
TALK.
WHAPP
ALL PRAISE...BROTHER BLOOD.
ALL RIGHT, ROSE. YOUR TURN.
NO.
NO, IT'S NOT ROSE--

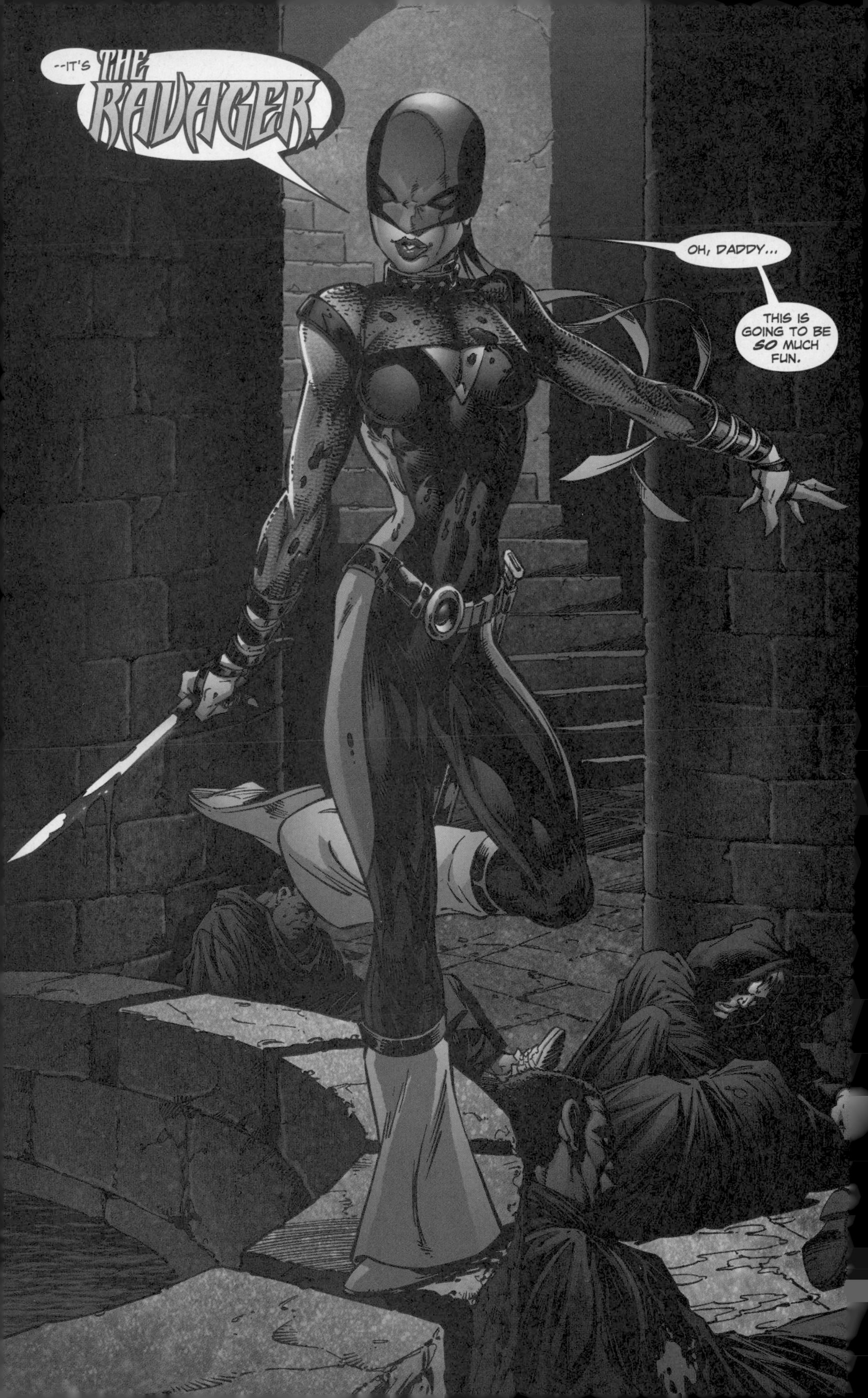
--IT'S THE RAVAGER.
OH, DADDY...
THIS IS GOING TO BE SO MUCH FUN.

Teen Titans

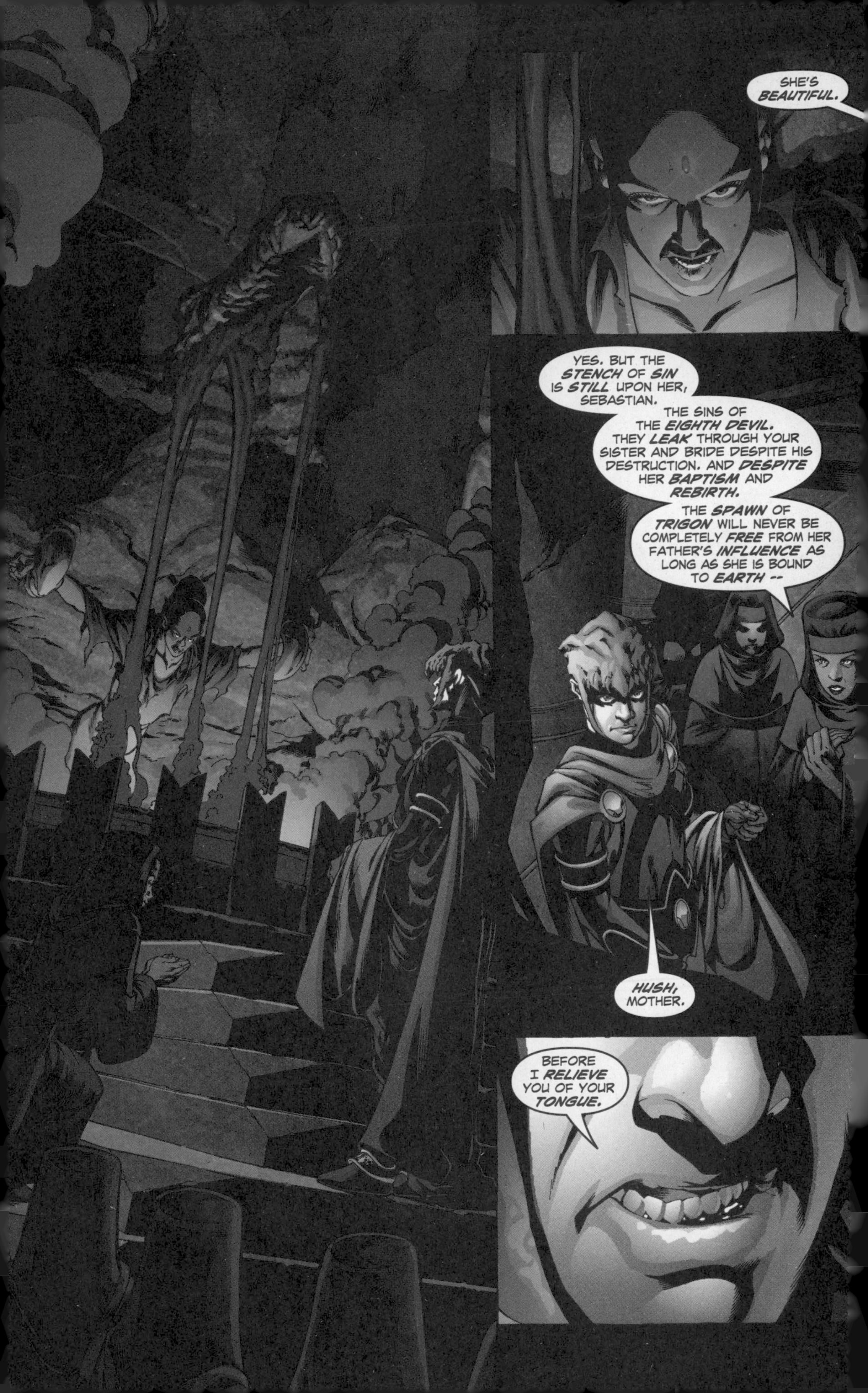
SHE'S BEAUTIFUL.
YES. BUT THE STENCH OF SIN IS STILL UPON HER, SEBASTIAN.
THE SINS OF THE EIGHTH DEVIL. THEY LEAK THROUGH YOUR SISTER AND BRIDE DESPITE HIS DESTRUCTION. AND DESPITE HER BAPTISM AND REBIRTH.
THE SPAWN OF TRIGON WILL NEVER BE COMPLETELY FREE FROM HER FATHER'S INFLUENCE AS LONG AS SHE IS BOUND TO EARTH --
HUSH, MOTHER.
BEFORE I RELIEVE YOU OF YOUR TONGUE.

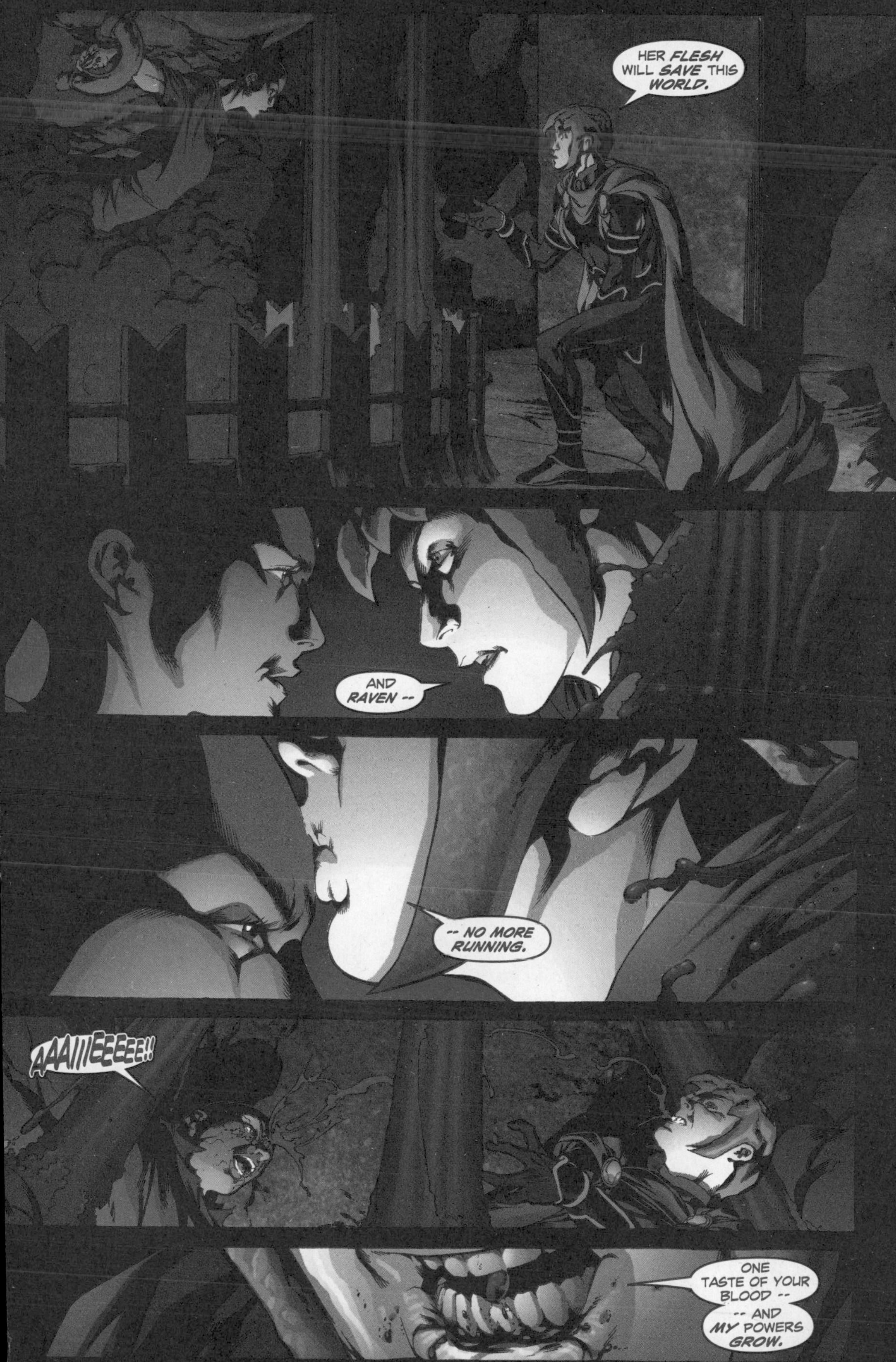
HER FLESH WILL SAVE THIS WORLD.
AND RAVEN --
-- NO MORE RUNNING.
AAAIIIEEEEE!!
ONE TASTE OF YOUR BLOOD --
-- AND MY POWERS GROW.

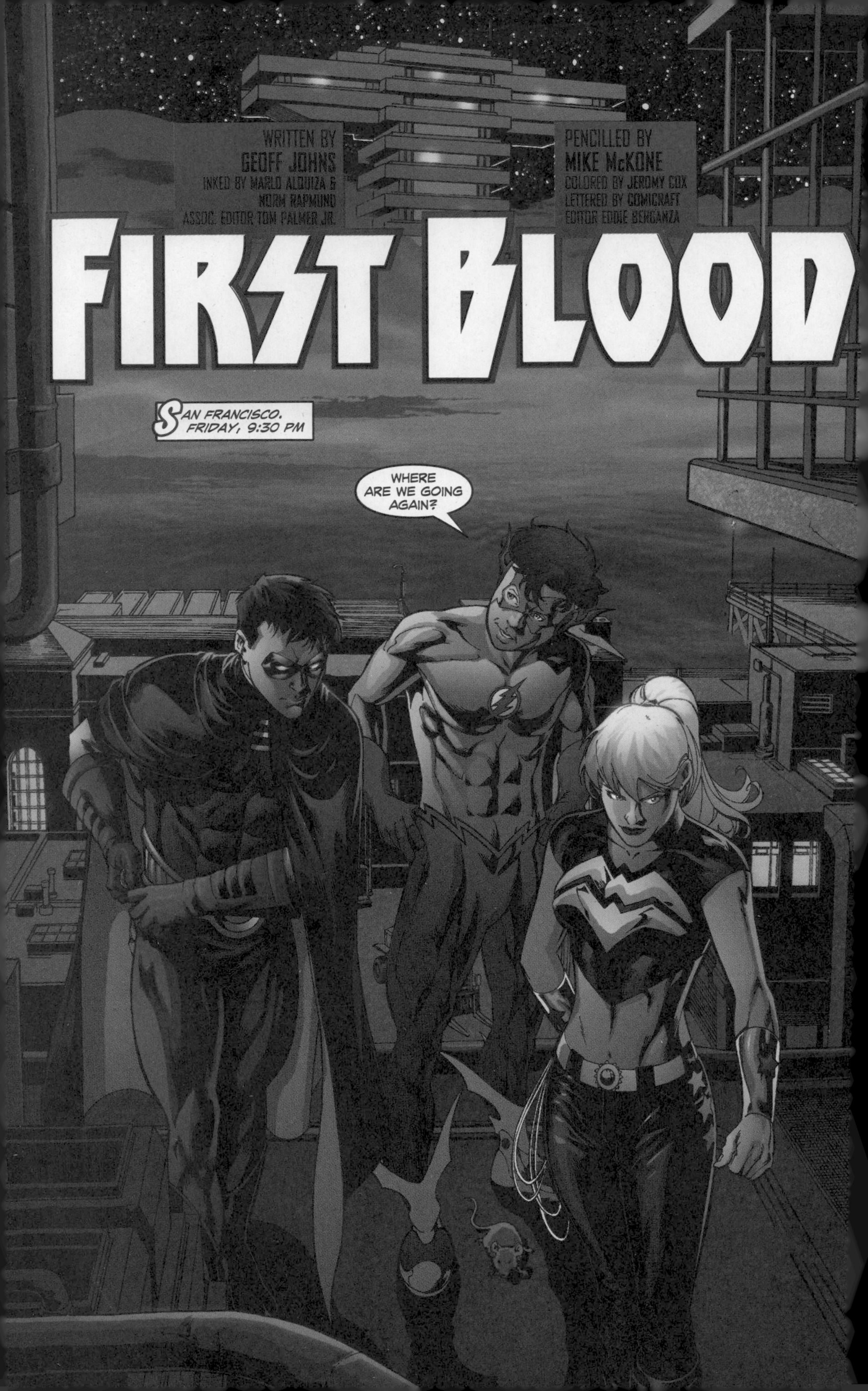
WRITTEN BY
GEOFF JOHNS
INKED BY MARLO ALQUIZA &
NORM RAPMUND
ASSOC. EDITOR TOM PALMER JR.
PENCILLED BY
MIKE McKONE
COLORED BY JEROMY COX
LETTERED BY COMICRAFT
EDITOR EDDIE BERGANZA
FIRST BLOOD
SAN FRANCISCO. FRIDAY, 9:30 PM
WHERE ARE WE GOING AGAIN?

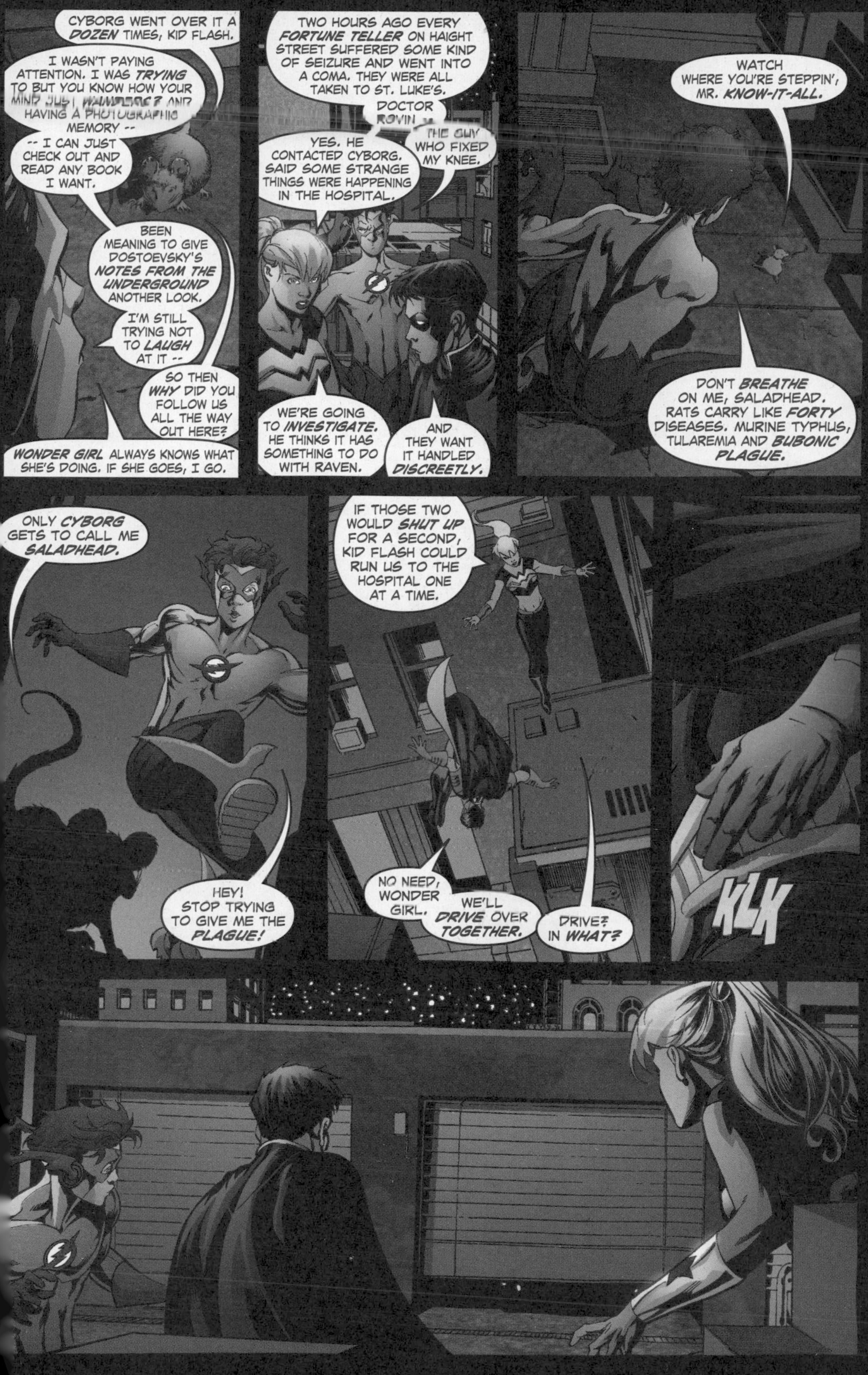
CYBORG WENT OVER IT A DOZEN TIMES, KID FLASH.
I WASN'T PAYING ATTENTION. I WAS TRYING TO BUT YOU KNOW HOW YOUR MIND JUST AND HAVING A PHOTOGRAPHIC MEMORY --
-- I CAN JUST CHECK OUT AND READ ANY BOOK I WANT.
BEEN MEANING TO GIVE DOSTOEVSKY'S NOTES FROM THE UNDERGROUND ANOTHER LOOK.
I'M STILL TRYING NOT TO LAUGH AT IT --
SO THEN WHY DID YOU FOLLOW US ALL THE WAY OUT HERE?
WONDER GIRL ALWAYS KNOWS WHAT SHE'S DOING. IF SHE GOES, I GO.
TWO HOURS AGO EVERY FORTUNE TELLER ON HAIGHT STREET SUFFERED SOME KIND OF SEIZURE AND WENT INTO A COMA. THEY WERE ALL TAKEN TO ST. LUKE'S.
DOCTOR ROVIN --
THE GUY WHO FIXED MY KNEE.
YES. HE CONTACTED CYBORG. SAID SOME STRANGE THINGS WERE HAPPENING IN THE HOSPITAL.
WE'RE GOING TO INVESTIGATE. HE THINKS IT HAS SOMETHING TO DO WITH RAVEN.
AND THEY WANT IT HANDLED DISCREETLY.
WATCH WHERE YOU'RE STEPPIN', MR. KNOW-IT-ALL.
DON'T BREATHE ON ME, SALADHEAD. RATS CARRY LIKE FORTY DISEASES. MURINE TYPHUS, TULAREMIA AND BUBONIC PLAGUE.
ONLY CYBORG GETS TO CALL ME SALADHEAD.
HEY! STOP TRYING TO GIVE ME THE PLAGUE!
IF THOSE TWO WOULD SHUT UP FOR A SECOND, KID FLASH COULD RUN US TO THE HOSPITAL ONE AT A TIME.
NO NEED, WONDER GIRL.
WE'LL DRIVE OVER TOGETHER.
DRIVE? IN WHAT?
KLK

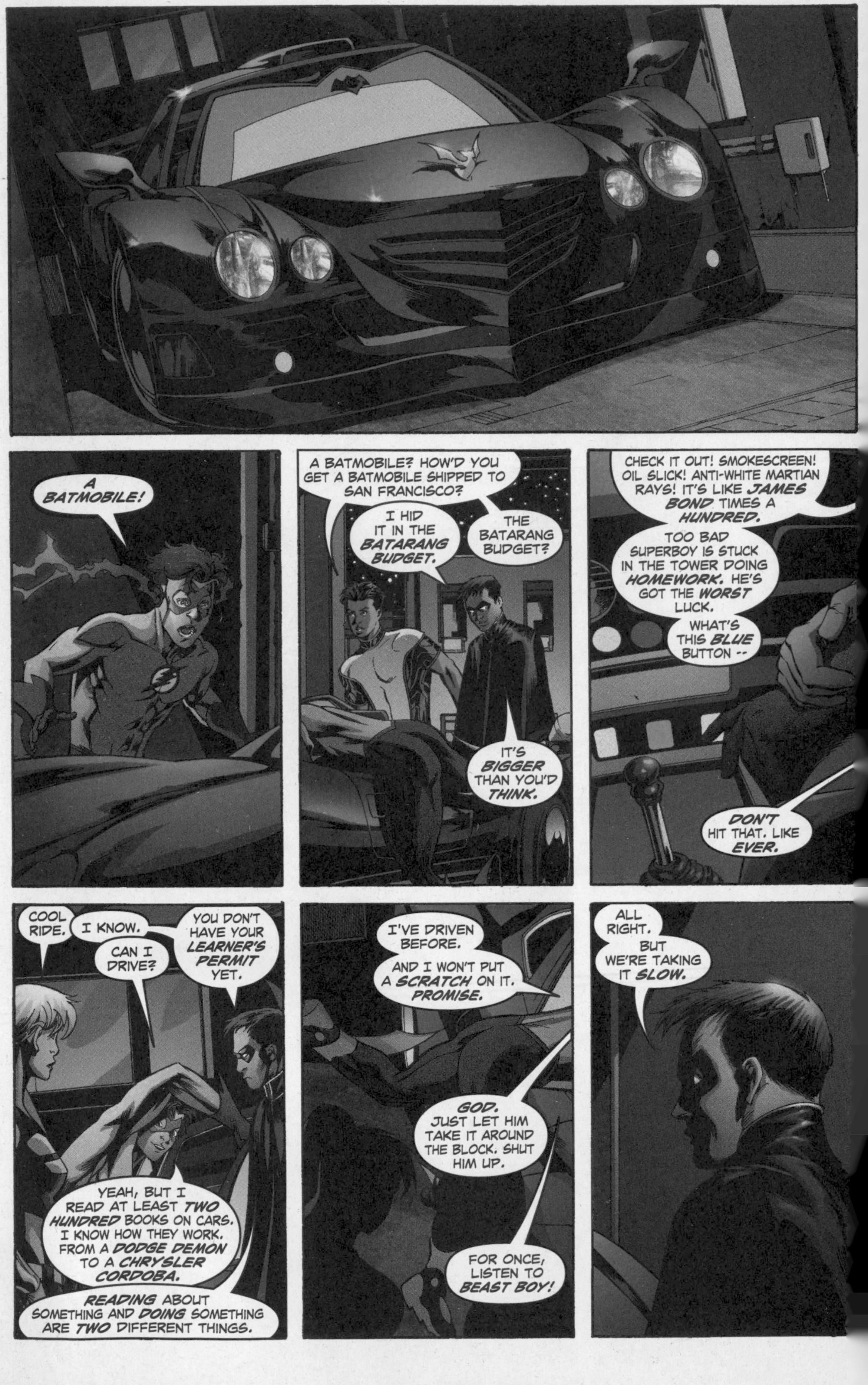
A BATMOBILE!
A BATMOBILE? HOW'D YOU GET A BATMOBILE SHIPPED TO SAN FRANCISCO?
I HID IT IN THE BATARANG BUDGET.
THE BATARANG BUDGET?
IT'S BIGGER THAN YOU'D THINK.
CHECK IT OUT! SMOKESCREEN! OIL SLICK! ANTI-WHITE MARTIAN RAYS! IT'S LIKE JAMES BOND TIMES A HUNDRED.
TOO BAD SUPERBOY IS STUCK IN THE TOWER DOING HOMEWORK. HE'S GOT THE WORST LUCK.
WHAT'S THIS BLUE BUTTON --
DON'T HIT THAT. LIKE EVER.
COOL RIDE.
I KNOW.
CAN I DRIVE?
YOU DON'T HAVE YOUR LEARNER'S PERMIT YET.
YEAH, BUT I READ AT LEAST TWO HUNDRED BOOKS ON CARS. I KNOW HOW THEY WORK. FROM A DODGE DEMON TO A CHRYSLER CORDOBA.
READING ABOUT SOMETHING AND DOING SOMETHING ARE TWO DIFFERENT THINGS.
I'VE DRIVEN BEFORE.
AND I WON'T PUT A SCRATCH ON IT. PROMISE.
GOD. JUST LET HIM TAKE IT AROUND THE BLOCK. SHUT HIM UP.
FOR ONCE, LISTEN TO BEAST BOY!
ALL RIGHT.
BUT WE'RE TAKING IT SLOW.

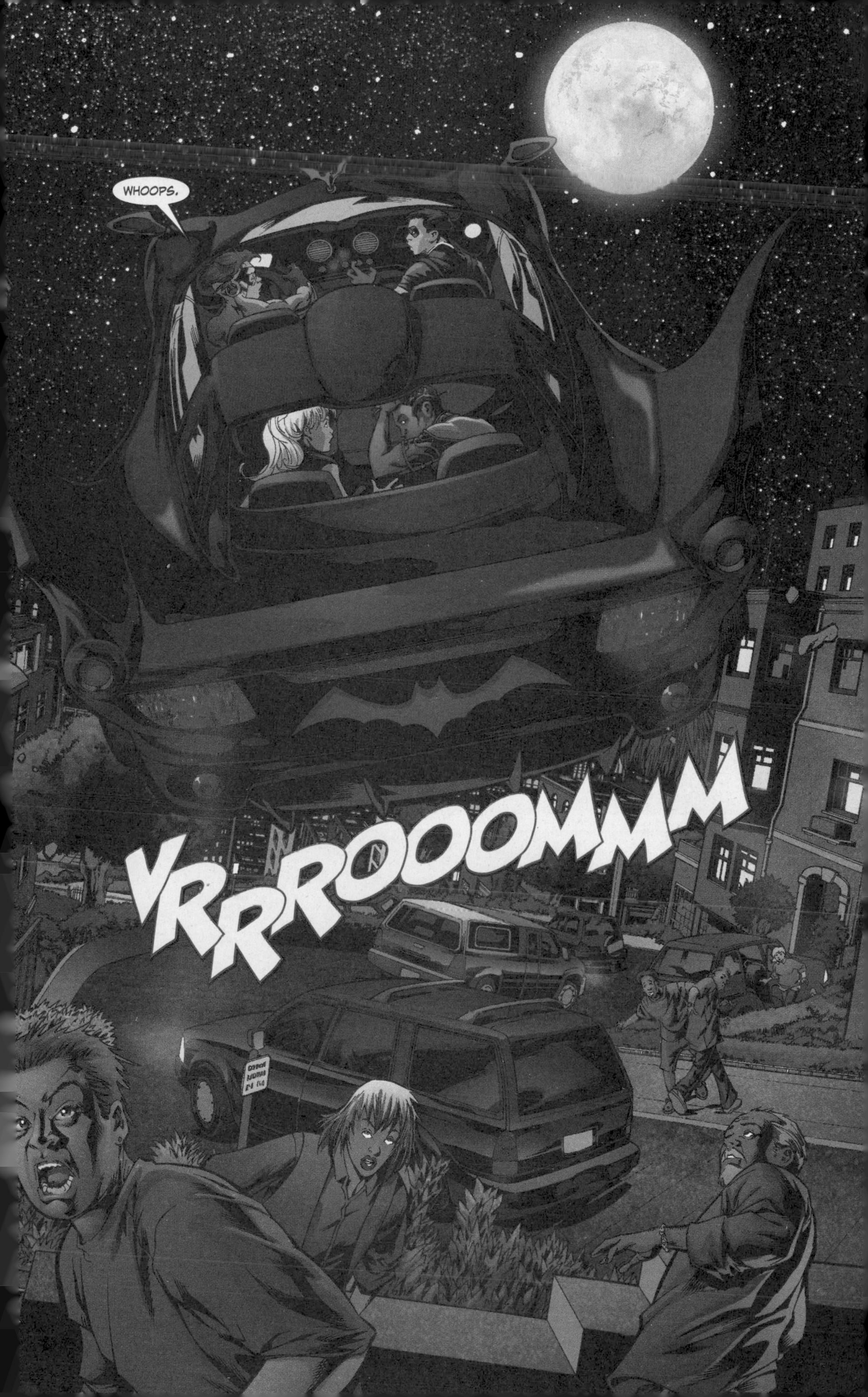
WHOOPS.
VRRROOOMMM

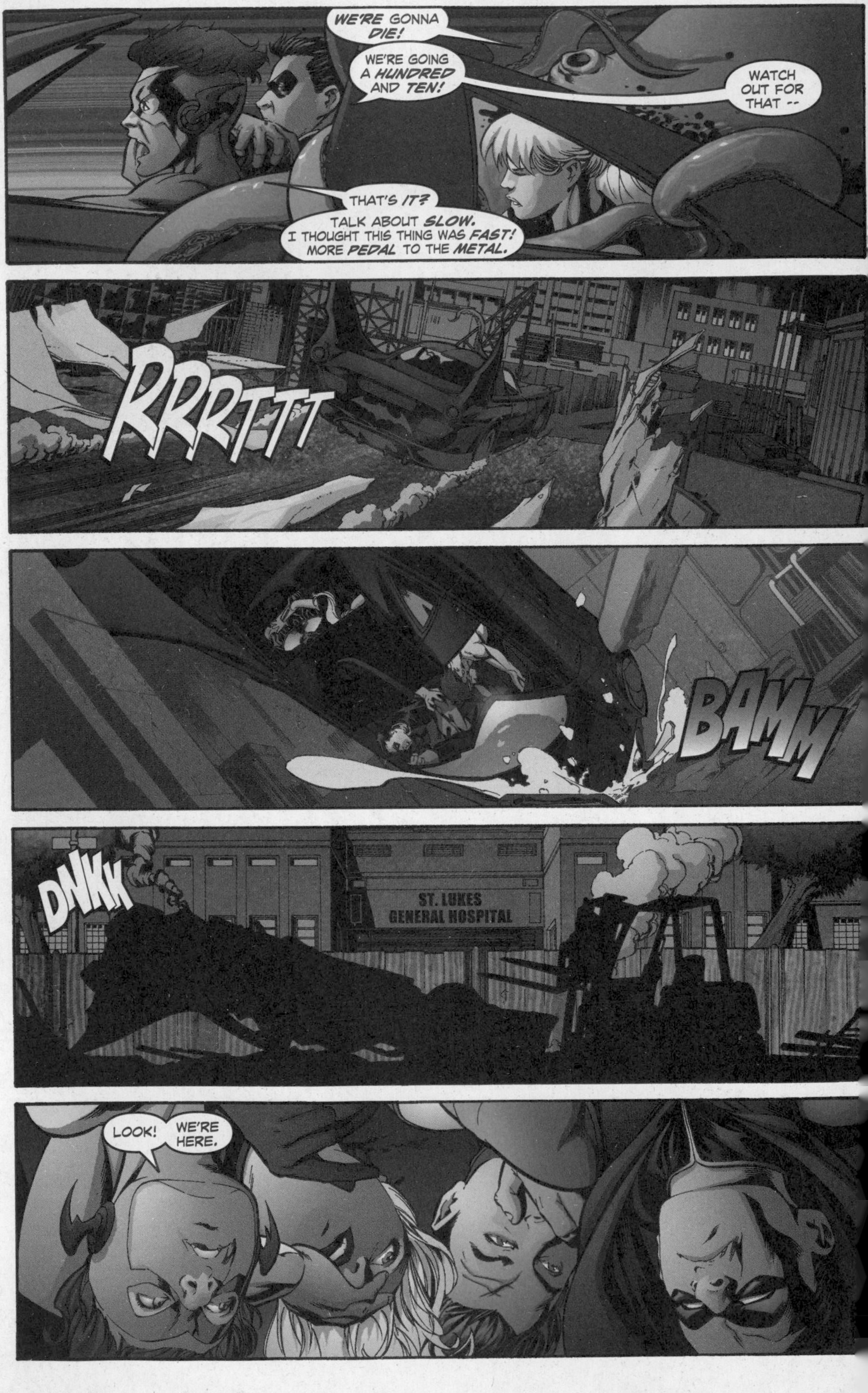
WE'RE GONNA DIE!
WE'RE GOING A HUNDRED AND TEN!
WATCH OUT FOR THAT --
THAT'S IT? TALK ABOUT SLOW. I THOUGHT THIS THING WAS FAST! MORE PEDAL TO THE METAL.
RRRTTT
BAMM
DNKK
ST. LUKES GENERAL HOSPITAL
LOOK!
WE'RE HERE.

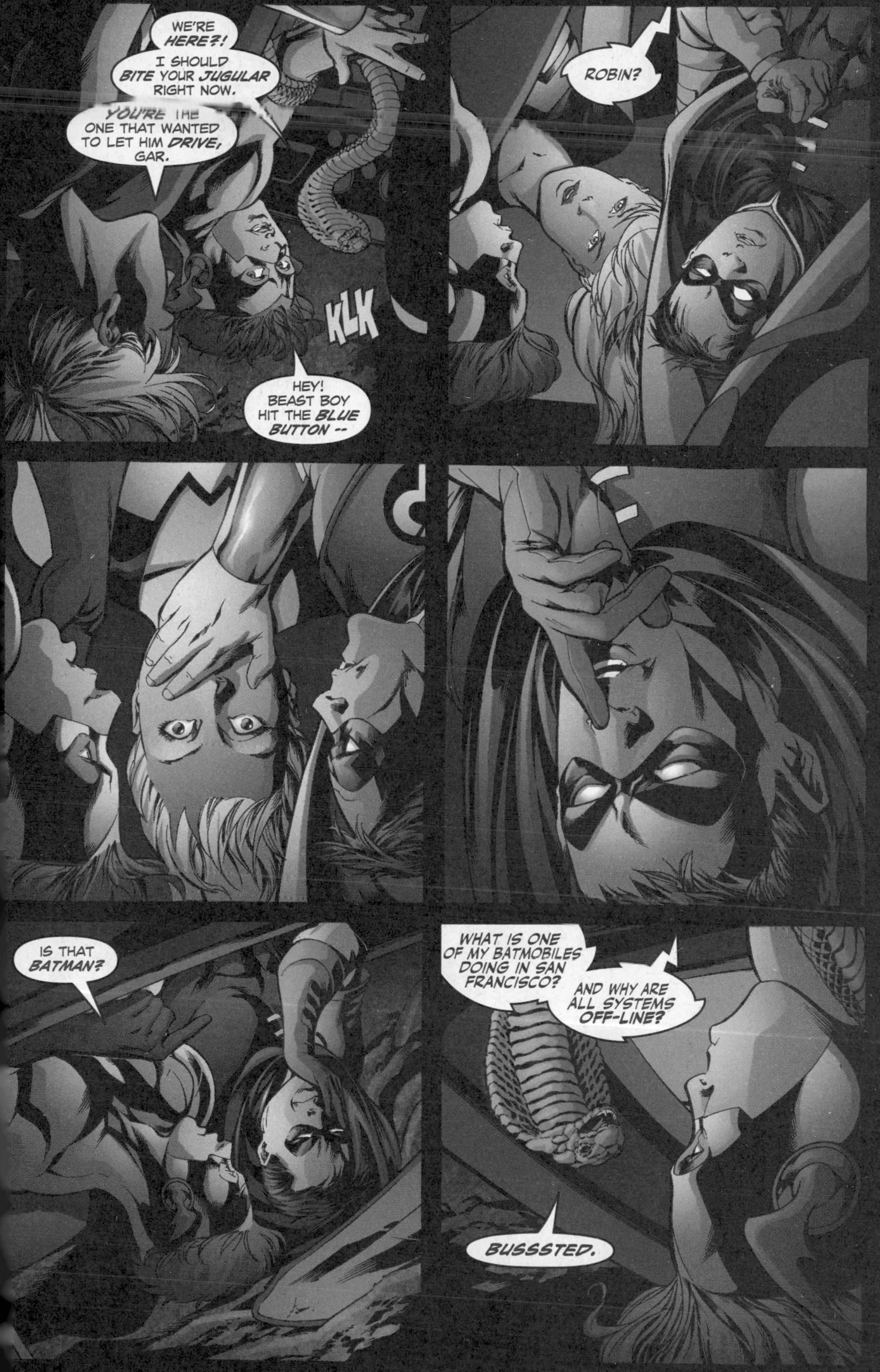
WE'RE HERE?! I SHOULD BITE YOUR JUGULAR RIGHT NOW.
YOU'RE THE ONE THAT WANTED TO LET HIM DRIVE, GAR.
KLK
HEY! BEAST BOY HIT THE BLUE BUTTON --
ROBIN?
IS THAT BATMAN?
WHAT IS ONE OF MY BATMOBILES DOING IN SAN FRANCISCO?
AND WHY ARE ALL SYSTEMS OFF-LINE?
BUSSSTED.

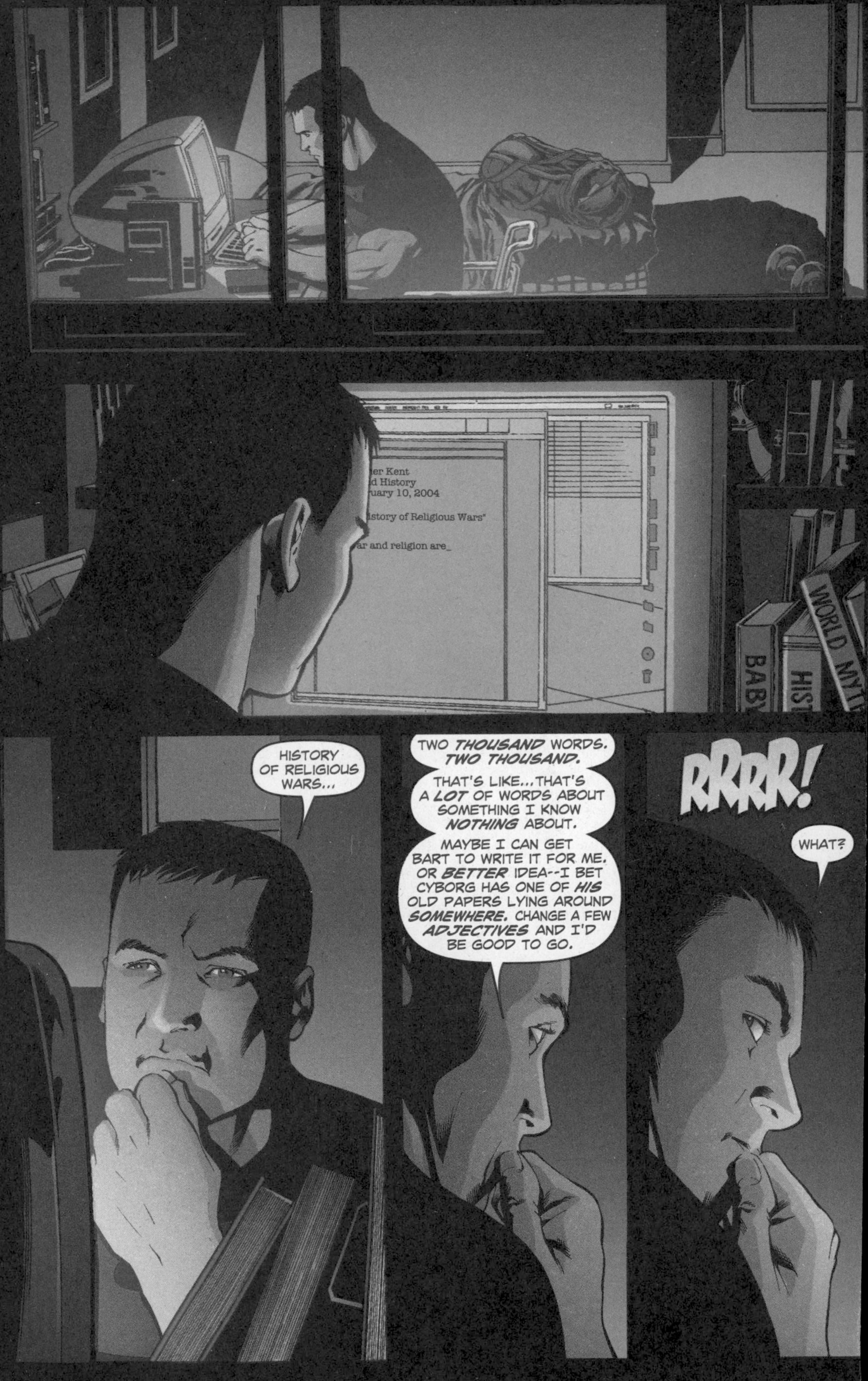

ier Kent
d History
uary 10, 2004
istory of Religious Wars"
ar and religion are_
WORLD MYT
BABY
HIST
HISTORY OF RELIGIOUS WARS...
TWO *THOUSAND* WORDS. *TWO THOUSAND.*
THAT'S LIKE...THAT'S A *LOT* OF WORDS ABOUT SOMETHING I KNOW *NOTHING* ABOUT.
MAYBE I CAN GET BART TO WRITE IT FOR ME. OR *BETTER* IDEA--I BET CYBORG HAS ONE OF *HIS* OLD PAPERS LYING AROUND *SOMEWHERE.* CHANGE A FEW *ADJECTIVES* AND I'D BE GOOD TO GO.
RRRR!
WHAT?

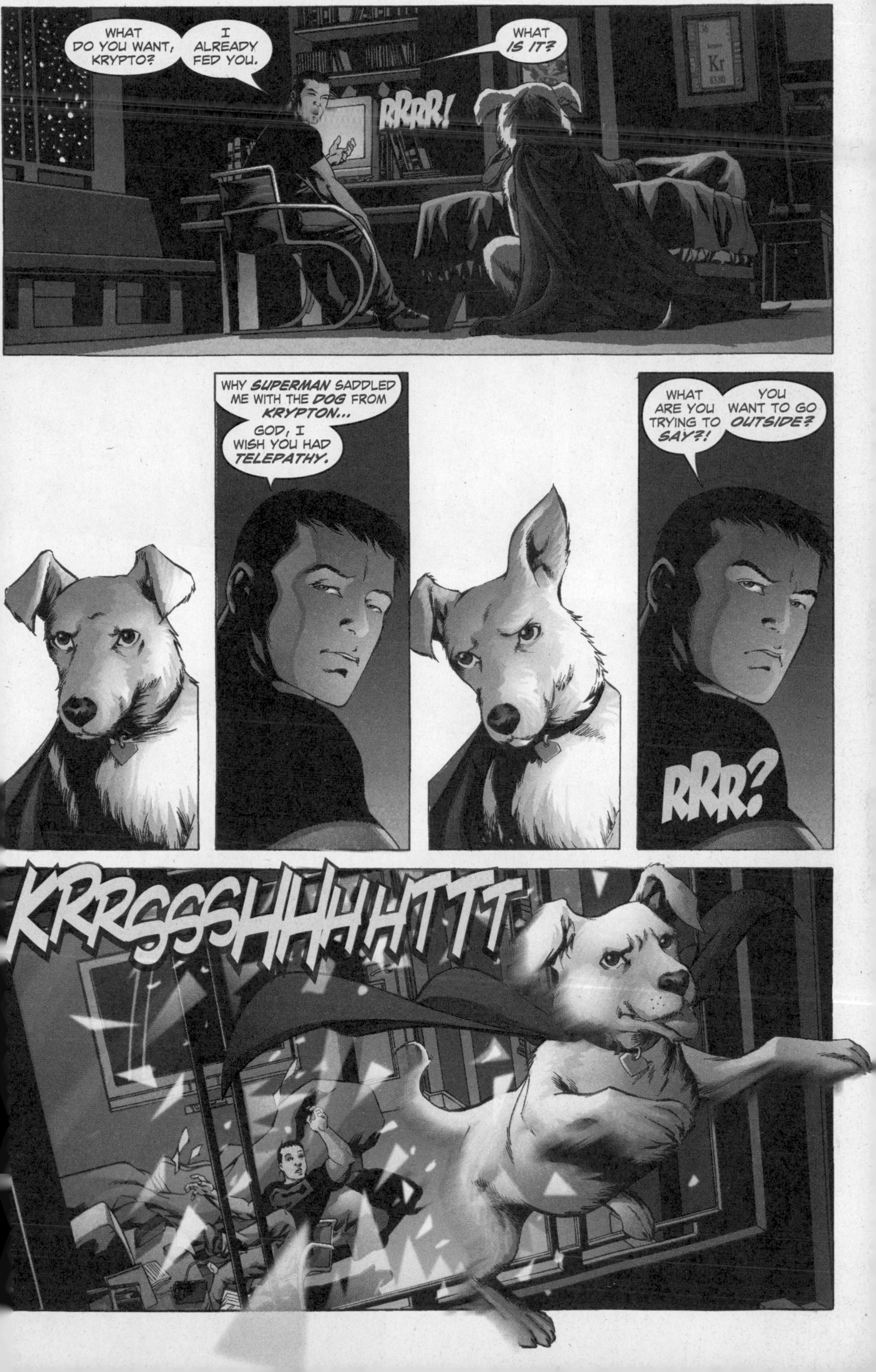
WHAT DO YOU WANT, KRYPTO?
I ALREADY FED YOU.
RRRR!
WHAT IS IT?
WHY SUPERMAN SADDLED ME WITH THE DOG FROM KRYPTON...
GOD, I WISH YOU HAD TELEPATHY.
WHAT ARE YOU TRYING TO SAY?!
YOU WANT TO GO OUTSIDE?
RRR?
KRRSSSHHHHTTT

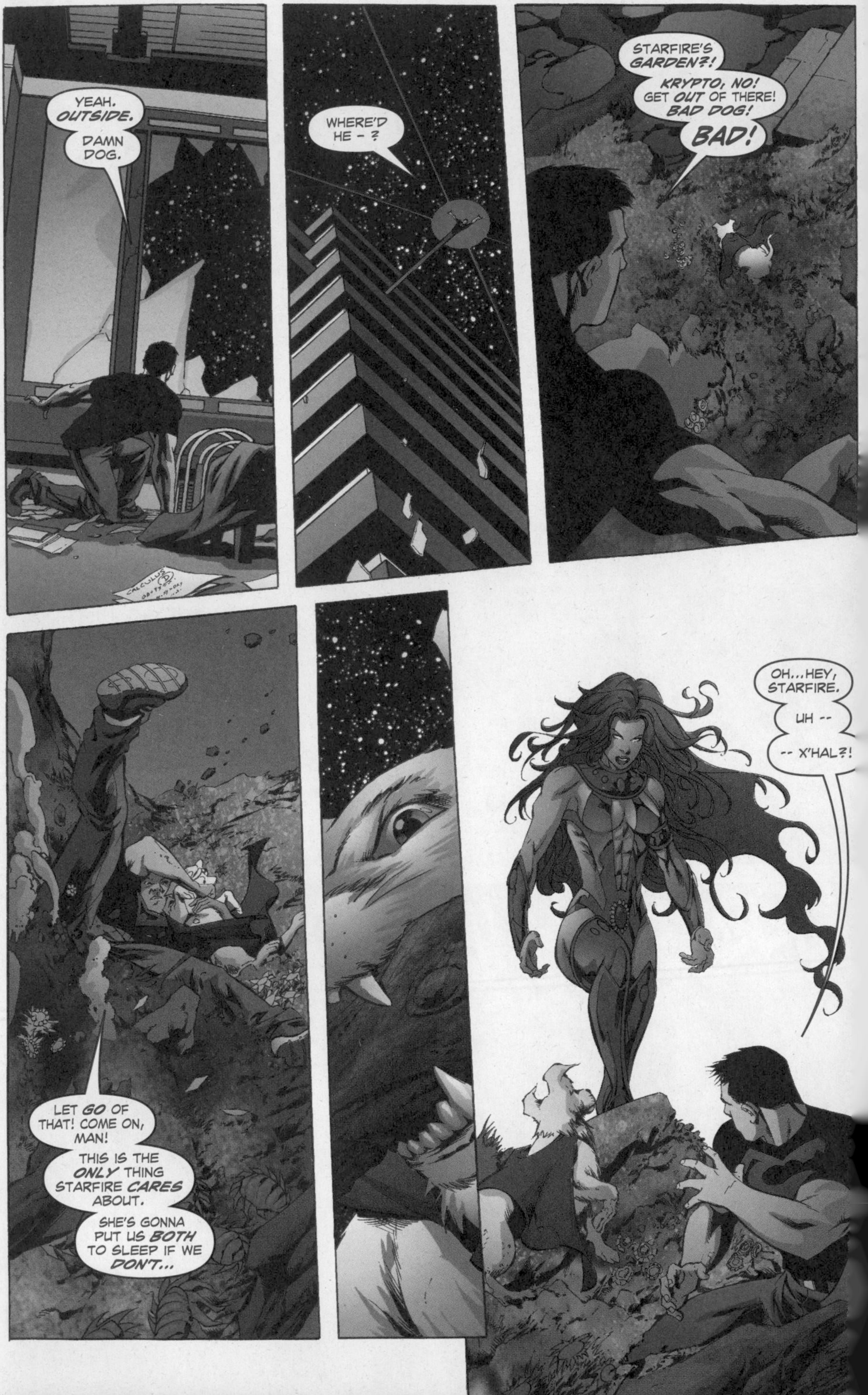
YEAH. OUTSIDE.
DAMN DOG.
WHERE'D HE - ?
STARFIRE'S GARDEN?!
KRYPTO, NO! GET OUT OF THERE! BAD DOG!
BAD!
LET GO OF THAT! COME ON, MAN!
THIS IS THE ONLY THING STARFIRE CARES ABOUT.
SHE'S GONNA PUT US BOTH TO SLEEP IF WE DON'T...
OH...HEY, STARFIRE.
UH --
-- X'HAL?!

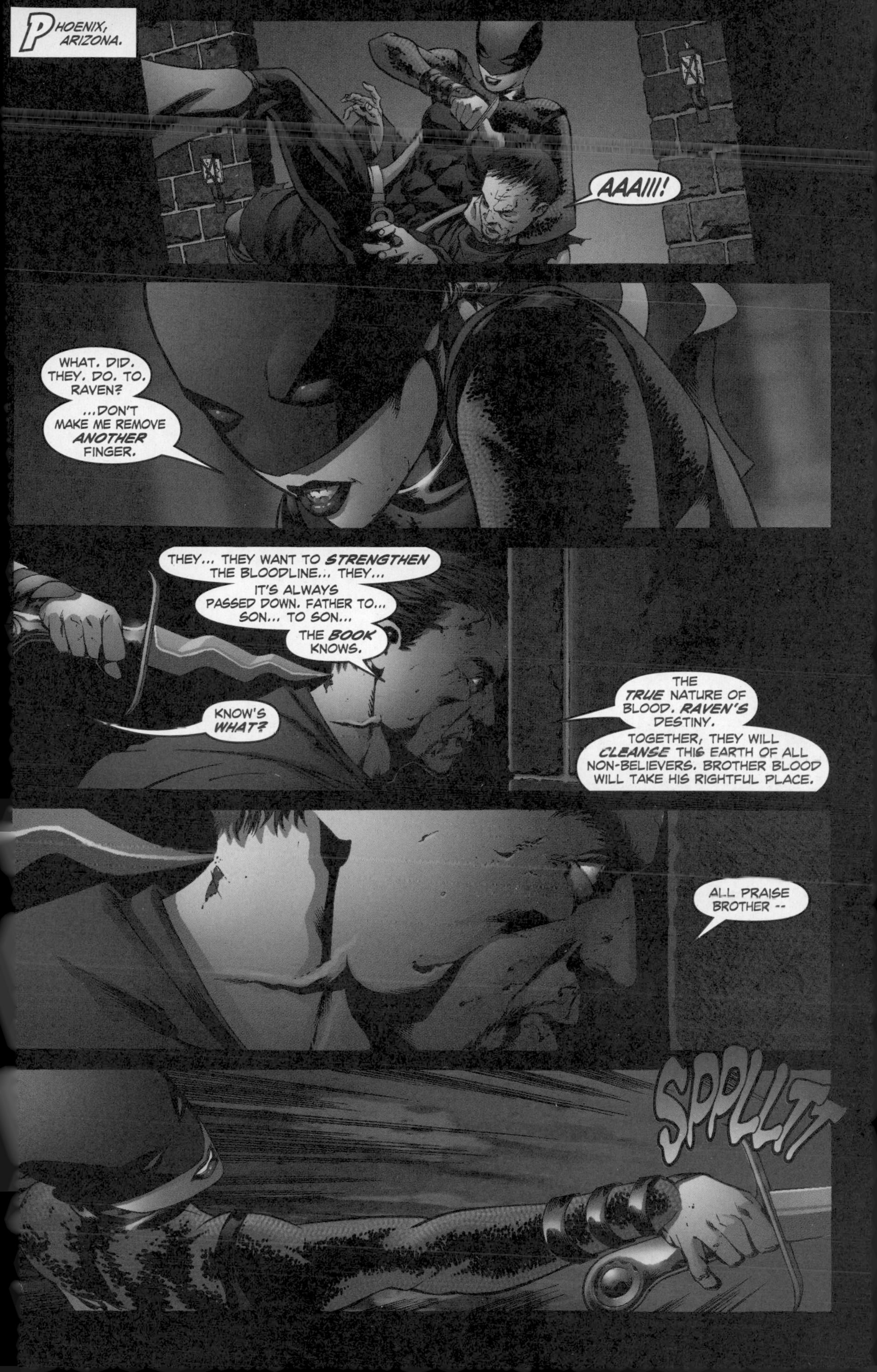
PHOENIX, ARIZONA.
AAAIII!
WHAT. DID. THEY. DO. TO. RAVEN?
...DON'T MAKE ME REMOVE ANOTHER FINGER.
THEY... THEY WANT TO STRENGTHEN THE BLOODLINE... THEY...
IT'S ALWAYS PASSED DOWN. FATHER TO... SON... TO SON...
THE BOOK KNOWS.
KNOW'S WHAT?
THE TRUE NATURE OF BLOOD. RAVEN'S DESTINY.
TOGETHER, THEY WILL CLEANSE THIS EARTH OF ALL NON-BELIEVERS. BROTHER BLOOD WILL TAKE HIS RIGHTFUL PLACE.
ALL PRAISE BROTHER --
SPPLLT

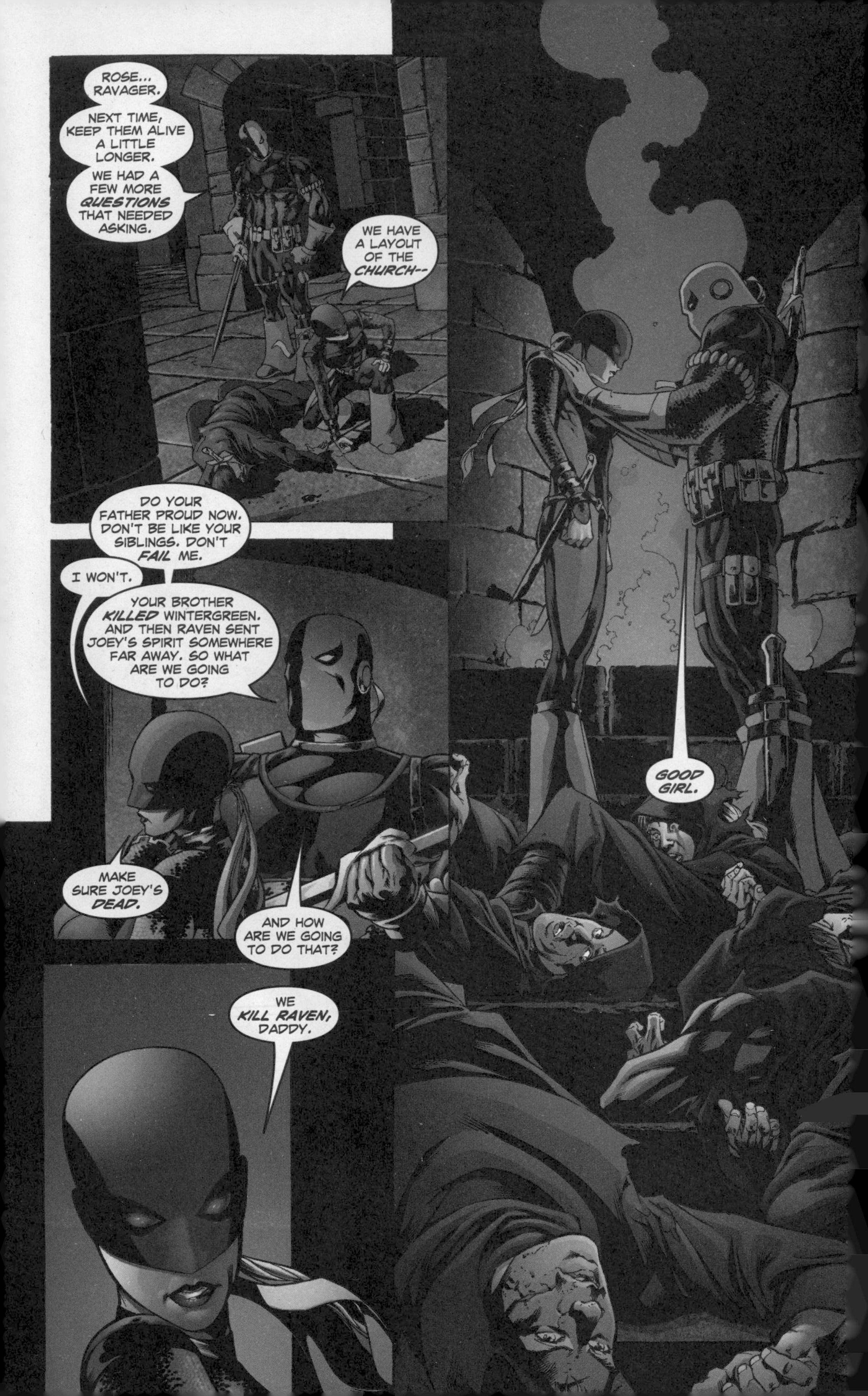
ROSE... RAVAGER.
NEXT TIME, KEEP THEM ALIVE A LITTLE LONGER.
WE HAD A FEW MORE QUESTIONS THAT NEEDED ASKING.
WE HAVE A LAYOUT OF THE CHURCH--
DO YOUR FATHER PROUD NOW. DON'T BE LIKE YOUR SIBLINGS. DON'T FAIL ME.
I WON'T.
GOOD GIRL.
YOUR BROTHER KILLED WINTERGREEN. AND THEN RAVEN SENT JOEY'S SPIRIT SOMEWHERE FAR AWAY. SO WHAT ARE WE GOING TO DO?
MAKE SURE JOEY'S DEAD.
AND HOW ARE WE GOING TO DO THAT?
WE KILL RAVEN, DADDY.

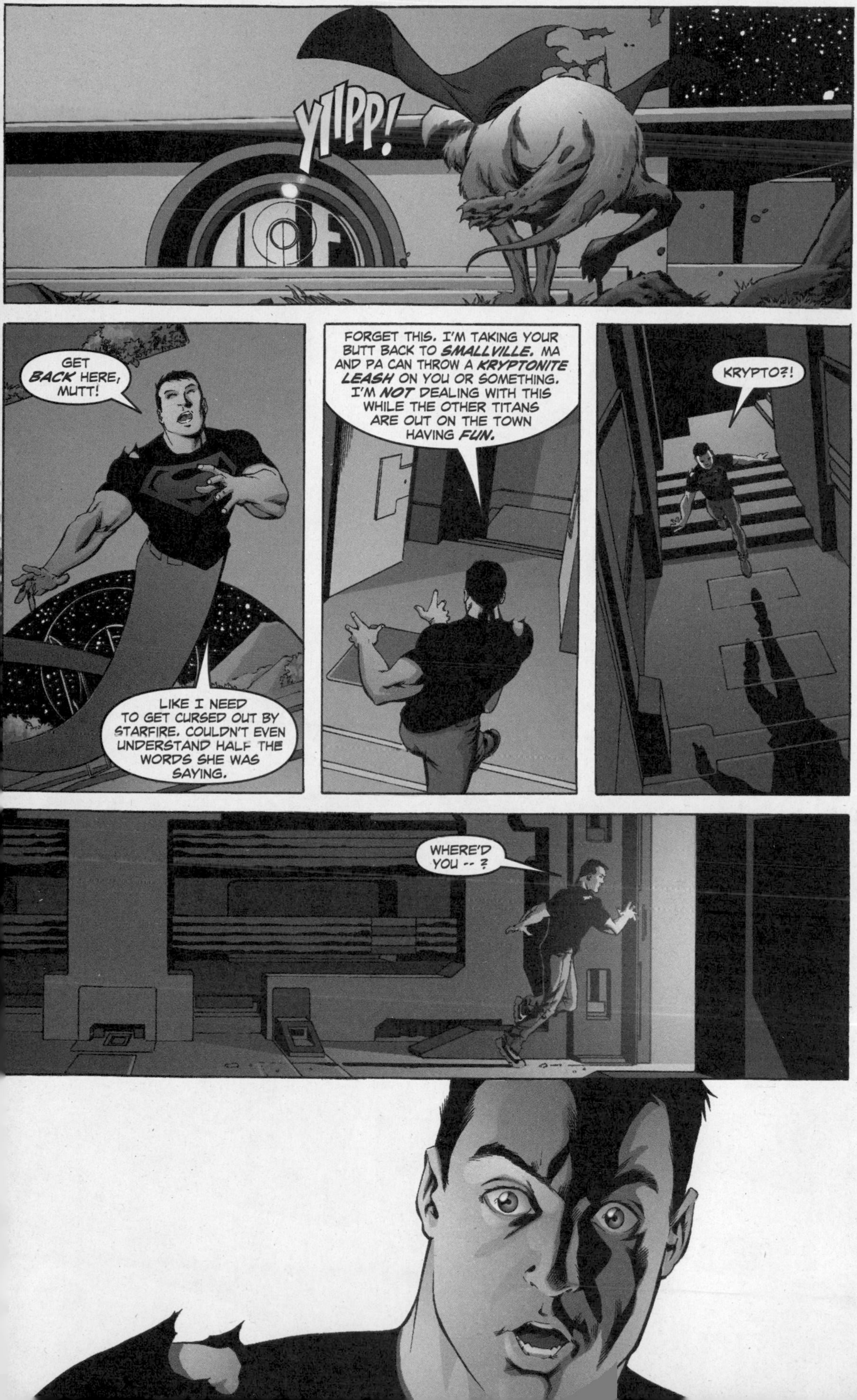
YIIPP!
GET BACK HERE, MUTT!
LIKE I NEED TO GET CURSED OUT BY STARFIRE. COULDN'T EVEN UNDERSTAND HALF THE WORDS SHE WAS SAYING.
FORGET THIS. I'M TAKING YOUR BUTT BACK TO SMALLVILLE. MA AND PA CAN THROW A KRYPTONITE LEASH ON YOU OR SOMETHING. I'M NOT DEALING WITH THIS WHILE THE OTHER TITANS ARE OUT ON THE TOWN HAVING FUN.
KRYPTO?!
WHERE'D YOU -- ?

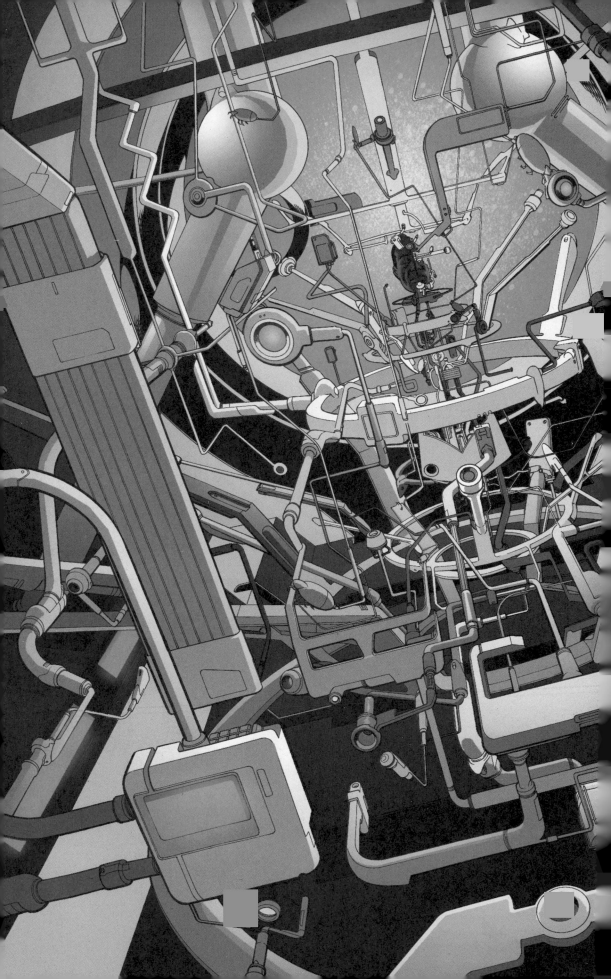

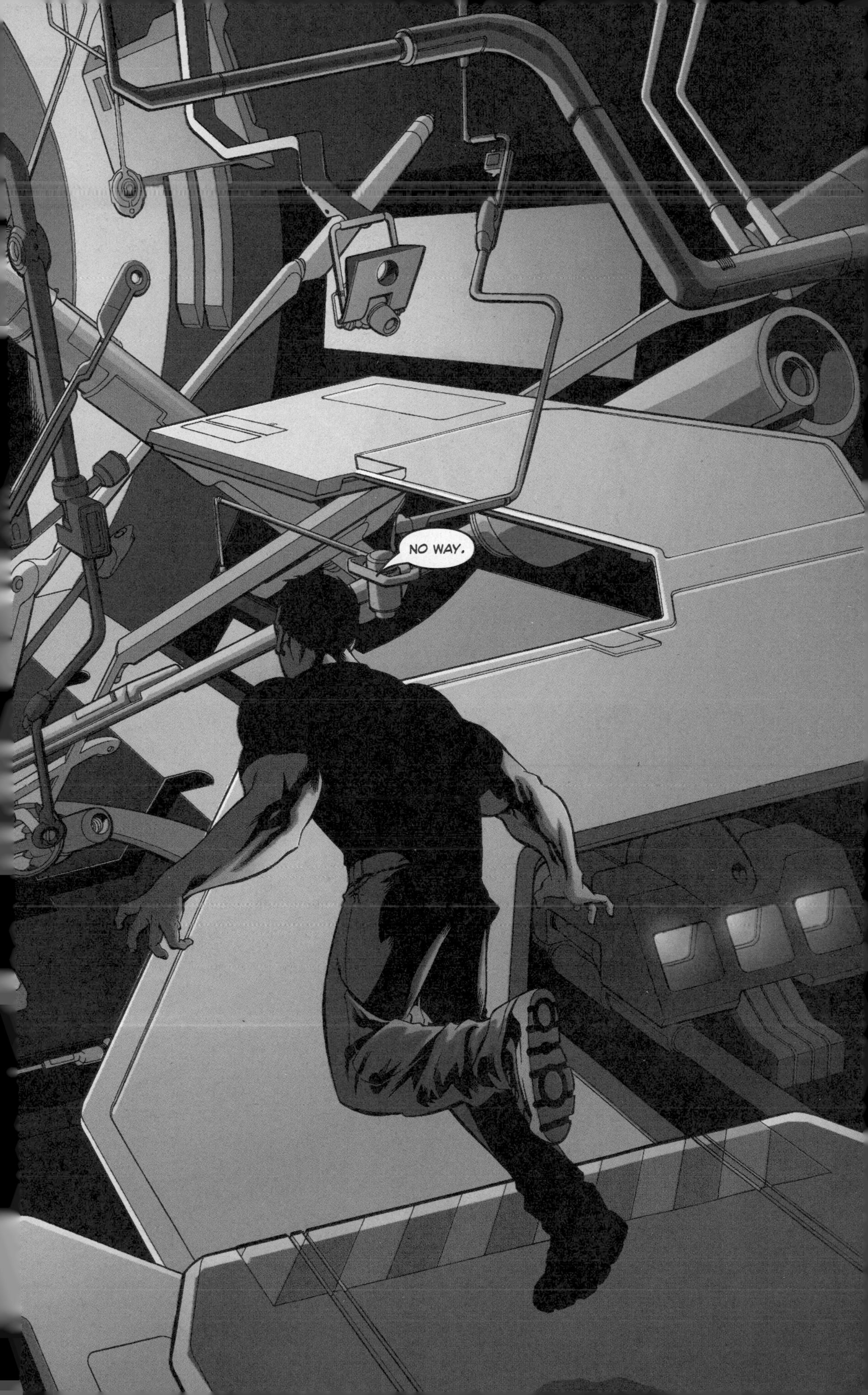
NO WAY.

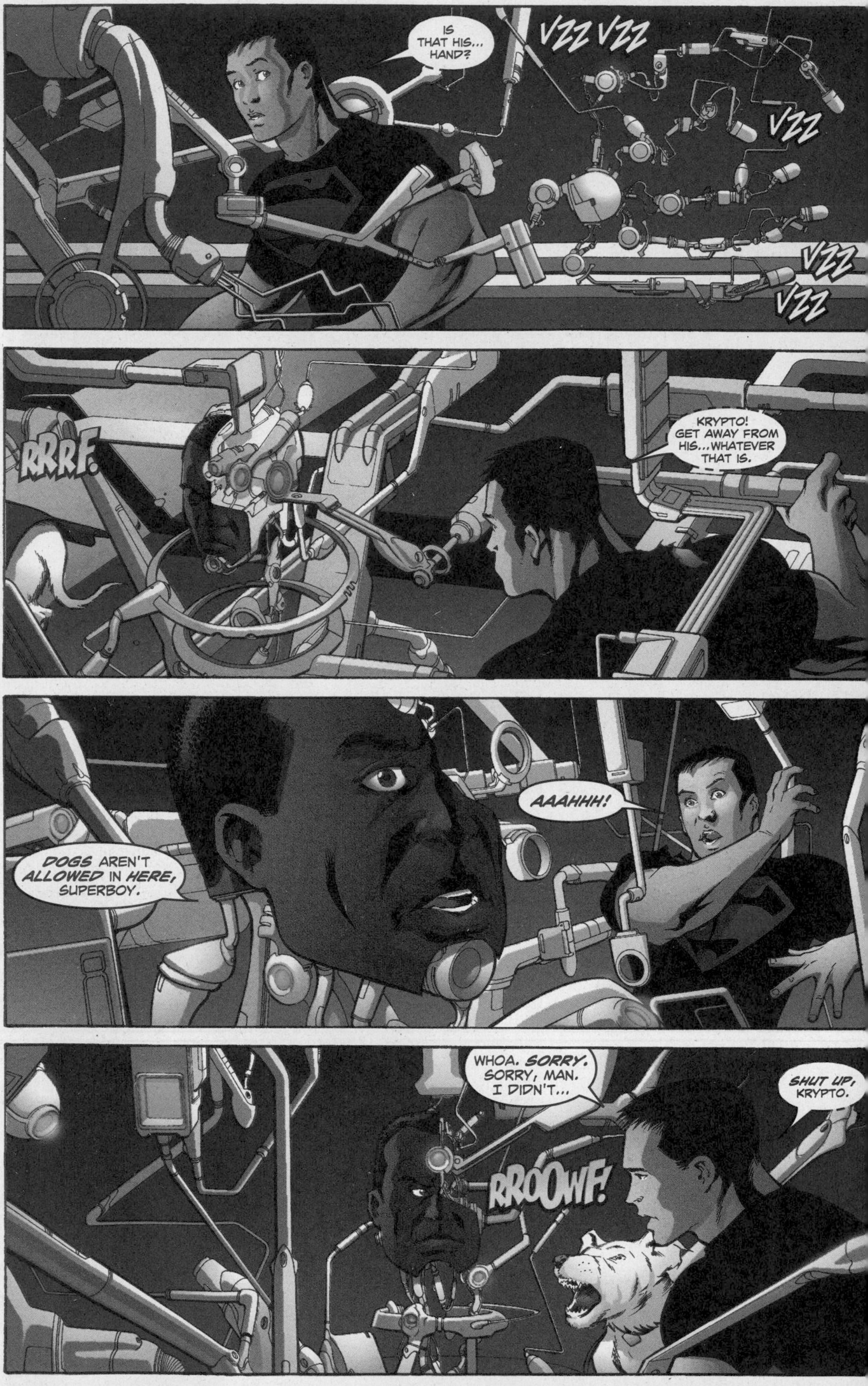
IS THAT HIS... HAND?
VZZ VZZ
VZZ
VZZ
VZZ
RRRF.
KRYPTO! GET AWAY FROM HIS...WHATEVER THAT IS.
AAAHHH!
DOGS AREN'T ALLOWED IN HERE, SUPERBOY.
WHOA. SORRY. SORRY, MAN. I DIDN'T...
SHUT UP, KRYPTO.
RROOWF!

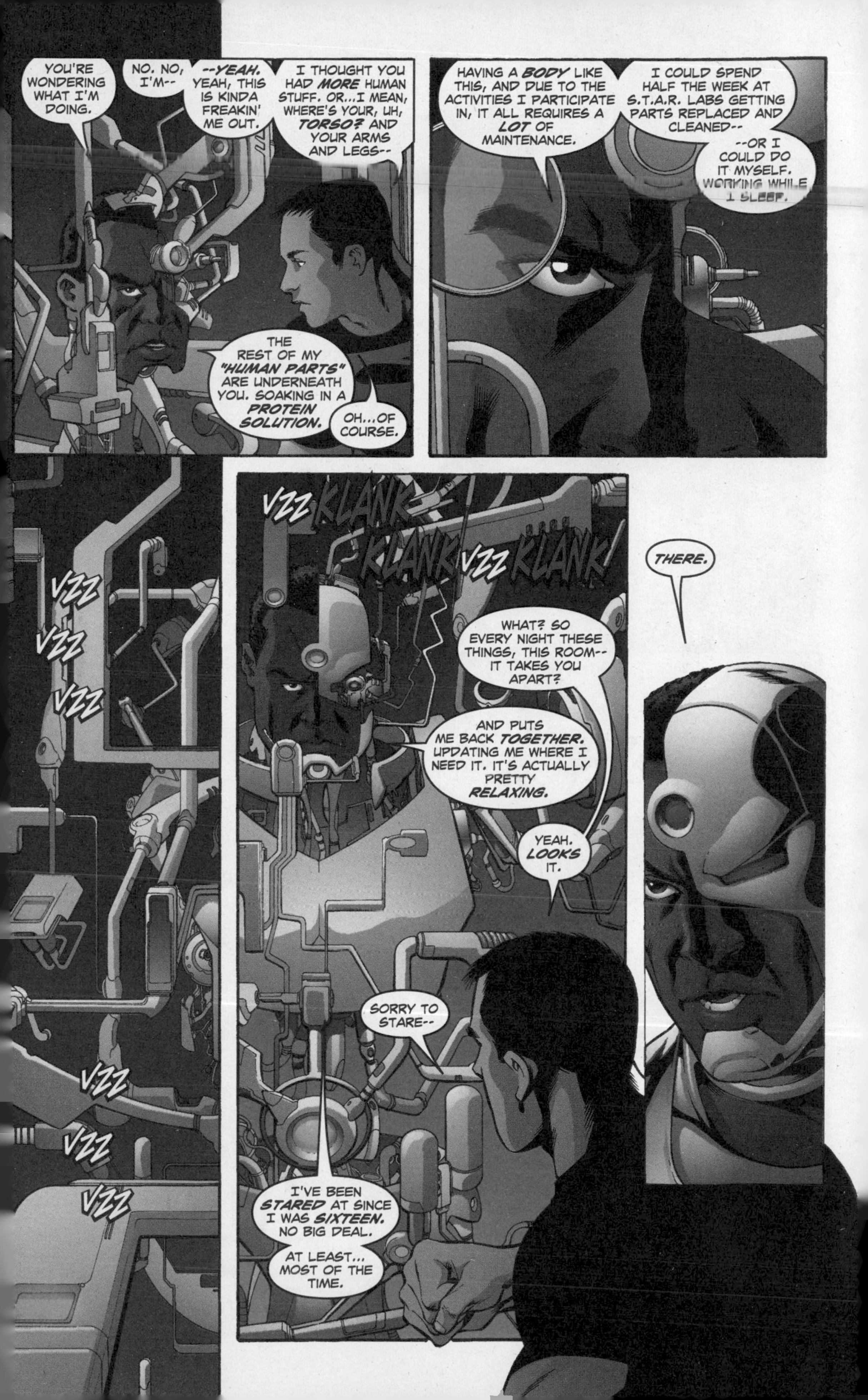

YOU'RE WONDERING WHAT I'M DOING.
NO. NO, I'M--
--YEAH. YEAH, THIS IS KINDA FREAKIN' ME OUT.
I THOUGHT YOU HAD MORE HUMAN STUFF. OR...I MEAN, WHERE'S YOUR, UH, TORSO? AND YOUR ARMS AND LEGS--
THE REST OF MY "HUMAN PARTS" ARE UNDERNEATH YOU. SOAKING IN A PROTEIN SOLUTION.
OH...OF COURSE.
HAVING A BODY LIKE THIS, AND DUE TO THE ACTIVITIES I PARTICIPATE IN, IT ALL REQUIRES A LOT OF MAINTENANCE.
I COULD SPEND HALF THE WEEK AT S.T.A.R. LABS GETTING PARTS REPLACED AND CLEANED--
--OR I COULD DO IT MYSELF. WORKING WHILE I SLEEP.
VZZ
VZZ
VZZ
VZZ KLANK
KLANK
VZZ KLANK
WHAT? SO EVERY NIGHT THESE THINGS, THIS ROOM-- IT TAKES YOU APART?
AND PUTS ME BACK TOGETHER. UPDATING ME WHERE I NEED IT. IT'S ACTUALLY PRETTY RELAXING.
YEAH. LOOKS IT.
SORRY TO STARE--
I'VE BEEN STARED AT SINCE I WAS SIXTEEN. NO BIG DEAL.
AT LEAST... MOST OF THE TIME.
VZZ
VZZ
VZZ
THERE.

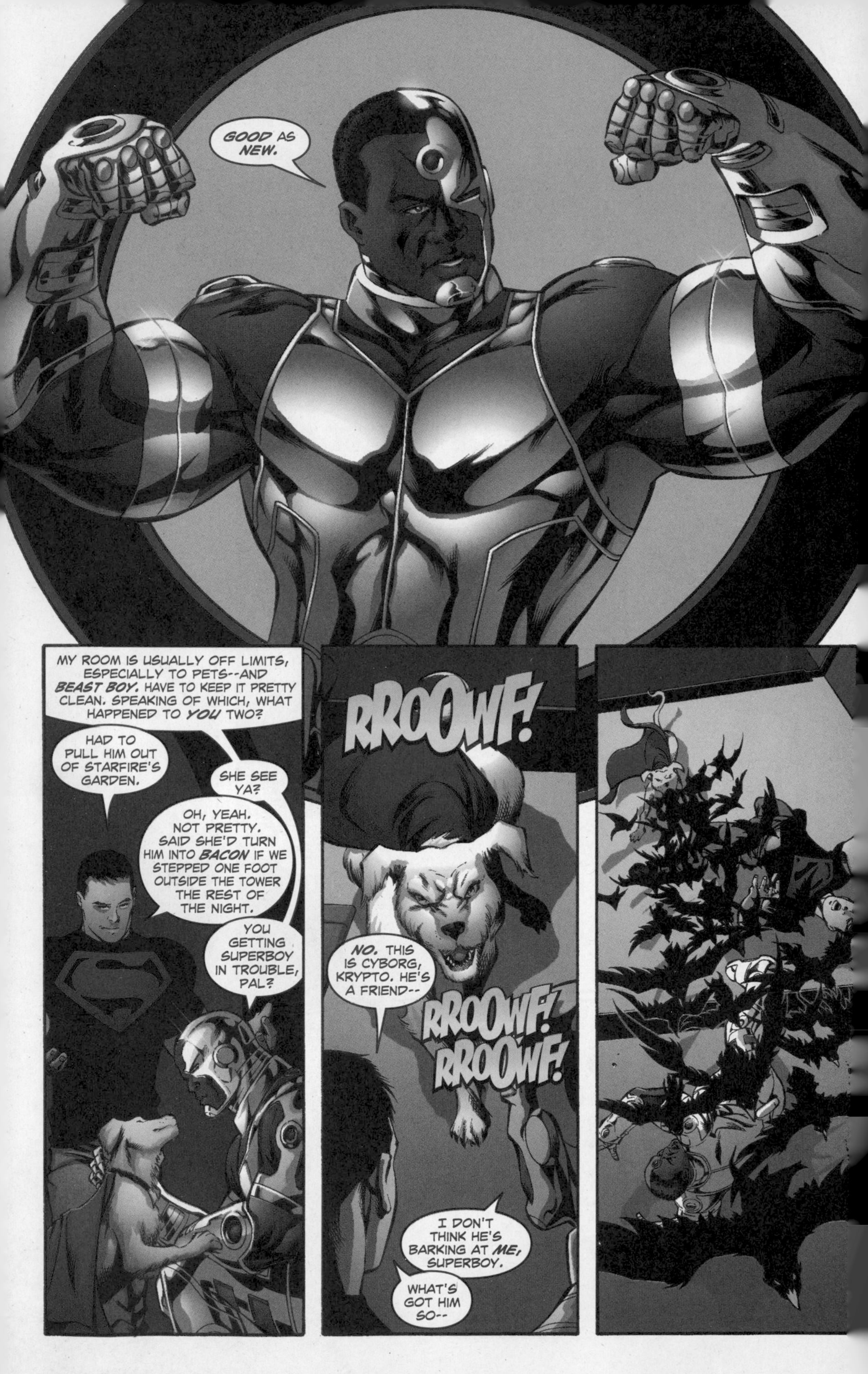
GOOD AS NEW.
MY ROOM IS USUALLY OFF LIMITS, ESPECIALLY TO PETS--AND BEAST BOY. HAVE TO KEEP IT PRETTY CLEAN. SPEAKING OF WHICH, WHAT HAPPENED TO YOU TWO?
HAD TO PULL HIM OUT OF STARFIRE'S GARDEN.
SHE SEE YA?
OH, YEAH. NOT PRETTY. SAID SHE'D TURN HIM INTO BACON IF WE STEPPED ONE FOOT OUTSIDE THE TOWER THE REST OF THE NIGHT.
YOU GETTING SUPERBOY IN TROUBLE, PAL?
RROOWF!
NO. THIS IS CYBORG, KRYPTO. HE'S A FRIEND--
RROOWF! RROOWF!
I DON'T THINK HE'S BARKING AT ME, SUPERBOY.
WHAT'S GOT HIM SO--

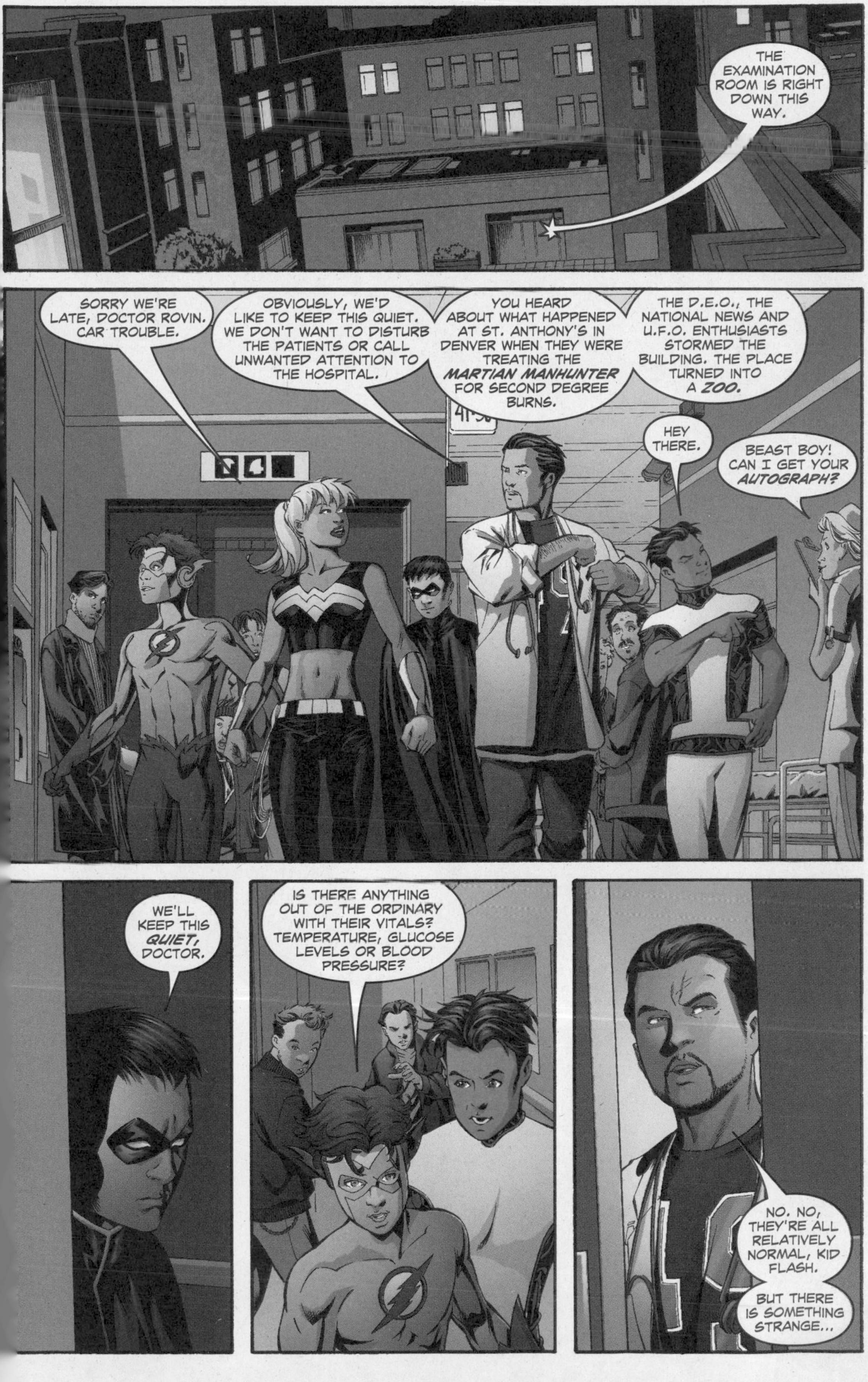
THE EXAMINATION ROOM IS RIGHT DOWN THIS WAY.
SORRY WE'RE LATE, DOCTOR ROVIN. CAR TROUBLE.
OBVIOUSLY, WE'D LIKE TO KEEP THIS QUIET. WE DON'T WANT TO DISTURB THE PATIENTS OR CALL UNWANTED ATTENTION TO THE HOSPITAL.
YOU HEARD ABOUT WHAT HAPPENED AT ST. ANTHONY'S IN DENVER WHEN THEY WERE TREATING THE MARTIAN MANHUNTER FOR SECOND DEGREE BURNS.
THE D.E.O., THE NATIONAL NEWS AND U.F.O. ENTHUSIASTS STORMED THE BUILDING. THE PLACE TURNED INTO A ZOO.
HEY THERE.
BEAST BOY! CAN I GET YOUR AUTOGRAPH?
WE'LL KEEP THIS QUIET, DOCTOR.
IS THERE ANYTHING OUT OF THE ORDINARY WITH THEIR VITALS? TEMPERATURE, GLUCOSE LEVELS OR BLOOD PRESSURE?
NO. NO, THEY'RE ALL RELATIVELY NORMAL, KID FLASH.
BUT THERE IS SOMETHING STRANGE...

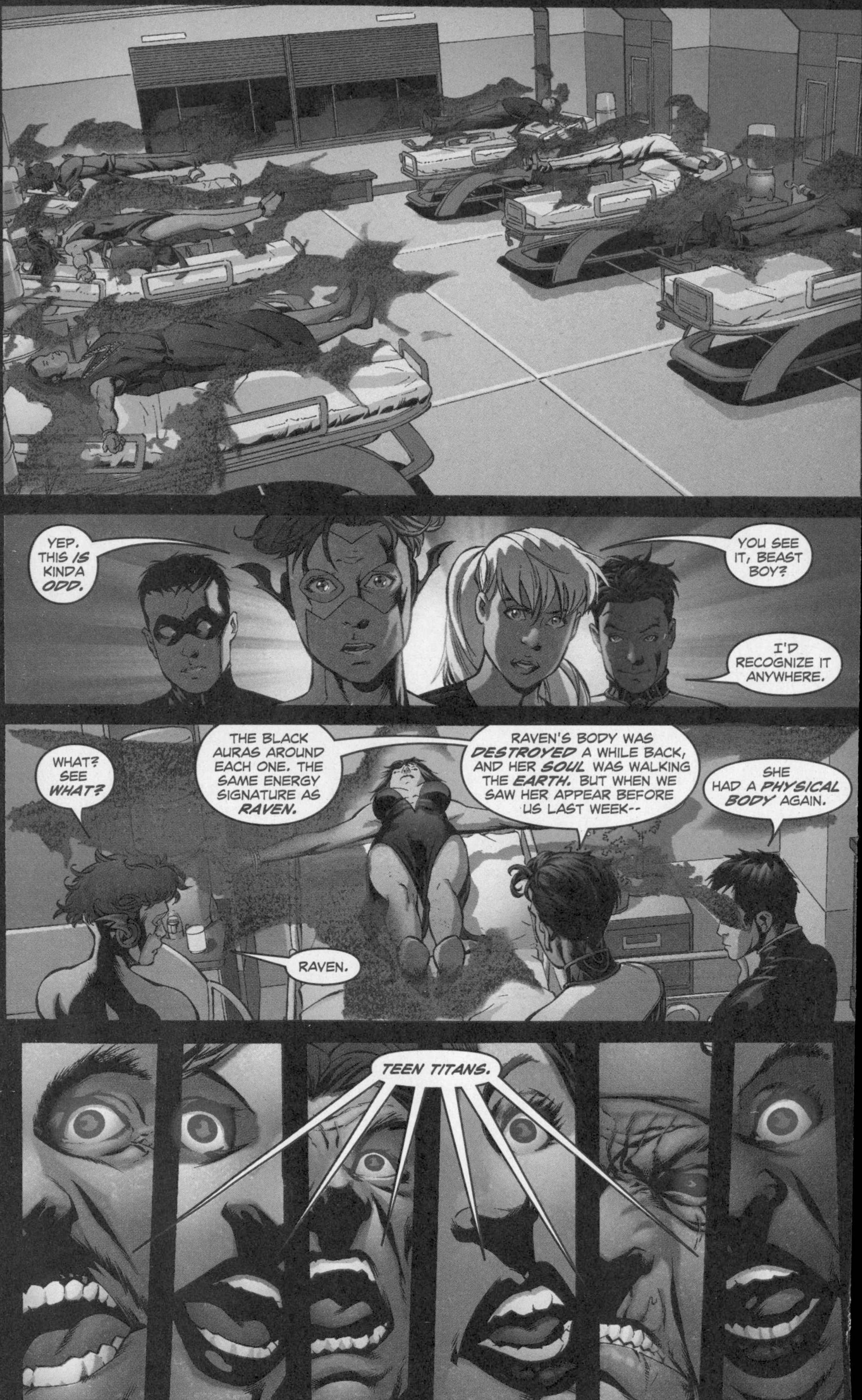
YEP. THIS *IS* KINDA *ODD.*
YOU SEE IT, BEAST BOY?
I'D RECOGNIZE IT ANYWHERE.
WHAT? SEE *WHAT?*
THE BLACK AURAS AROUND EACH ONE. THE SAME ENERGY SIGNATURE AS *RAVEN.*
RAVEN.
RAVEN'S BODY WAS *DESTROYED* A WHILE BACK, AND HER *SOUL* WAS WALKING THE *EARTH.* BUT WHEN WE SAW HER APPEAR BEFORE US LAST WEEK--
SHE HAD A *PHYSICAL BODY* AGAIN.
TEEN TITANS.

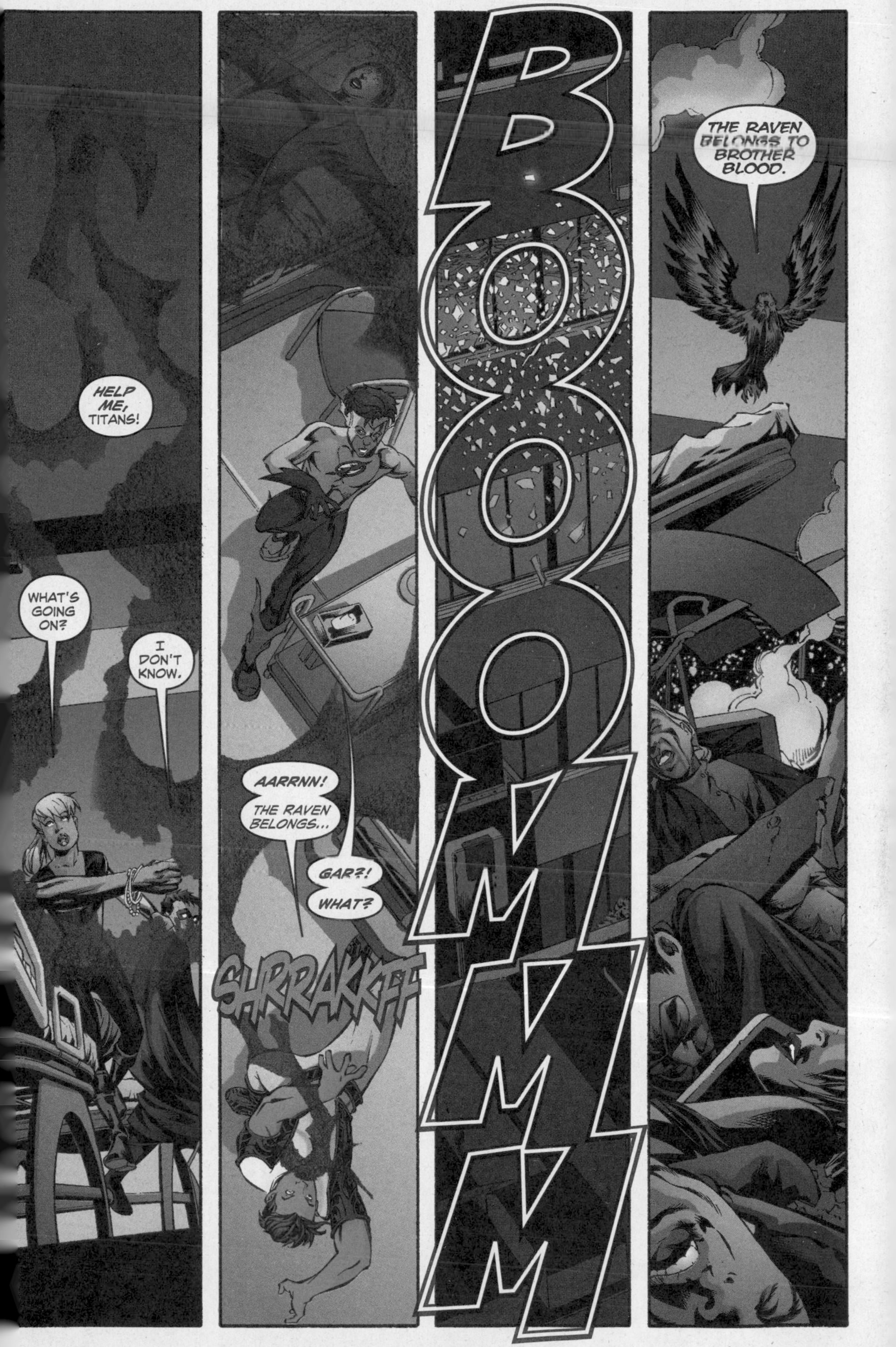

HELP ME, TITANS!
WHAT'S GOING ON?
I DON'T KNOW.
AARRNN!
THE RAVEN BELONGS...
GAR?!
WHAT?
SHRRAKKFF
BOOOMMMM
THE RAVEN BELONGS TO BROTHER BLOOD.

Teen Titans

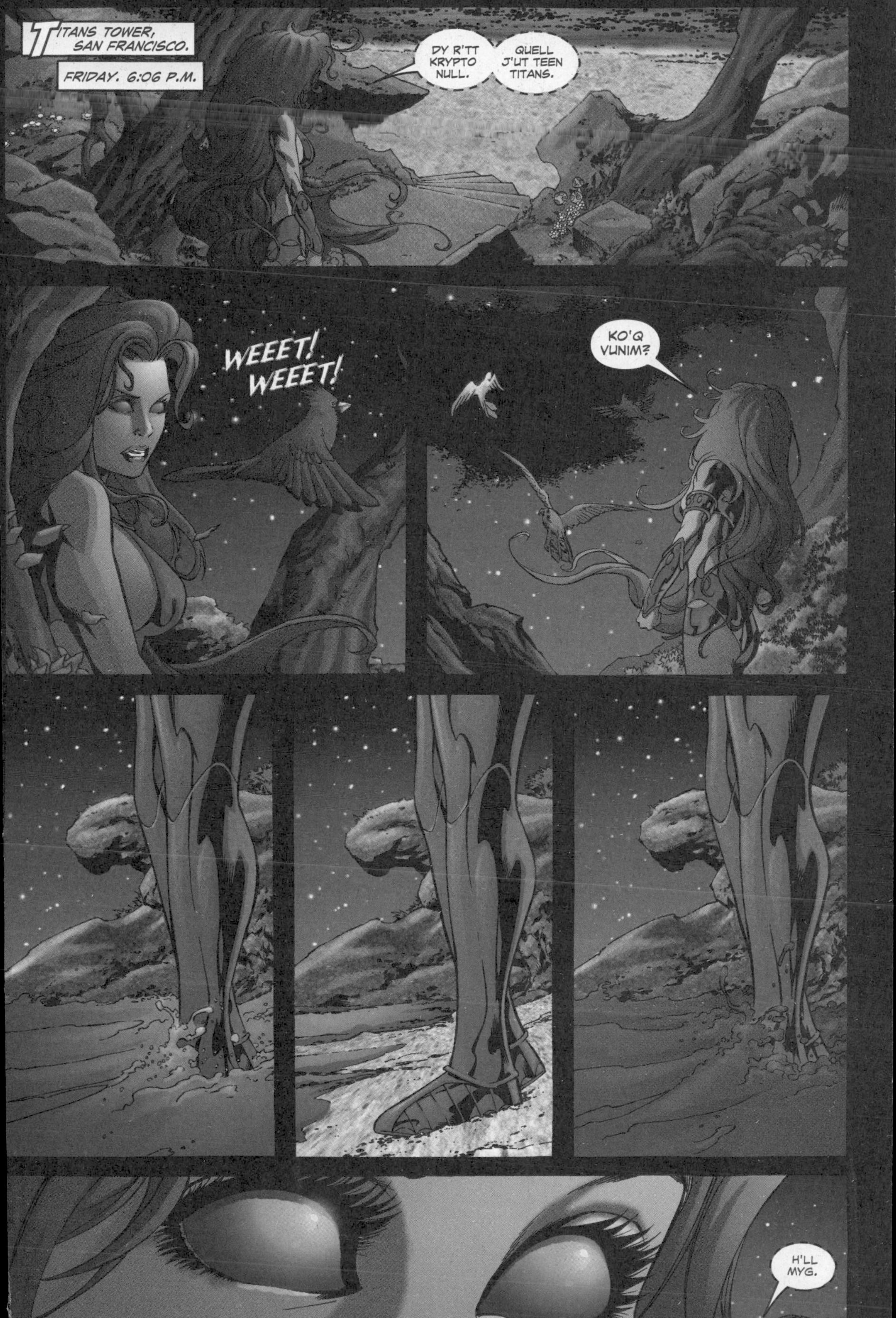
TITANS TOWER, SAN FRANCISCO.
FRIDAY. 6:06 P.M.
DY R'TT KRYPTO NULL.
QUELL J'UT TEEN TITANS.
WEEET! WEEET!
KO'Q VUNIM?
H'LL MYG.

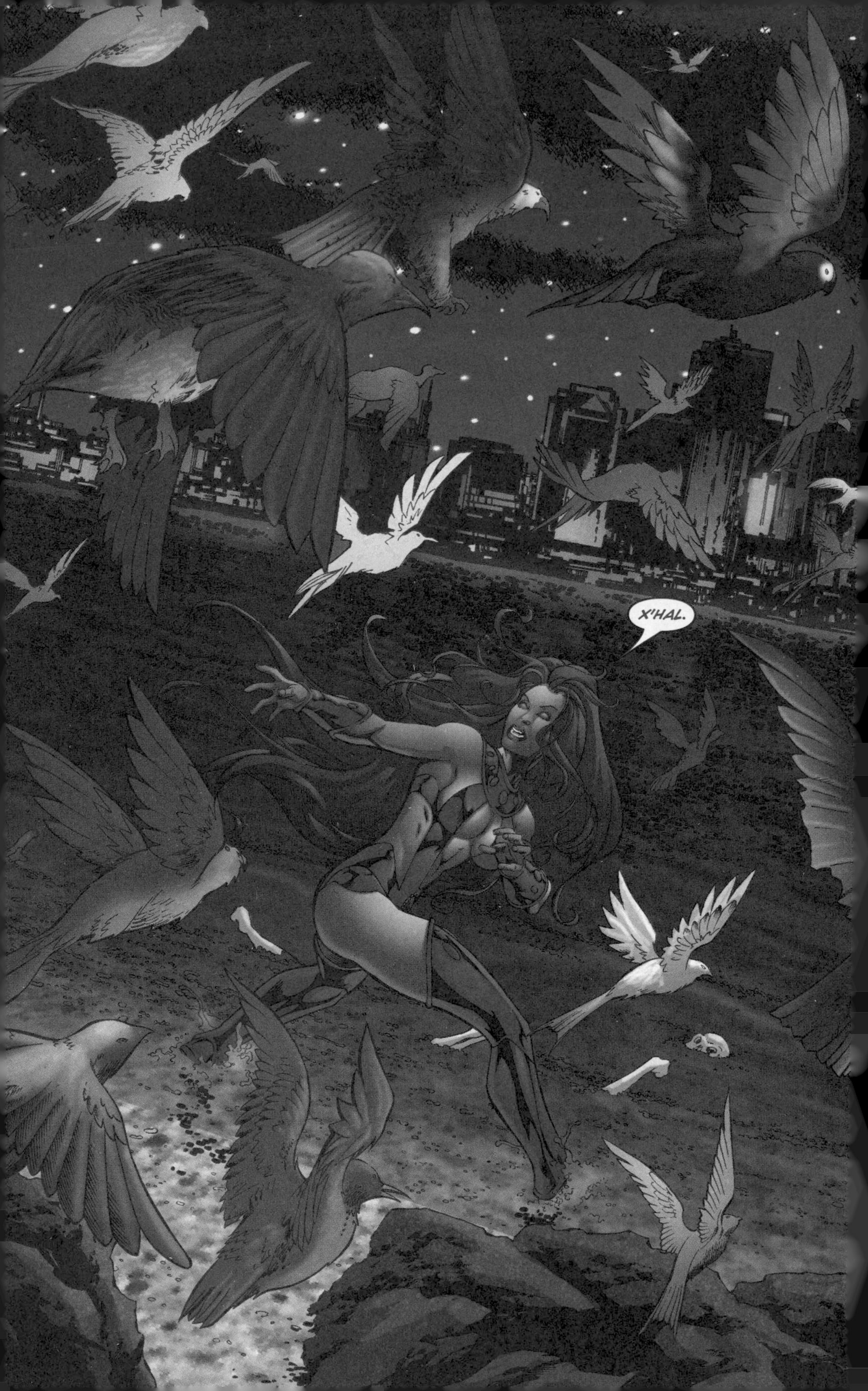
X'HAL.

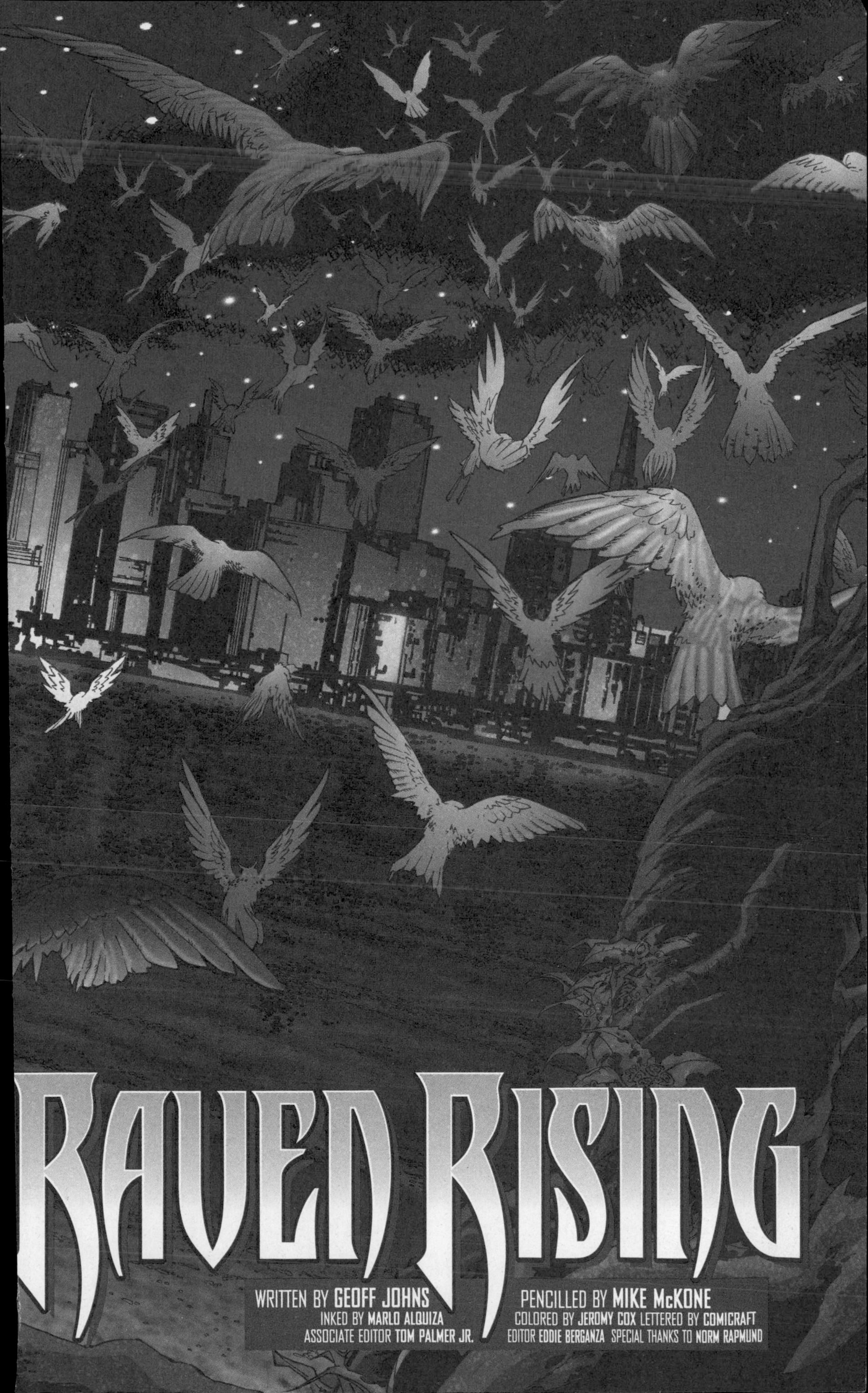
RAVEN RISING
WRITTEN BY GEOFF JOHNS
PENCILLED BY MIKE McKONE
INKED BY MARLO ALQUIZA
COLORED BY JEROMY COX LETTERED BY COMICRAFT
ASSOCIATE EDITOR TOM PALMER JR.
EDITOR EDDIE BERGANZA SPECIAL THANKS TO NORM RAPMUND

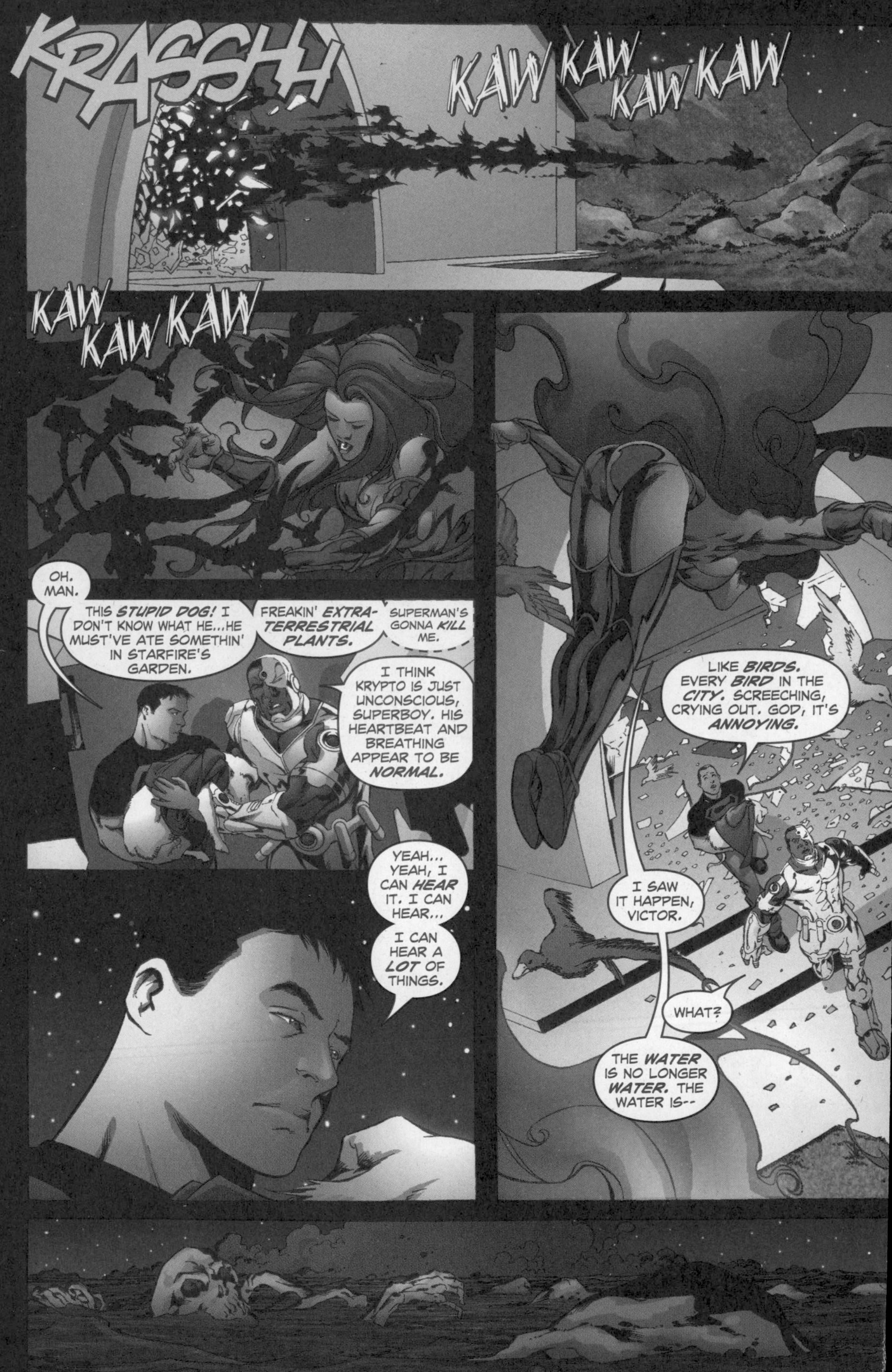
KRASSHH
KAW KAW KAW KAW
KAW KAW KAW
OH. MAN.
THIS STUPID DOG! I DON'T KNOW WHAT HE...HE MUST'VE ATE SOMETHIN' IN STARFIRE'S GARDEN.
FREAKIN' EXTRA-TERRESTRIAL PLANTS.
SUPERMAN'S GONNA KILL ME.
I THINK KRYPTO IS JUST UNCONSCIOUS, SUPERBOY. HIS HEARTBEAT AND BREATHING APPEAR TO BE NORMAL.
YEAH... YEAH, I CAN HEAR IT. I CAN HEAR...
I CAN HEAR A LOT OF THINGS.
LIKE BIRDS. EVERY BIRD IN THE CITY. SCREECHING, CRYING OUT. GOD, IT'S ANNOYING.
I SAW IT HAPPEN, VICTOR.
WHAT?
THE WATER IS NO LONGER WATER. THE WATER IS--

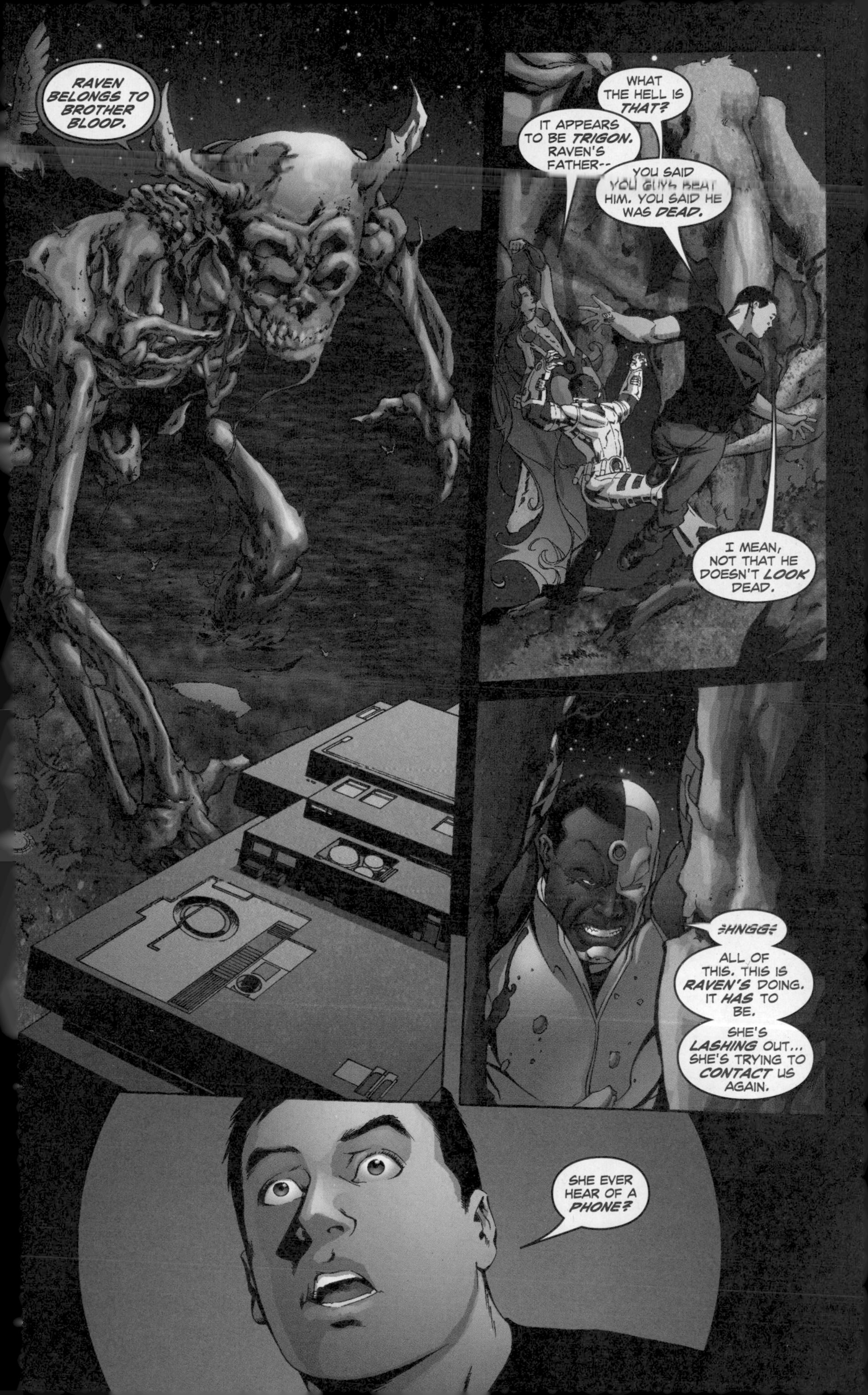
RAVEN BELONGS TO BROTHER BLOOD.
WHAT THE HELL IS THAT?
IT APPEARS TO BE TRIGON. RAVEN'S FATHER--
YOU SAID YOU GUYS BEAT HIM. YOU SAID HE WAS DEAD.
I MEAN, NOT THAT HE DOESN'T LOOK DEAD.
SHNGG
ALL OF THIS. THIS IS RAVEN'S DOING. IT HAS TO BE.
SHE'S LASHING OUT... SHE'S TRYING TO CONTACT US AGAIN.
SHE EVER HEAR OF A PHONE?

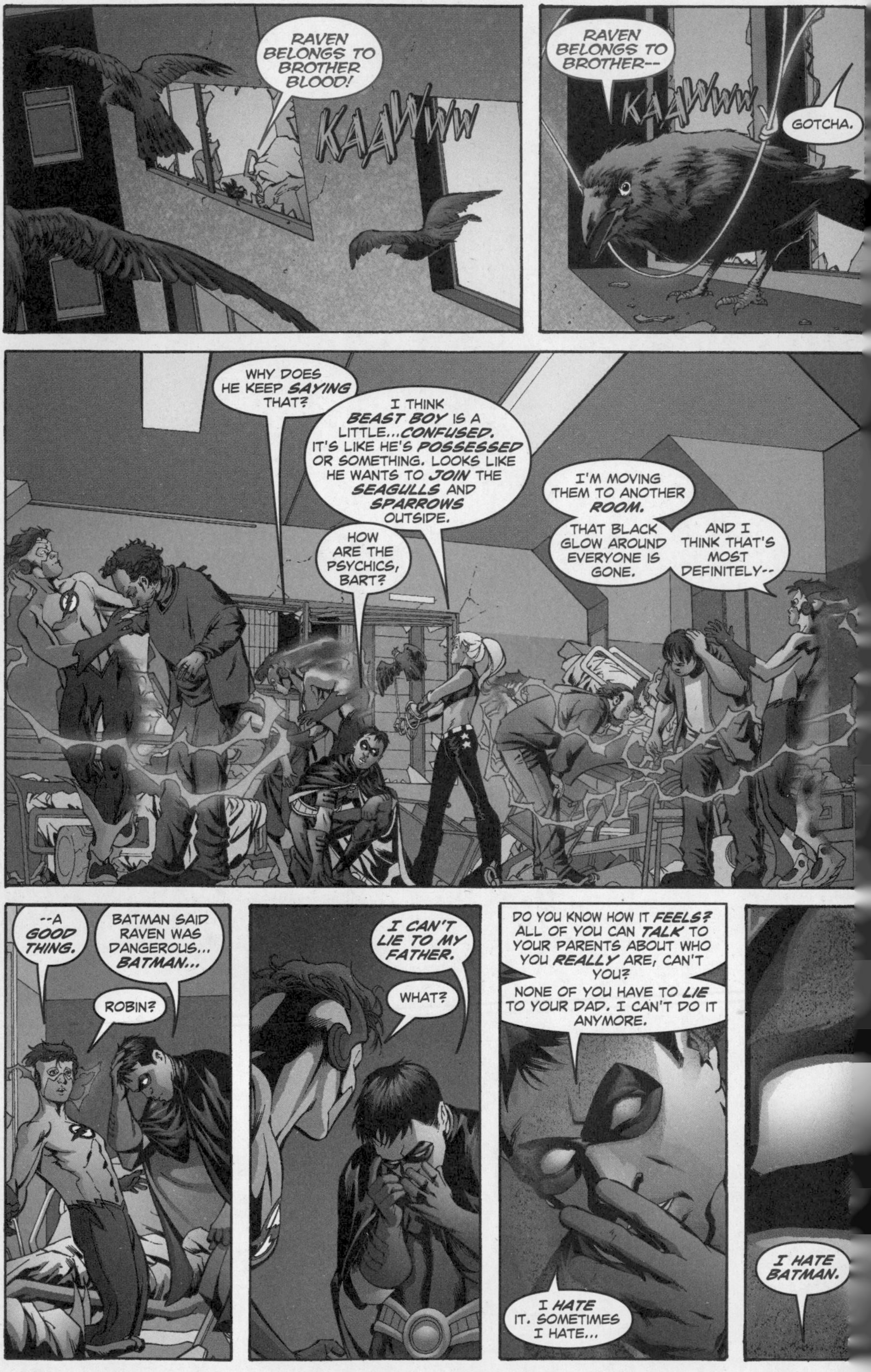
RAVEN BELONGS TO BROTHER BLOOD!
KAAWWW
RAVEN BELONGS TO BROTHER--
KAAWWW
GOTCHA.
WHY DOES HE KEEP SAYING THAT?
I THINK BEAST BOY IS A LITTLE...CONFUSED. IT'S LIKE HE'S POSSESSED OR SOMETHING. LOOKS LIKE HE WANTS TO JOIN THE SEAGULLS AND SPARROWS OUTSIDE.
HOW ARE THE PSYCHICS, BART?
I'M MOVING THEM TO ANOTHER ROOM.
THAT BLACK GLOW AROUND EVERYONE IS GONE.
AND I THINK THAT'S MOST DEFINITELY--
--A GOOD THING.
BATMAN SAID RAVEN WAS DANGEROUS... BATMAN...
ROBIN?
I CAN'T LIE TO MY FATHER.
WHAT?
DO YOU KNOW HOW IT FEELS? ALL OF YOU CAN TALK TO YOUR PARENTS ABOUT WHO YOU REALLY ARE, CAN'T YOU?
NONE OF YOU HAVE TO LIE TO YOUR DAD. I CAN'T DO IT ANYMORE.
I HATE IT. SOMETIMES I HATE...
I HATE BATMAN.

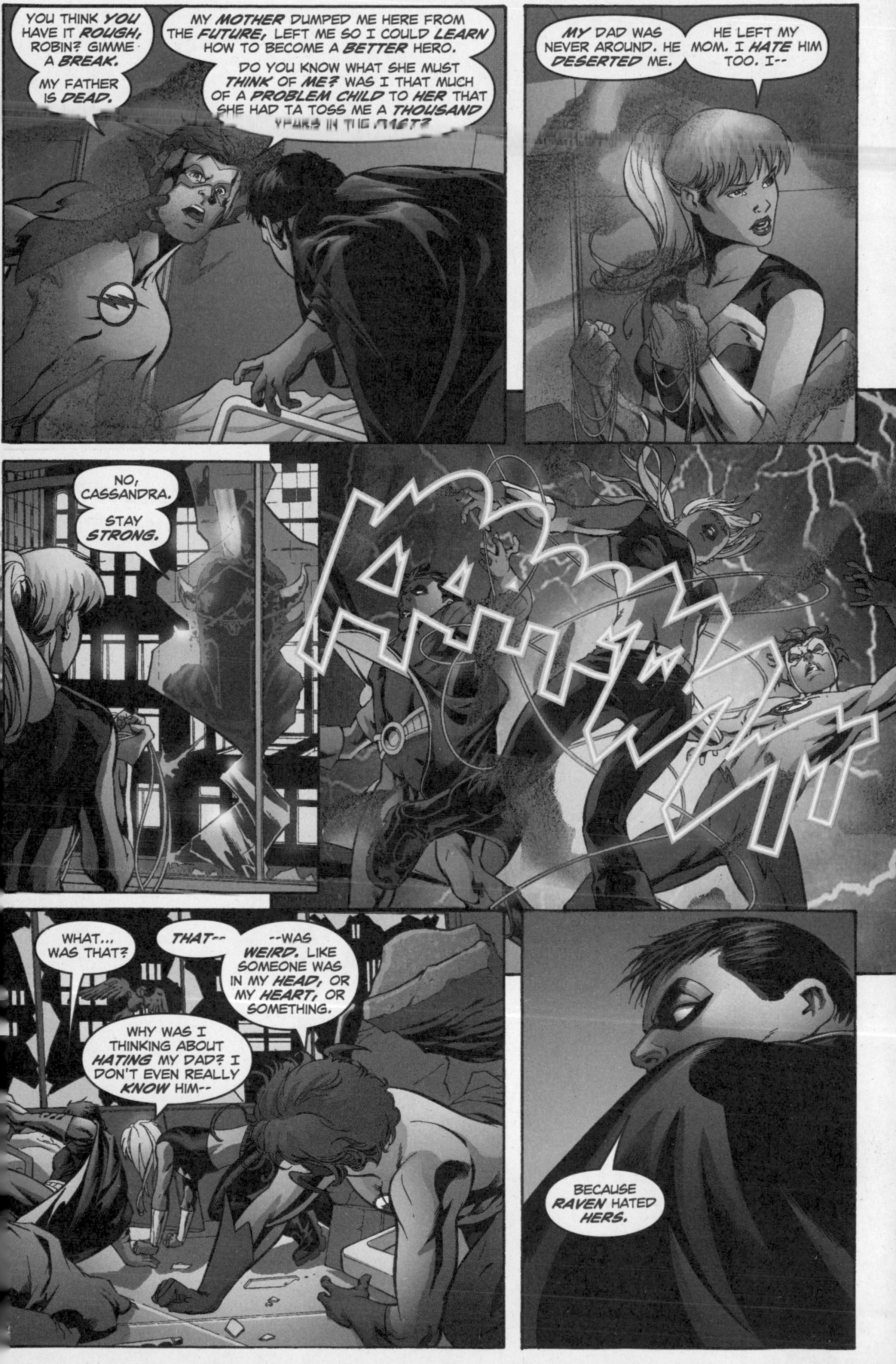

YOU THINK YOU HAVE IT ROUGH, ROBIN? GIMME A BREAK.
MY FATHER IS DEAD.
MY MOTHER DUMPED ME HERE FROM THE FUTURE, LEFT ME SO I COULD LEARN HOW TO BECOME A BETTER HERO.
DO YOU KNOW WHAT SHE MUST THINK OF ME? WAS I THAT MUCH OF A PROBLEM CHILD TO HER THAT SHE HAD TA TOSS ME A THOUSAND
MY DAD WAS NEVER AROUND. HE DESERTED ME.
HE LEFT MY MOM. I HATE HIM TOO. I--
NO, CASSANDRA.
STAY STRONG.
WHAT... WAS THAT?
THAT--
--WAS WEIRD. LIKE SOMEONE WAS IN MY HEAD, OR MY HEART, OR SOMETHING.
WHY WAS I THINKING ABOUT HATING MY DAD? I DON'T EVEN REALLY KNOW HIM--
BECAUSE RAVEN HATED HERS.

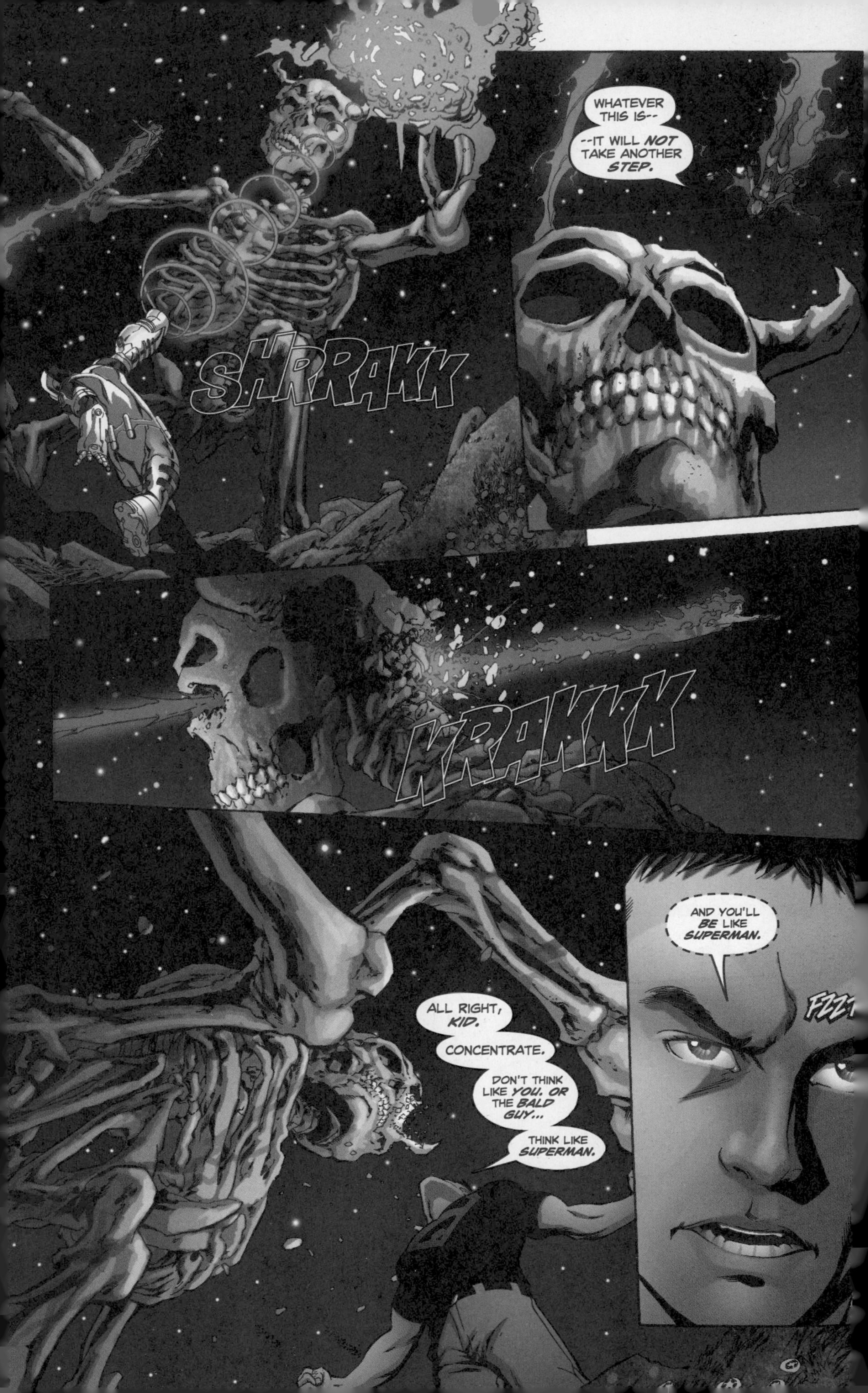
SHRRAKK
WHATEVER THIS IS--
--IT WILL NOT TAKE ANOTHER STEP.
KRAKKK
AND YOU'LL BE LIKE SUPERMAN.
ALL RIGHT, KID.
CONCENTRATE.
DON'T THINK LIKE YOU. OR THE BALD GUY...
THINK LIKE SUPERMAN.

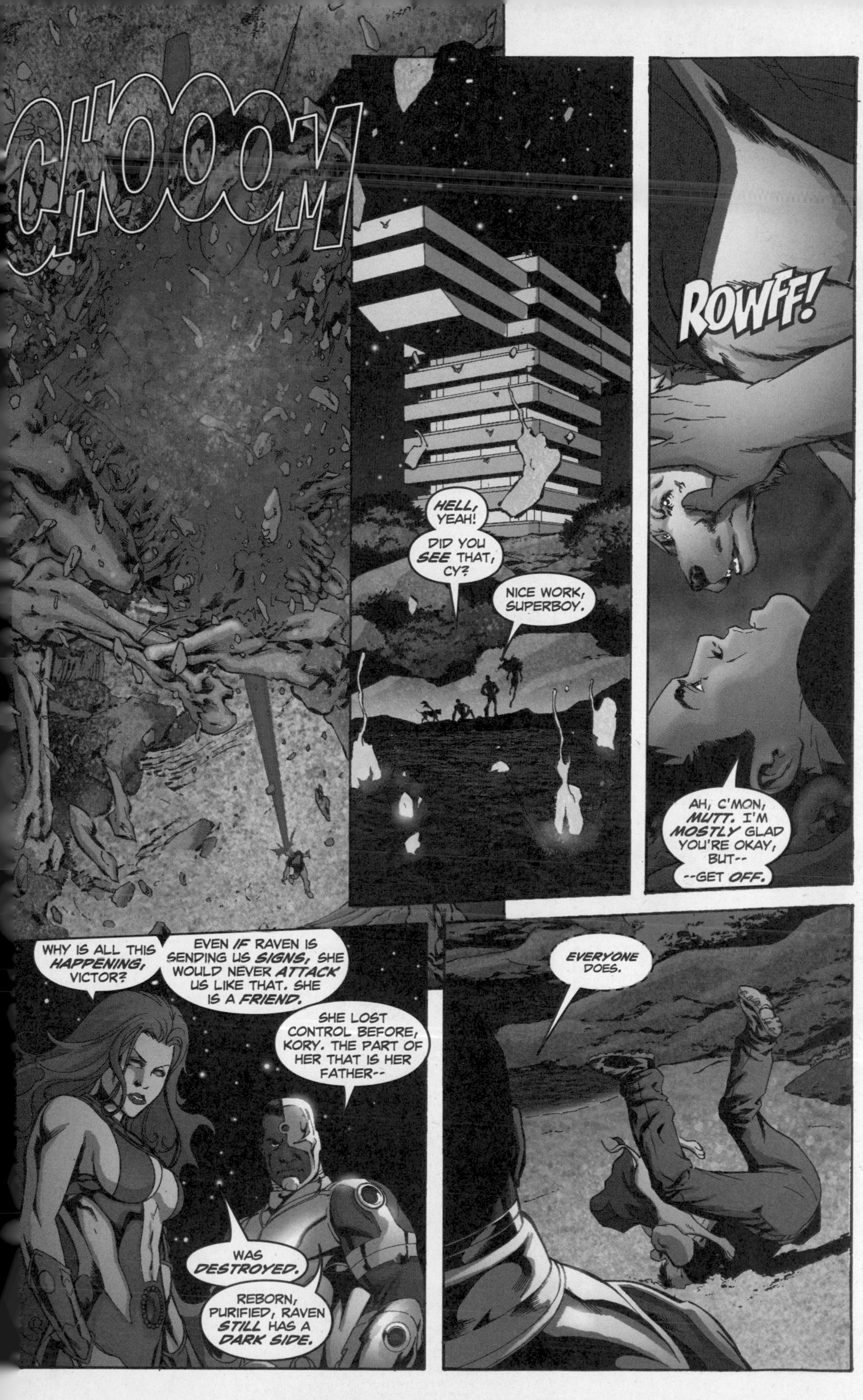
CHOOOM
HELL, YEAH!
DID YOU SEE THAT, CY?
NICE WORK, SUPERBOY.
ROWFF!
AH, C'MON, MUTT. I'M MOSTLY GLAD YOU'RE OKAY, BUT--
--GET OFF.
WHY IS ALL THIS HAPPENING, VICTOR?
EVEN IF RAVEN IS SENDING US SIGNS, SHE WOULD NEVER ATTACK US LIKE THAT. SHE IS A FRIEND.
SHE LOST CONTROL BEFORE, KORY. THE PART OF HER THAT IS HER FATHER--
WAS DESTROYED.
REBORN, PURIFIED, RAVEN STILL HAS A DARK SIDE.
EVERYONE DOES.

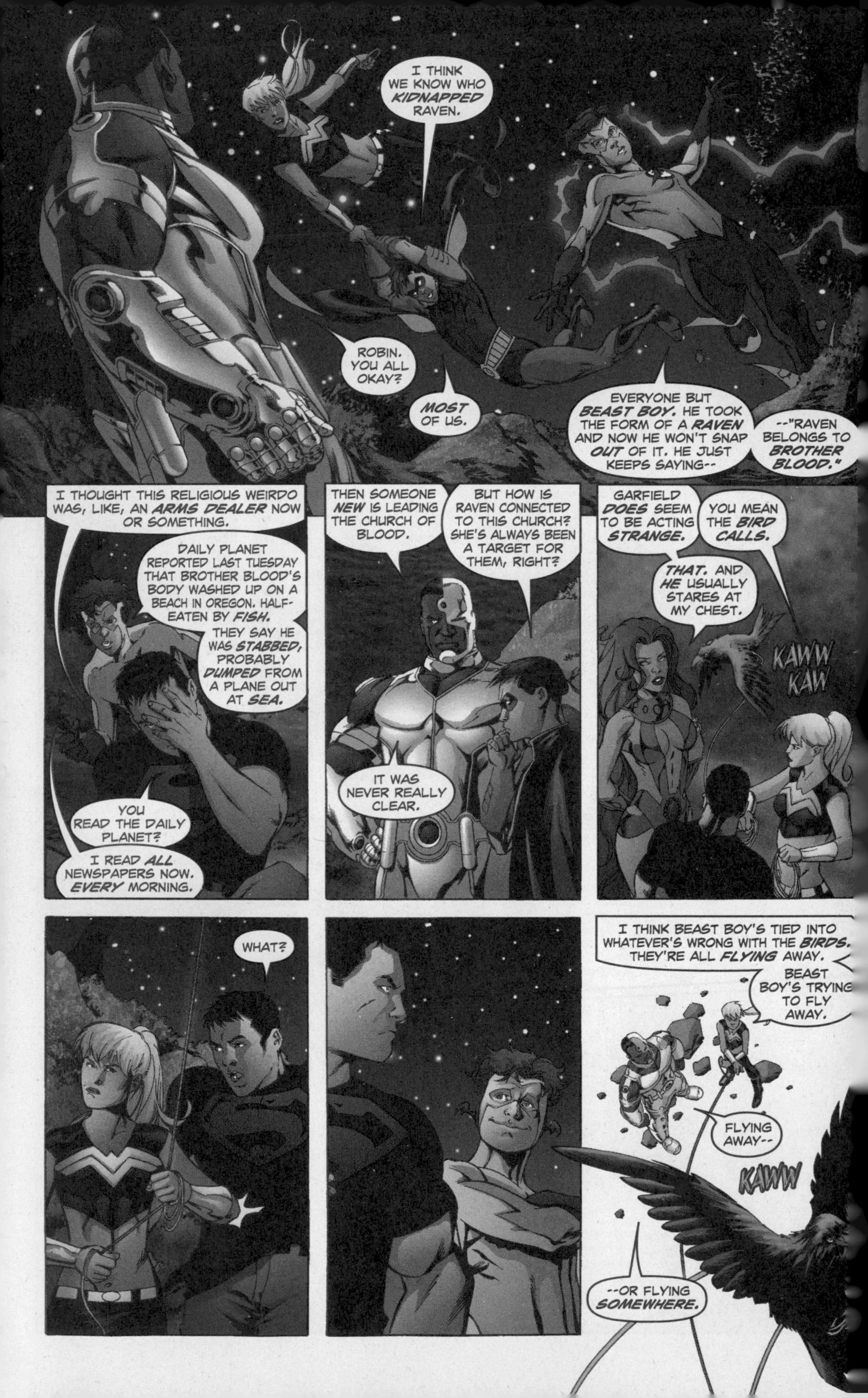

I THINK WE KNOW WHO KIDNAPPED RAVEN.
ROBIN. YOU ALL OKAY?
MOST OF US.
EVERYONE BUT BEAST BOY. HE TOOK THE FORM OF A RAVEN AND NOW HE WON'T SNAP OUT OF IT. HE JUST KEEPS SAYING--
--"RAVEN BELONGS TO BROTHER BLOOD."
I THOUGHT THIS RELIGIOUS WEIRDO WAS, LIKE, AN ARMS DEALER NOW OR SOMETHING.
DAILY PLANET REPORTED LAST TUESDAY THAT BROTHER BLOOD'S BODY WASHED UP ON A BEACH IN OREGON. HALF-EATEN BY FISH.
THEY SAY HE WAS STABBED, PROBABLY DUMPED FROM A PLANE OUT AT SEA.
YOU READ THE DAILY PLANET?
I READ ALL NEWSPAPERS NOW. EVERY MORNING.
THEN SOMEONE NEW IS LEADING THE CHURCH OF BLOOD.
BUT HOW IS RAVEN CONNECTED TO THIS CHURCH? SHE'S ALWAYS BEEN A TARGET FOR THEM, RIGHT?
IT WAS NEVER REALLY CLEAR.
GARFIELD DOES SEEM TO BE ACTING STRANGE.
YOU MEAN THE BIRD CALLS.
THAT. AND HE USUALLY STARES AT MY CHEST.
KAWW KAW
WHAT?
I THINK BEAST BOY'S TIED INTO WHATEVER'S WRONG WITH THE BIRDS. THEY'RE ALL FLYING AWAY.
BEAST BOY'S TRYING TO FLY AWAY.
FLYING AWAY--
KAWW
--OR FLYING SOMEWHERE.

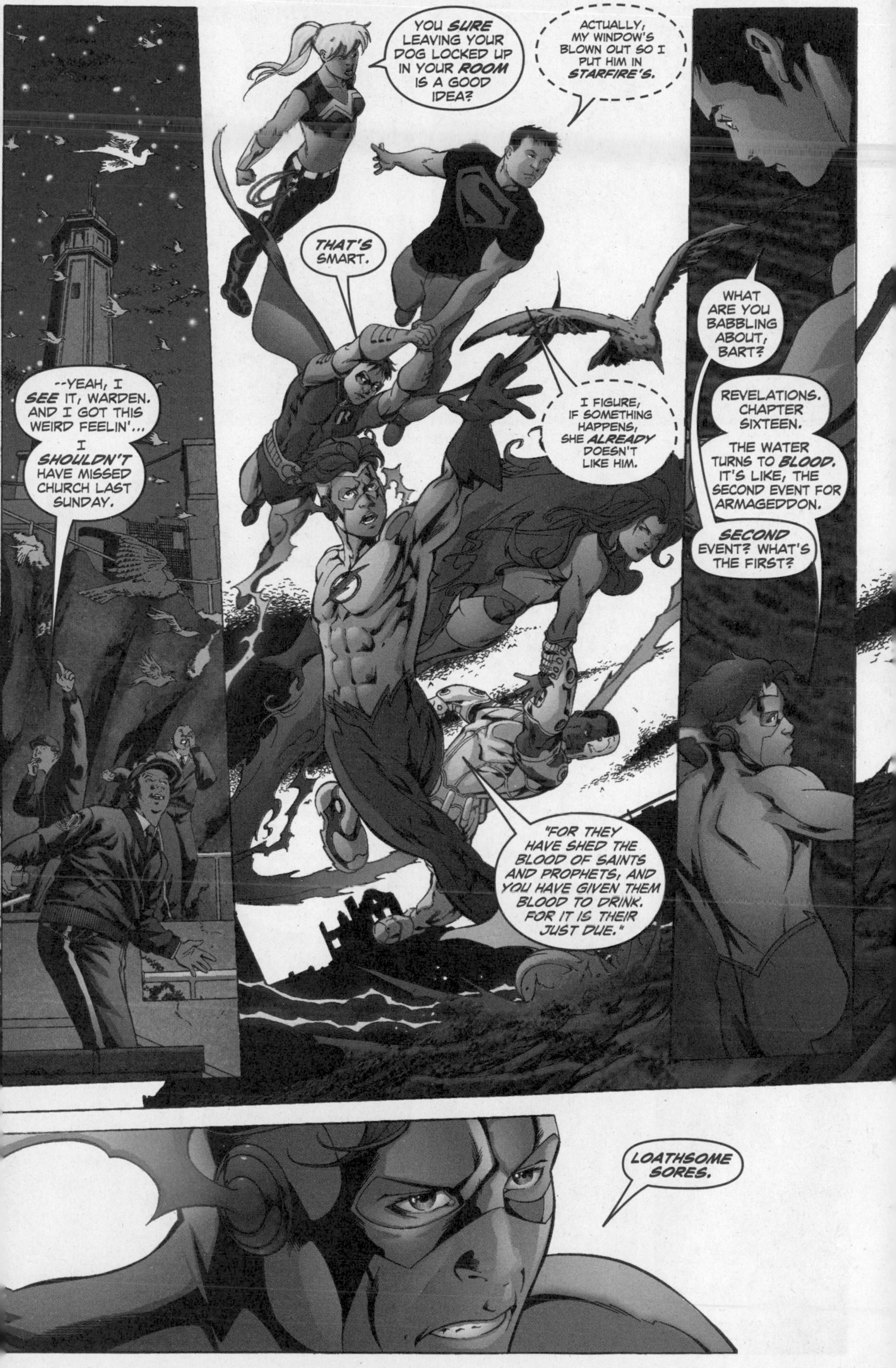

YOU SURE LEAVING YOUR DOG LOCKED UP IN YOUR ROOM IS A GOOD IDEA?
ACTUALLY, MY WINDOW'S BLOWN OUT SO I PUT HIM IN STARFIRE'S.
THAT'S SMART.
I FIGURE, IF SOMETHING HAPPENS, SHE ALREADY DOESN'T LIKE HIM.
--YEAH, I SEE IT, WARDEN. AND I GOT THIS WEIRD FEELIN'...
I SHOULDN'T HAVE MISSED CHURCH LAST SUNDAY.
"FOR THEY HAVE SHED THE BLOOD OF SAINTS AND PROPHETS, AND YOU HAVE GIVEN THEM BLOOD TO DRINK. FOR IT IS THEIR JUST DUE."
WHAT ARE YOU BABBLING ABOUT, BART?
REVELATIONS. CHAPTER SIXTEEN.
THE WATER TURNS TO BLOOD. IT'S LIKE, THE SECOND EVENT FOR ARMAGEDDON.
SECOND EVENT? WHAT'S THE FIRST?
LOATHSOME SORES.

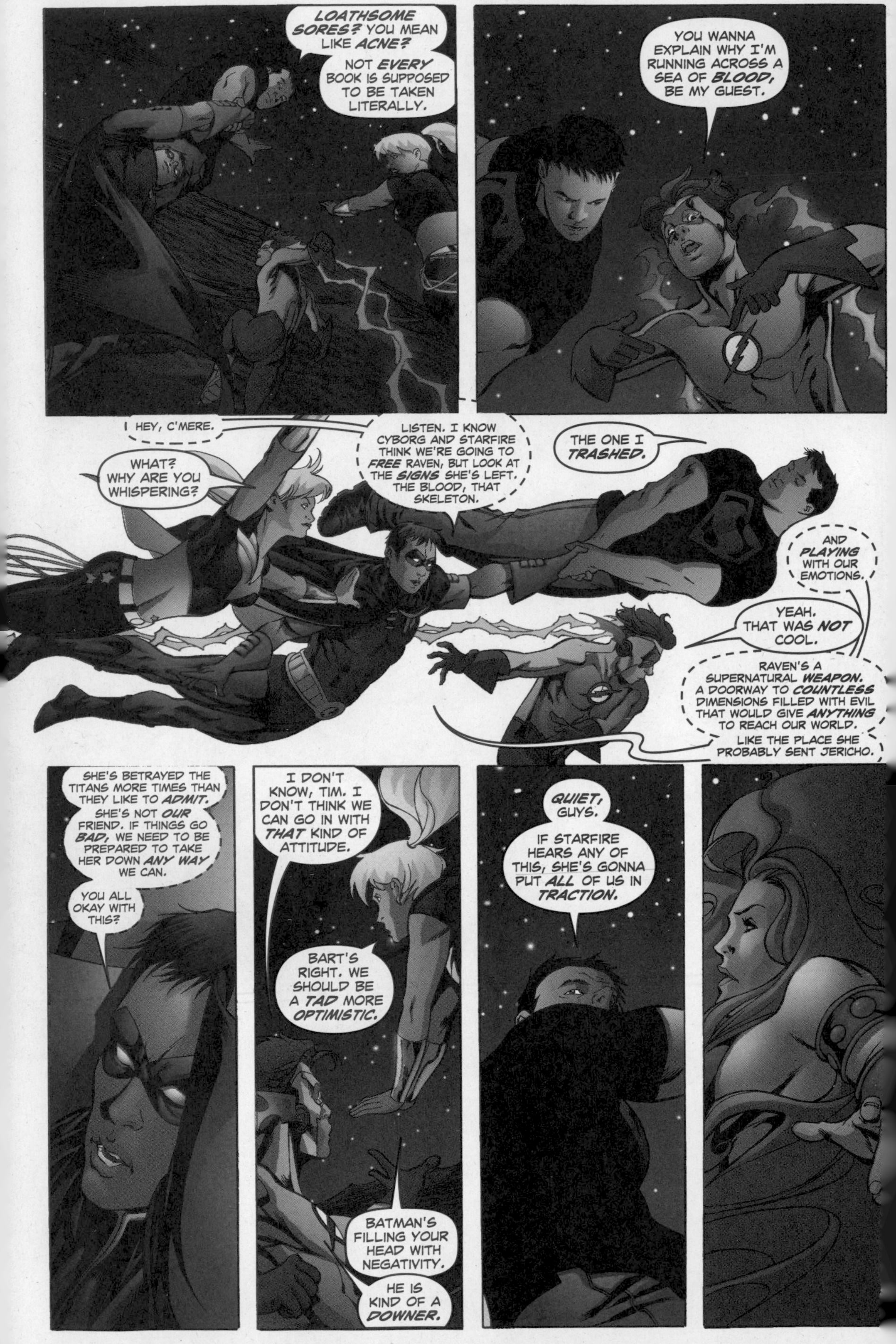
LOATHSOME SORES? YOU MEAN LIKE ACNE?
NOT EVERY BOOK IS SUPPOSED TO BE TAKEN LITERALLY.
YOU WANNA EXPLAIN WHY I'M RUNNING ACROSS A SEA OF BLOOD, BE MY GUEST.
HEY, C'MERE.
WHAT? WHY ARE YOU WHISPERING?
LISTEN. I KNOW CYBORG AND STARFIRE THINK WE'RE GOING TO FREE RAVEN, BUT LOOK AT THE SIGNS SHE'S LEFT. THE BLOOD, THAT SKELETON.
THE ONE I TRASHED.
AND PLAYING WITH OUR EMOTIONS.
YEAH. THAT WAS NOT COOL.
RAVEN'S A SUPERNATURAL WEAPON. A DOORWAY TO COUNTLESS DIMENSIONS FILLED WITH EVIL THAT WOULD GIVE ANYTHING TO REACH OUR WORLD.
LIKE THE PLACE SHE PROBABLY SENT JERICHO.
SHE'S BETRAYED THE TITANS MORE TIMES THAN THEY LIKE TO ADMIT. SHE'S NOT OUR FRIEND. IF THINGS GO BAD, WE NEED TO BE PREPARED TO TAKE HER DOWN ANY WAY WE CAN.
YOU ALL OKAY WITH THIS?
I DON'T KNOW, TIM. I DON'T THINK WE CAN GO IN WITH THAT KIND OF ATTITUDE.
BART'S RIGHT. WE SHOULD BE A TAD MORE OPTIMISTIC.
BATMAN'S FILLING YOUR HEAD WITH NEGATIVITY.
HE IS KIND OF A DOWNER.
QUIET, GUYS.
IF STARFIRE HEARS ANY OF THIS, SHE'S GONNA PUT ALL OF US IN TRACTION.

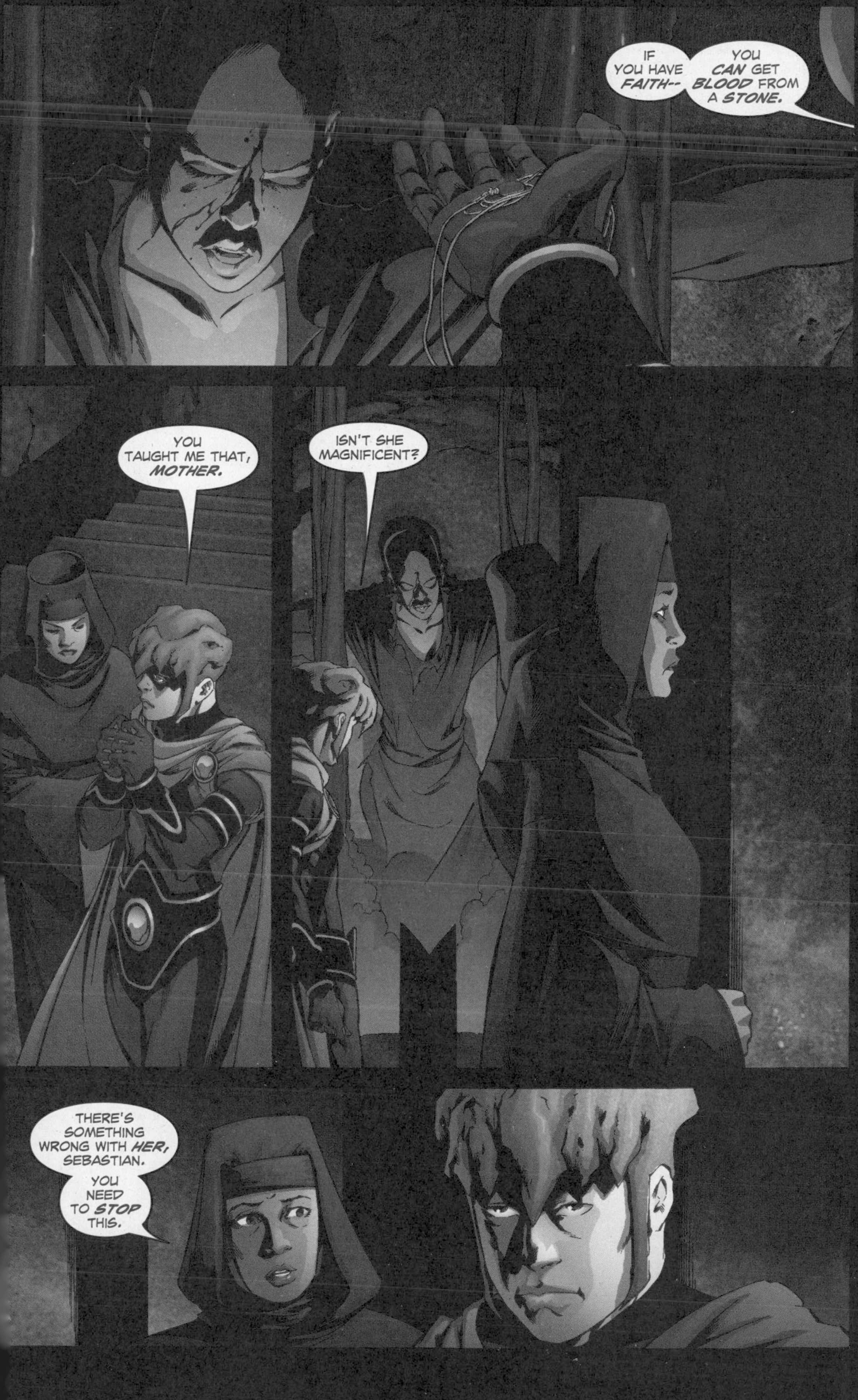
IF YOU HAVE FAITH--
YOU CAN GET BLOOD FROM A STONE.
YOU TAUGHT ME THAT, MOTHER.
ISN'T SHE MAGNIFICENT?
THERE'S SOMETHING WRONG WITH HER, SEBASTIAN.
YOU NEED TO STOP THIS.

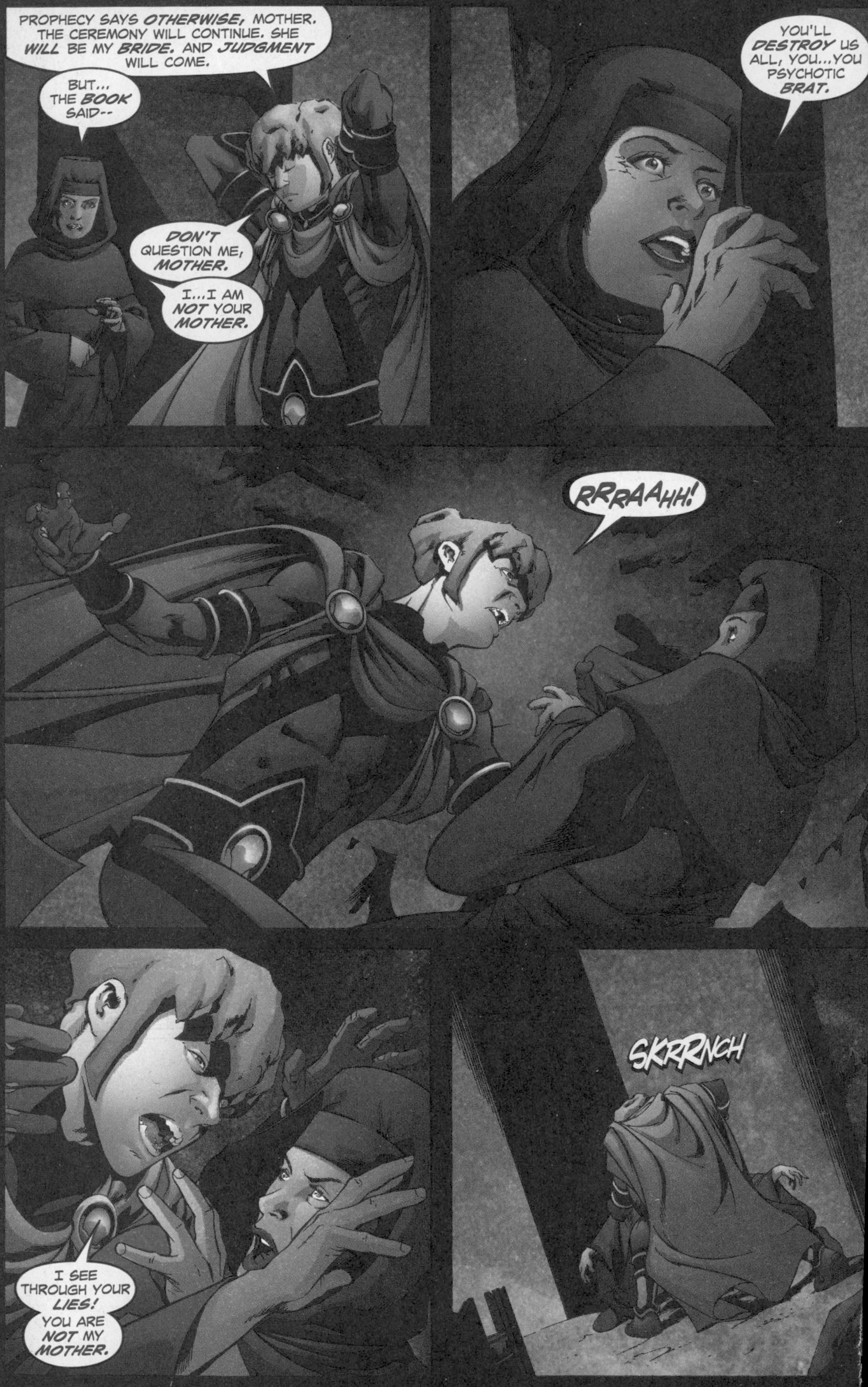
PROPHECY SAYS OTHERWISE, MOTHER. THE CEREMONY WILL CONTINUE. SHE WILL BE MY BRIDE. AND JUDGMENT WILL COME.
BUT... THE BOOK SAID--
DON'T QUESTION ME, MOTHER.
I...I AM NOT YOUR MOTHER.
YOU'LL DESTROY US ALL, YOU...YOU PSYCHOTIC BRAT.
RRRAAHH!
I SEE THROUGH YOUR LIES! YOU ARE NOT MY MOTHER.
SKRRNCH

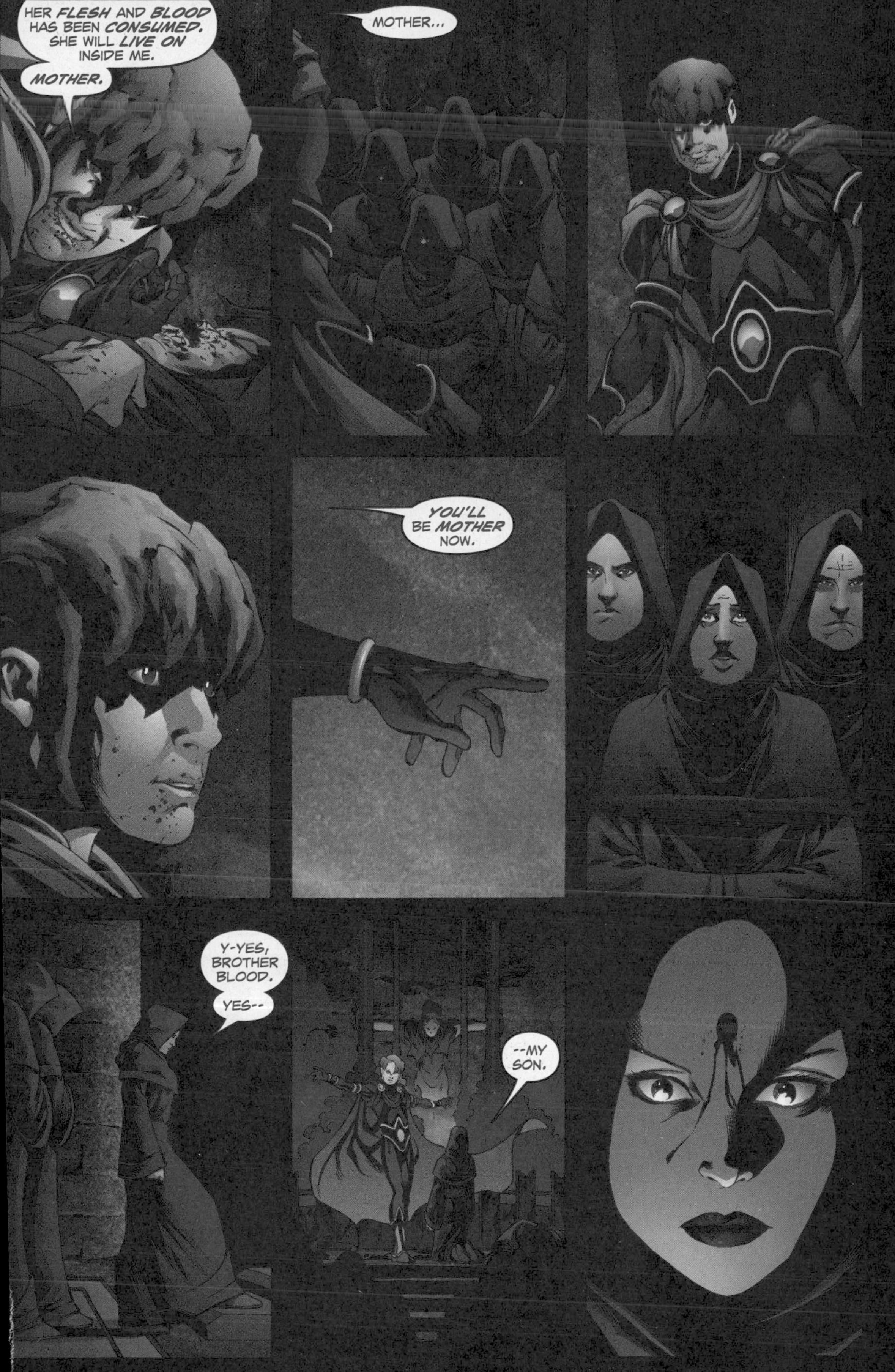
HER FLESH AND BLOOD HAS BEEN CONSUMED. SHE WILL LIVE ON INSIDE ME.
MOTHER.
MOTHER...
YOU'LL BE MOTHER NOW.
Y-YES, BROTHER BLOOD.
YES--
--MY SON.

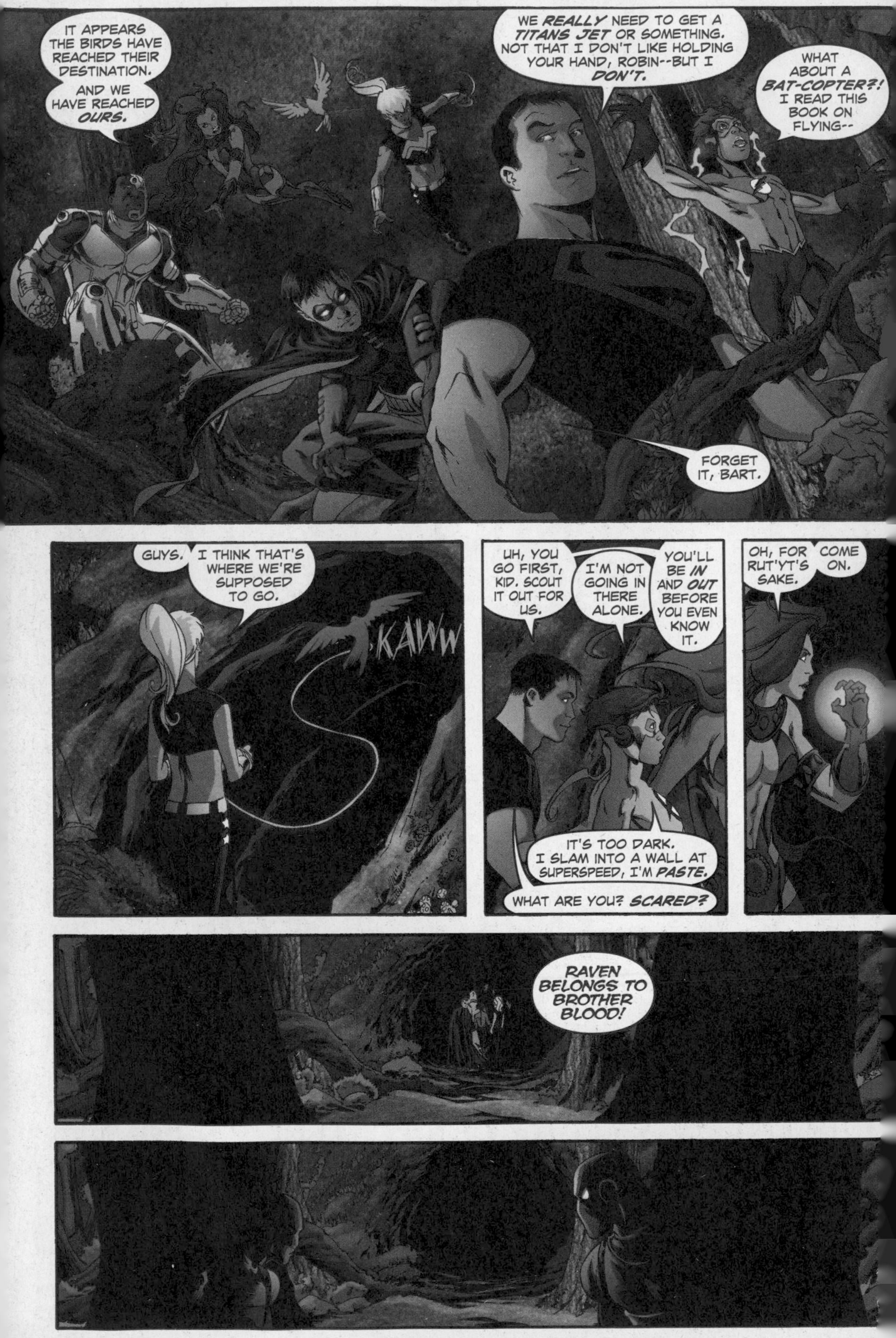
IT APPEARS THE BIRDS HAVE REACHED THEIR DESTINATION.
AND WE HAVE REACHED OURS.
WE REALLY NEED TO GET A TITANS JET OR SOMETHING. NOT THAT I DON'T LIKE HOLDING YOUR HAND, ROBIN--BUT I DON'T.
WHAT ABOUT A BAT-COPTER?! I READ THIS BOOK ON FLYING--
FORGET IT, BART.
GUYS.
I THINK THAT'S WHERE WE'RE SUPPOSED TO GO.
KAWW
UH, YOU GO FIRST, KID. SCOUT IT OUT FOR US.
I'M NOT GOING IN THERE ALONE.
YOU'LL BE IN AND OUT BEFORE YOU EVEN KNOW IT.
IT'S TOO DARK. I SLAM INTO A WALL AT SUPERSPEED, I'M PASTE.
WHAT ARE YOU? SCARED?
OH, FOR RUT'YT'S SAKE.
COME ON.
RAVEN BELONGS TO BROTHER BLOOD!

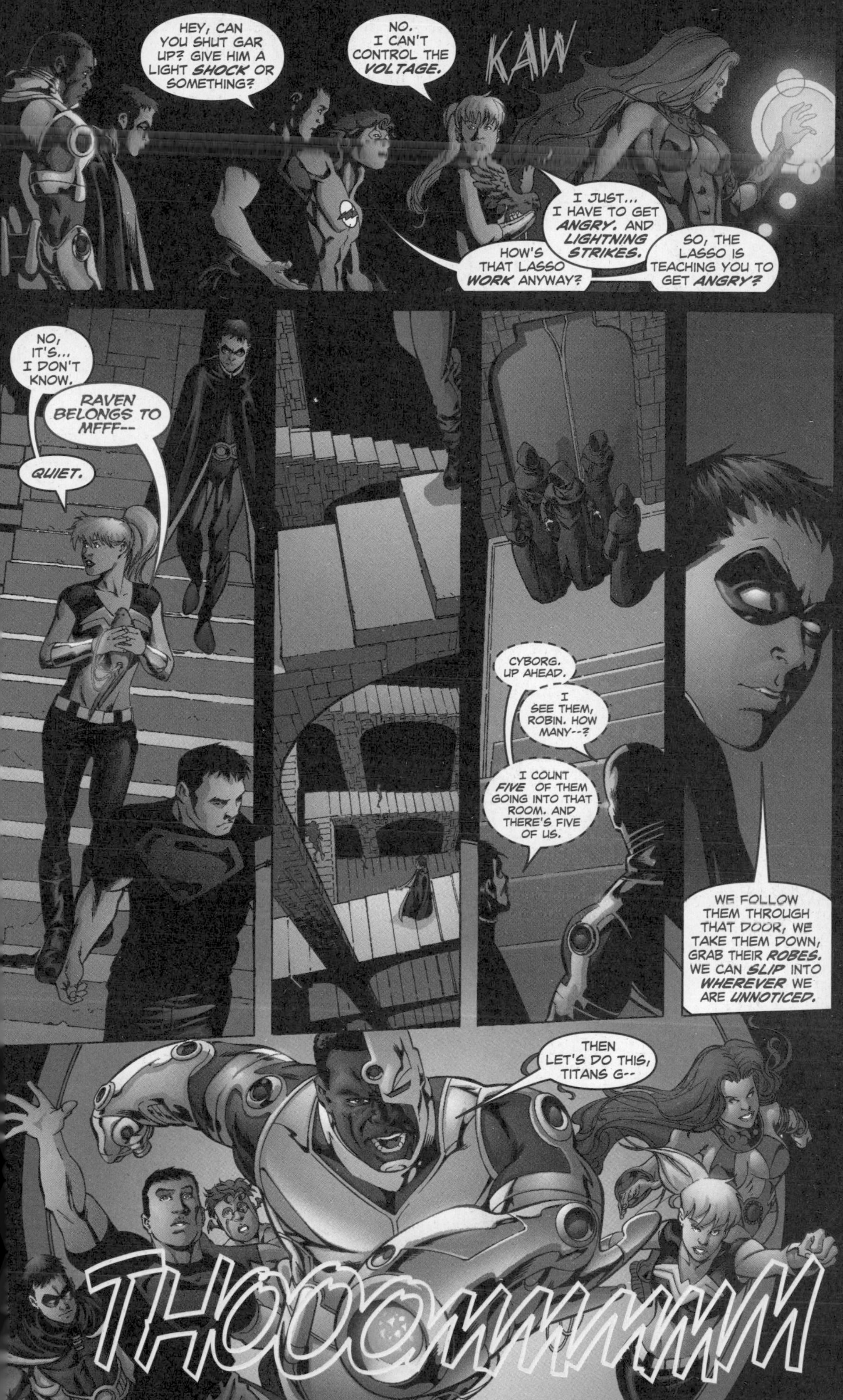
HEY, CAN YOU SHUT GAR UP? GIVE HIM A LIGHT SHOCK OR SOMETHING?
NO. I CAN'T CONTROL THE VOLTAGE.
KAW
I JUST... I HAVE TO GET ANGRY. AND LIGHTNING STRIKES.
HOW'S THAT LASSO WORK ANYWAY?
SO, THE LASSO IS TEACHING YOU TO GET ANGRY?
NO, IT'S... I DON'T KNOW.
RAVEN BELONGS TO MFFF--
QUIET.
CYBORG. UP AHEAD.
I SEE THEM, ROBIN. HOW MANY--?
I COUNT FIVE OF THEM GOING INTO THAT ROOM. AND THERE'S FIVE OF US.
WE FOLLOW THEM THROUGH THAT DOOR, WE TAKE THEM DOWN, GRAB THEIR ROBES. WE CAN SLIP INTO WHEREVER WE ARE UNNOTICED.
THEN LET'S DO THIS, TITANS G--
THOOOMMMMM

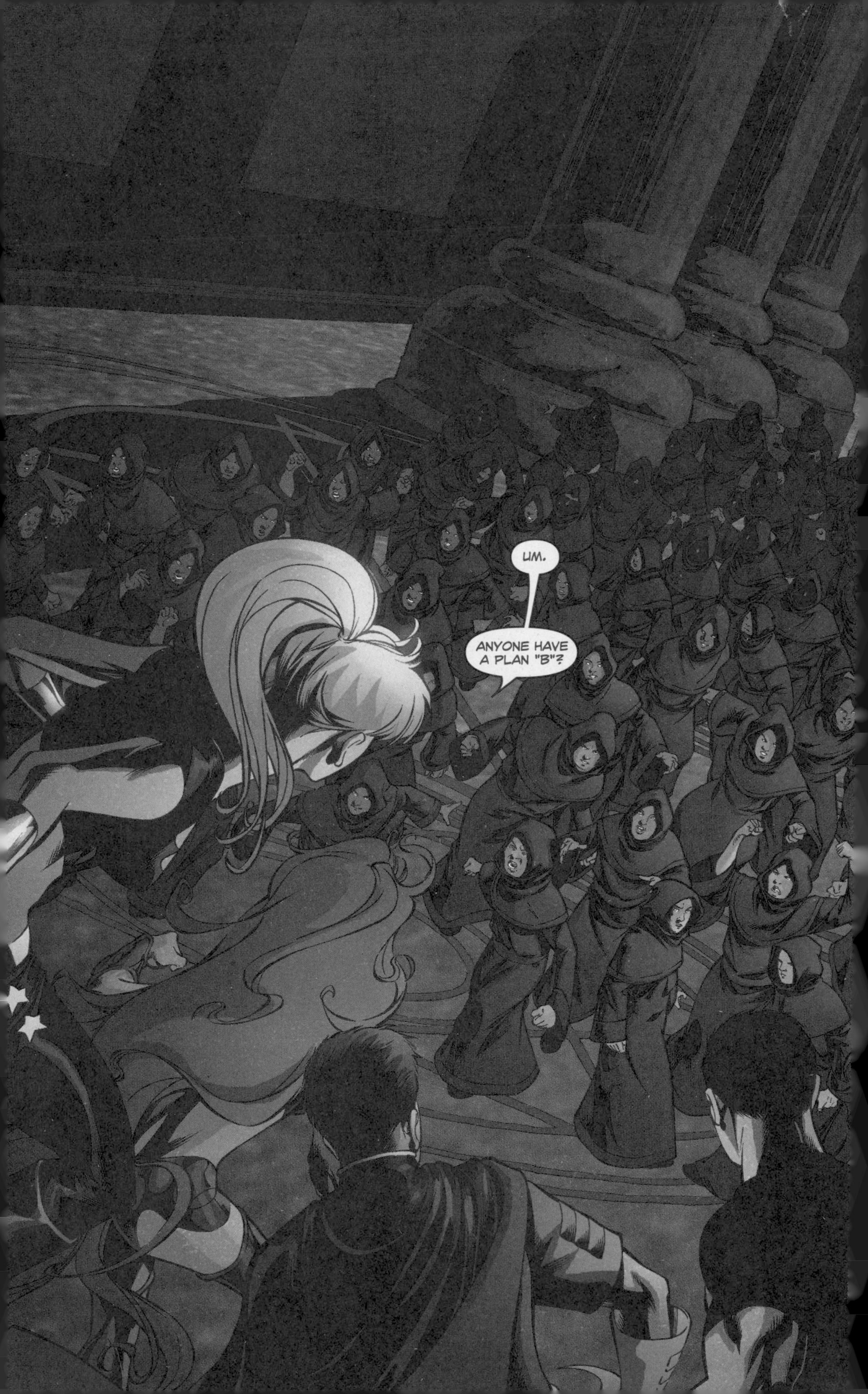
UM.
ANYONE HAVE A PLAN "B"?

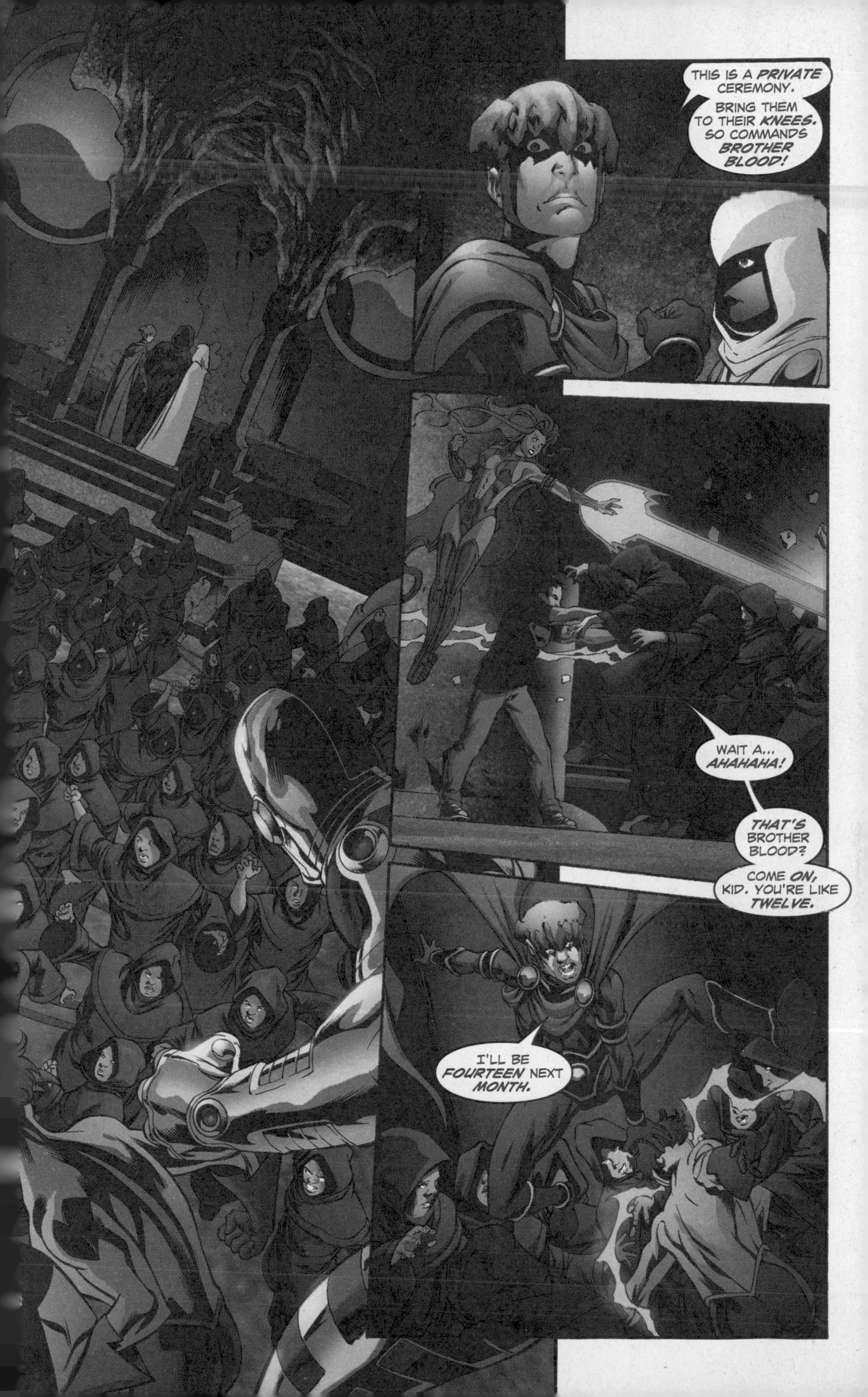
THIS IS A *PRIVATE* CEREMONY.
BRING THEM TO THEIR ***KNEES.*** SO COMMANDS ***BROTHER BLOOD!***
WAIT A... ***AHAHAHA!***
THAT'S BROTHER BLOOD?
COME ***ON,*** KID. YOU'RE LIKE ***TWELVE.***
I'LL BE ***FOURTEEN*** NEXT ***MONTH.***

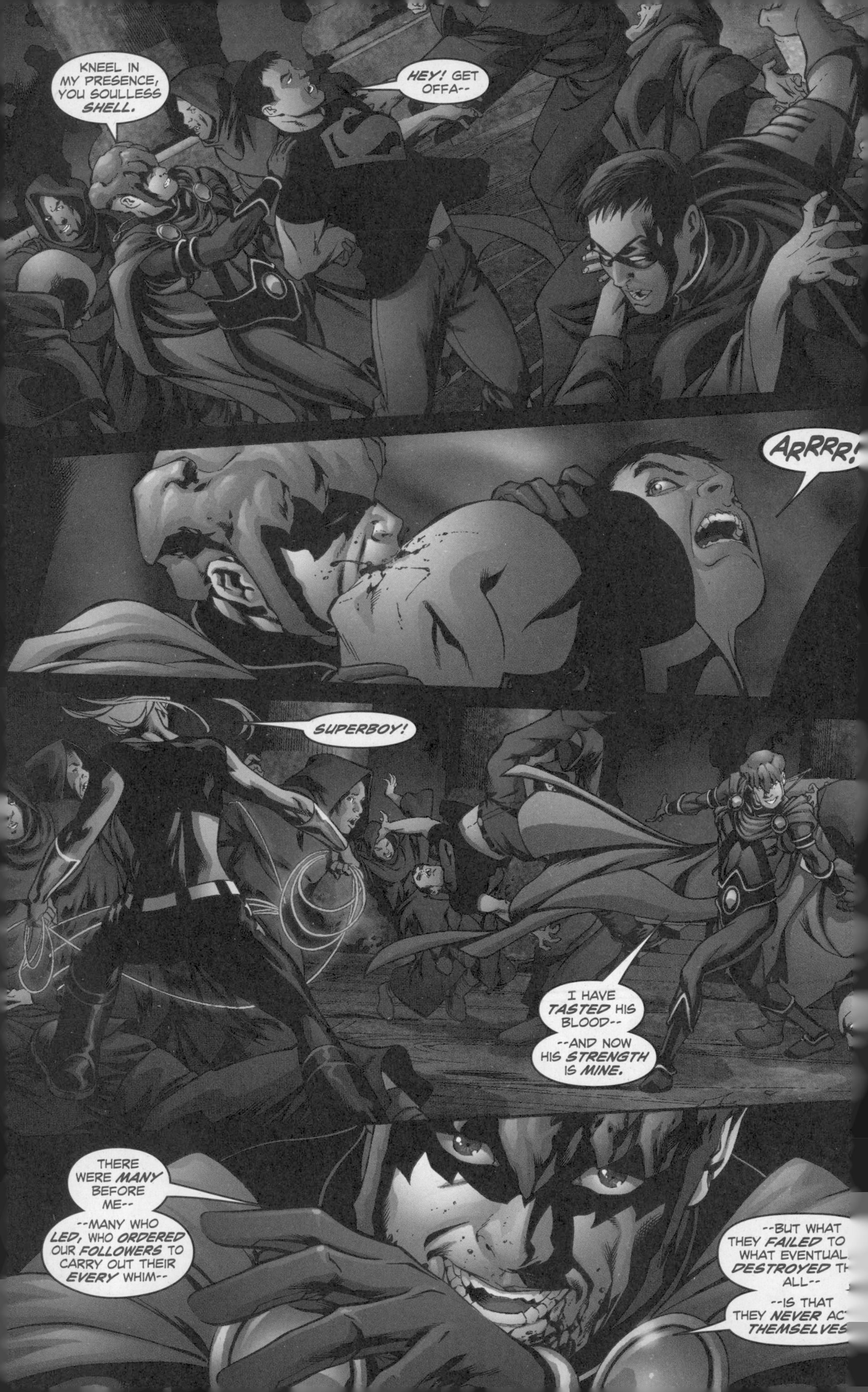
KNEEL IN MY PRESENCE, YOU SOULLESS SHELL.
HEY! GET OFFA--
ARRRR!
SUPERBOY!
I HAVE TASTED HIS BLOOD--
--AND NOW HIS STRENGTH IS MINE.
THERE WERE MANY BEFORE ME--
--MANY WHO LED, WHO ORDERED OUR FOLLOWERS TO CARRY OUT THEIR EVERY WHIM--
--BUT WHAT THEY FAILED TO
--IS THAT THEY NEVER ACT

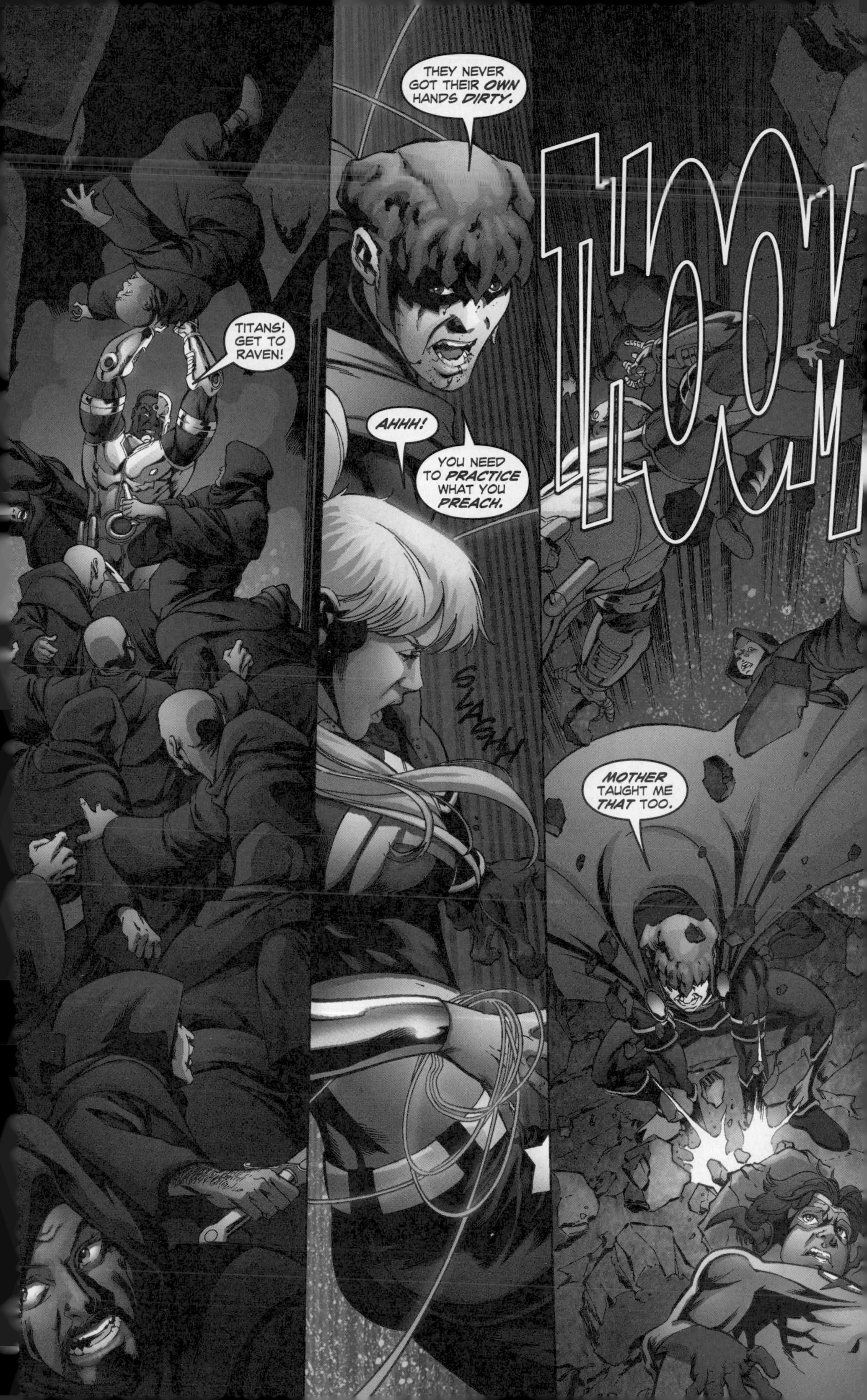
TITANS! GET TO RAVEN!
THEY NEVER GOT THEIR OWN HANDS DIRTY.
AHHH!
YOU NEED TO PRACTICE WHAT YOU PREACH.
THOOM
MOTHER TAUGHT ME THAT TOO.

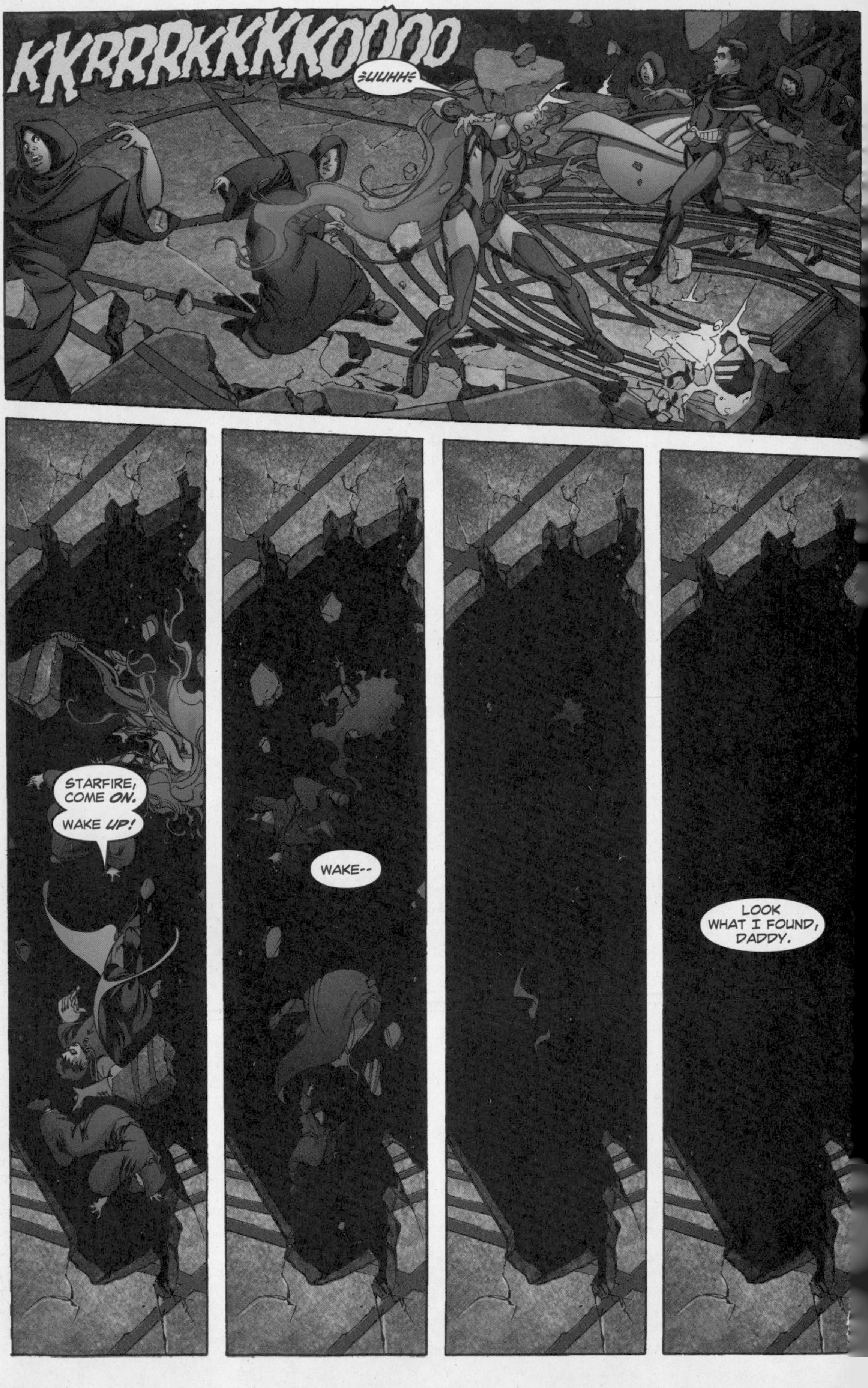
KKRRRKKKKOOOO
UUUHH
STARFIRE, COME ON.
WAKE UP!
WAKE--
LOOK WHAT I FOUND, DADDY.

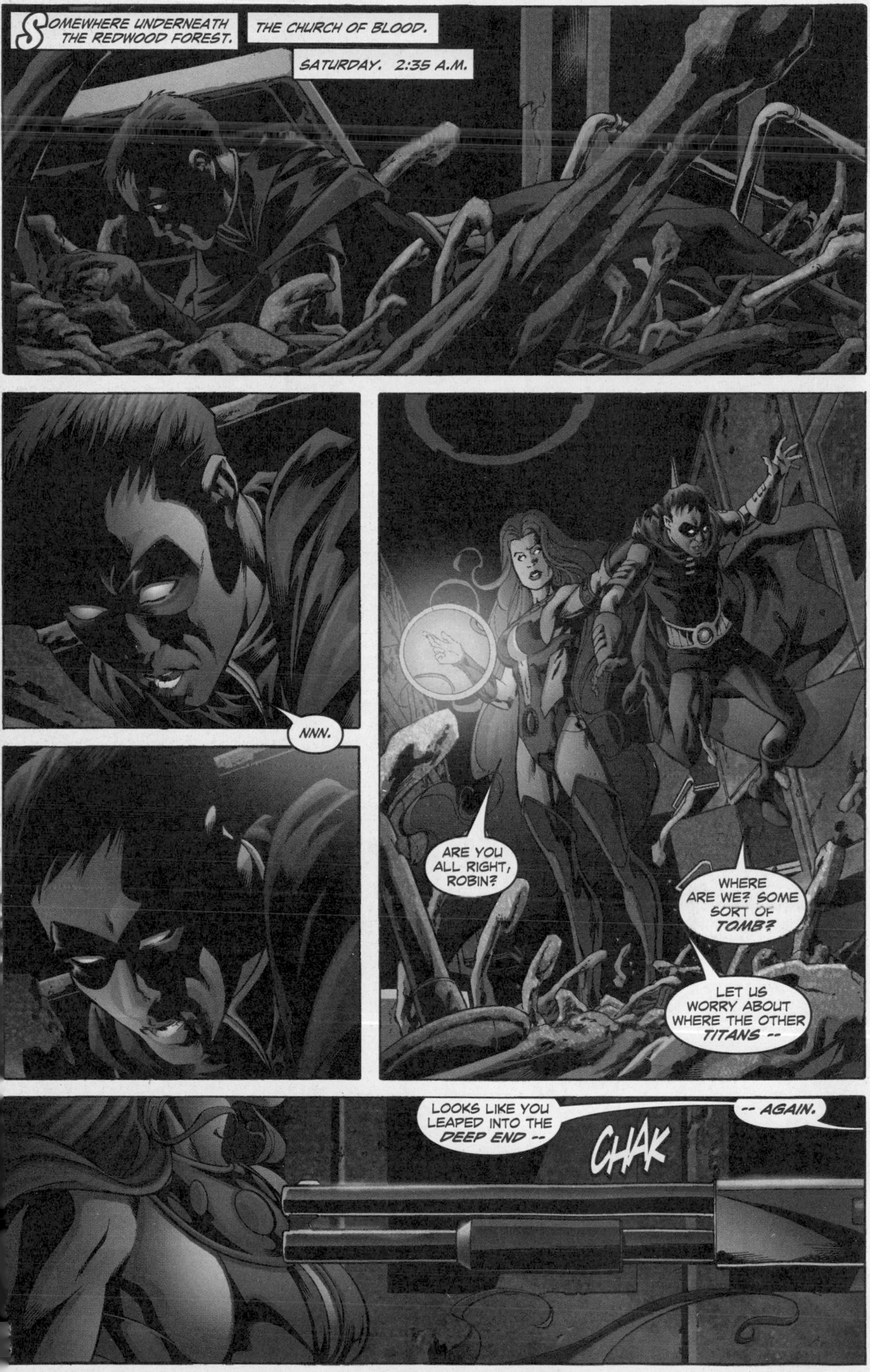
SOMEWHERE UNDERNEATH THE REDWOOD FOREST.
THE CHURCH OF BLOOD.
SATURDAY. 2:35 A.M.
NNN.
ARE YOU ALL RIGHT, ROBIN?
WHERE ARE WE? SOME SORT OF TOMB?
LET US WORRY ABOUT WHERE THE OTHER TITANS --
LOOKS LIKE YOU LEAPED INTO THE DEEP END --
-- AGAIN.
CHAK

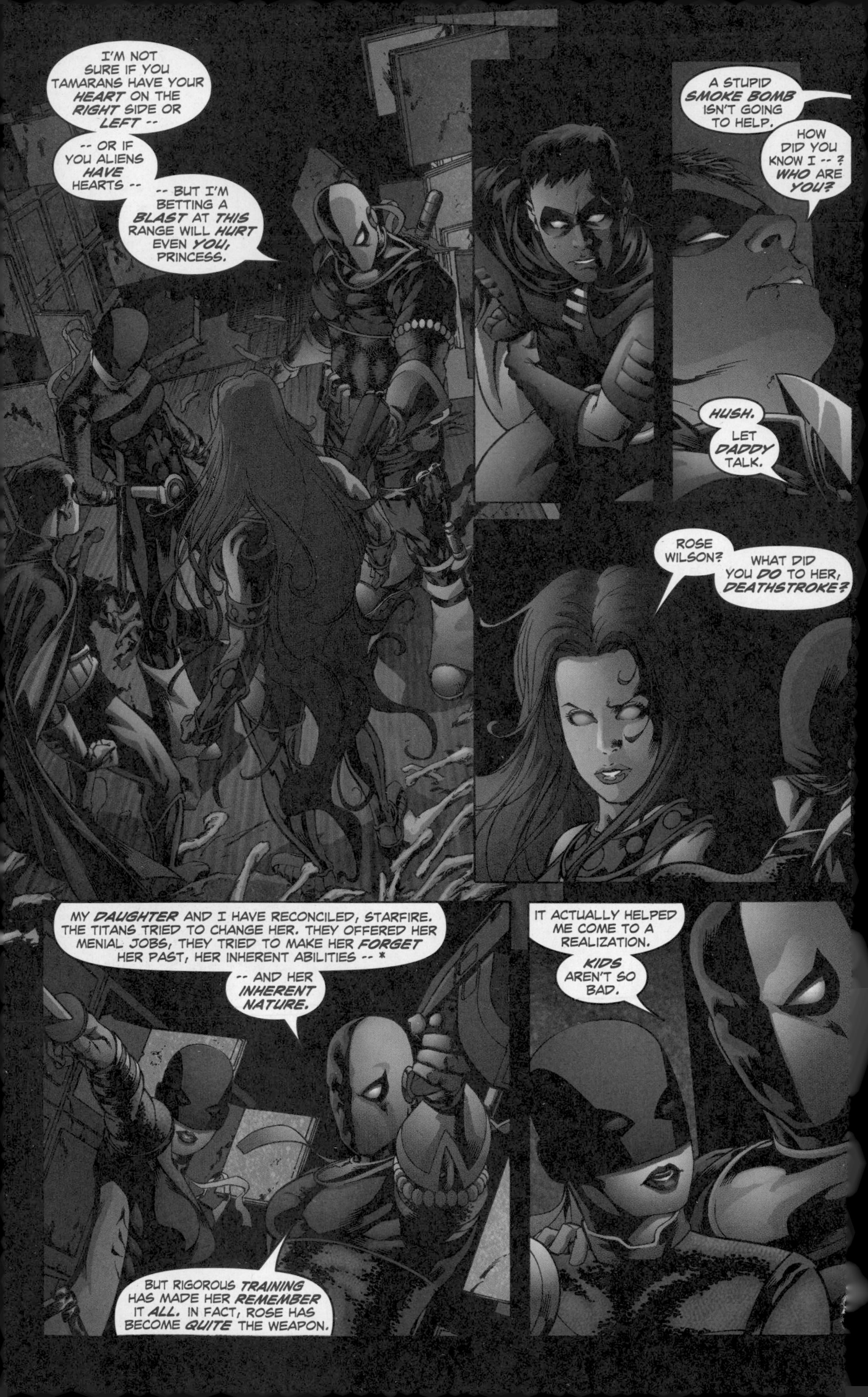
I'M NOT SURE IF YOU TAMARANS HAVE YOUR HEART ON THE RIGHT SIDE OR LEFT --
-- OR IF YOU ALIENS HAVE HEARTS --
-- BUT I'M BETTING A BLAST AT THIS RANGE WILL HURT EVEN YOU, PRINCESS.
A STUPID SMOKE BOMB ISN'T GOING TO HELP.
HOW DID YOU KNOW I -- ? WHO ARE YOU?
HUSH.
LET DADDY TALK.
ROSE WILSON?
WHAT DID YOU DO TO HER, DEATHSTROKE?
MY DAUGHTER AND I HAVE RECONCILED, STARFIRE. THE TITANS TRIED TO CHANGE HER. THEY OFFERED HER MENIAL JOBS, THEY TRIED TO MAKE HER FORGET HER PAST, HER INHERENT ABILITIES -- *
-- AND HER INHERENT NATURE.
BUT RIGOROUS TRAINING HAS MADE HER REMEMBER IT ALL. IN FACT, ROSE HAS BECOME QUITE THE WEAPON.
IT ACTUALLY HELPED ME COME TO A REALIZATION.
KIDS AREN'T SO BAD.

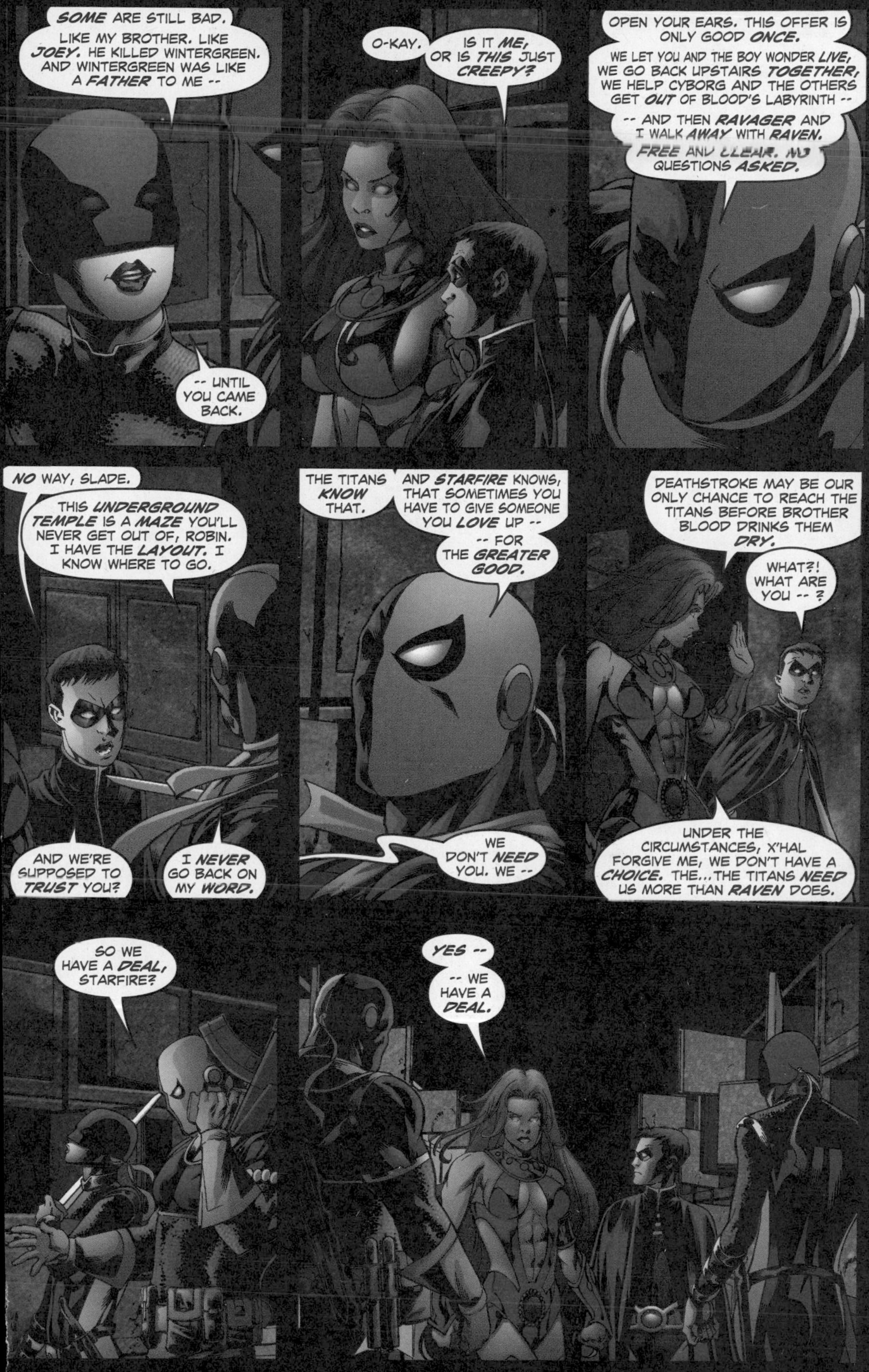
SOME ARE STILL BAD.
LIKE MY BROTHER. LIKE JOEY. HE KILLED WINTERGREEN. AND WINTERGREEN WAS LIKE A FATHER TO ME --
-- UNTIL YOU CAME BACK.
O-KAY.
IS IT ME, OR IS THIS JUST CREEPY?
OPEN YOUR EARS. THIS OFFER IS ONLY GOOD ONCE.
WE LET YOU AND THE BOY WONDER LIVE, WE GO BACK UPSTAIRS TOGETHER, WE HELP CYBORG AND THE OTHERS GET OUT OF BLOOD'S LABYRINTH --
-- AND THEN RAVAGER AND I WALK AWAY WITH RAVEN. FREE AND CLEAR. NO QUESTIONS ASKED.
NO WAY, SLADE.
THIS UNDERGROUND TEMPLE IS A MAZE YOU'LL NEVER GET OUT OF, ROBIN. I HAVE THE LAYOUT. I KNOW WHERE TO GO.
AND WE'RE SUPPOSED TO TRUST YOU?
I NEVER GO BACK ON MY WORD.
THE TITANS KNOW THAT.
AND STARFIRE KNOWS, THAT SOMETIMES YOU HAVE TO GIVE SOMEONE YOU LOVE UP --
-- FOR THE GREATER GOOD.
WE DON'T NEED YOU. WE --
DEATHSTROKE MAY BE OUR ONLY CHANCE TO REACH THE TITANS BEFORE BROTHER BLOOD DRINKS THEM DRY.
WHAT?! WHAT ARE YOU -- ?
UNDER THE CIRCUMSTANCES, X'HAL FORGIVE ME, WE DON'T HAVE A CHOICE. THE...THE TITANS NEED US MORE THAN RAVEN DOES.
SO WE HAVE A DEAL, STARFIRE?
YES --
-- WE HAVE A DEAL.

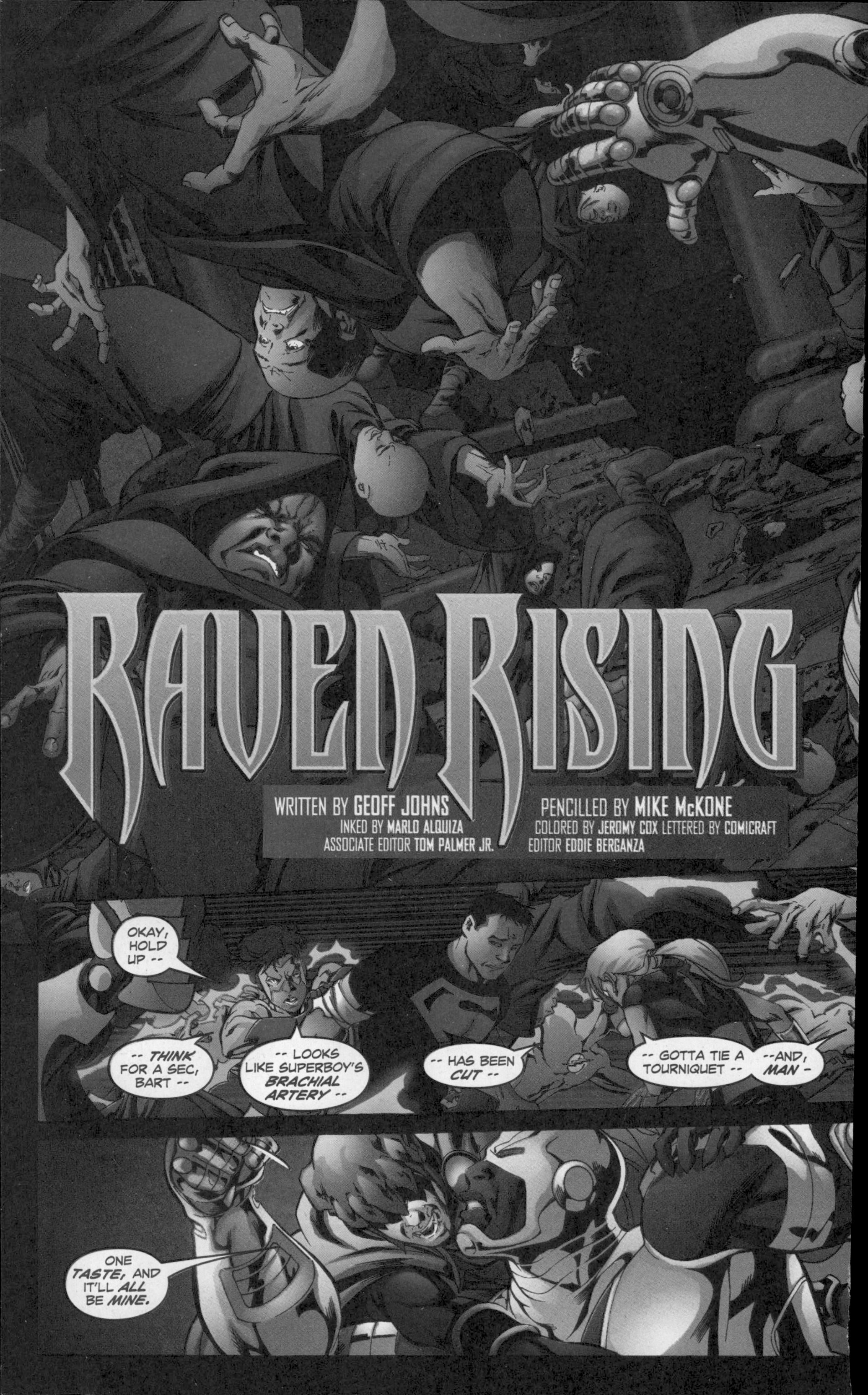
RAVEN RISING
WRITTEN BY GEOFF JOHNS PENCILLED BY MIKE McKONE
INKED BY MARLO ALQUIZA COLORED BY JEROMY COX LETTERED BY COMICRAFT
ASSOCIATE EDITOR TOM PALMER JR. EDITOR EDDIE BERGANZA
OKAY, HOLD UP --
-- THINK FOR A SEC, BART --
-- LOOKS LIKE SUPERBOY'S BRACHIAL ARTERY --
-- HAS BEEN CUT --
-- GOTTA TIE A TOURNIQUET --
--AND, MAN -
ONE TASTE, AND IT'LL ALL BE MINE.

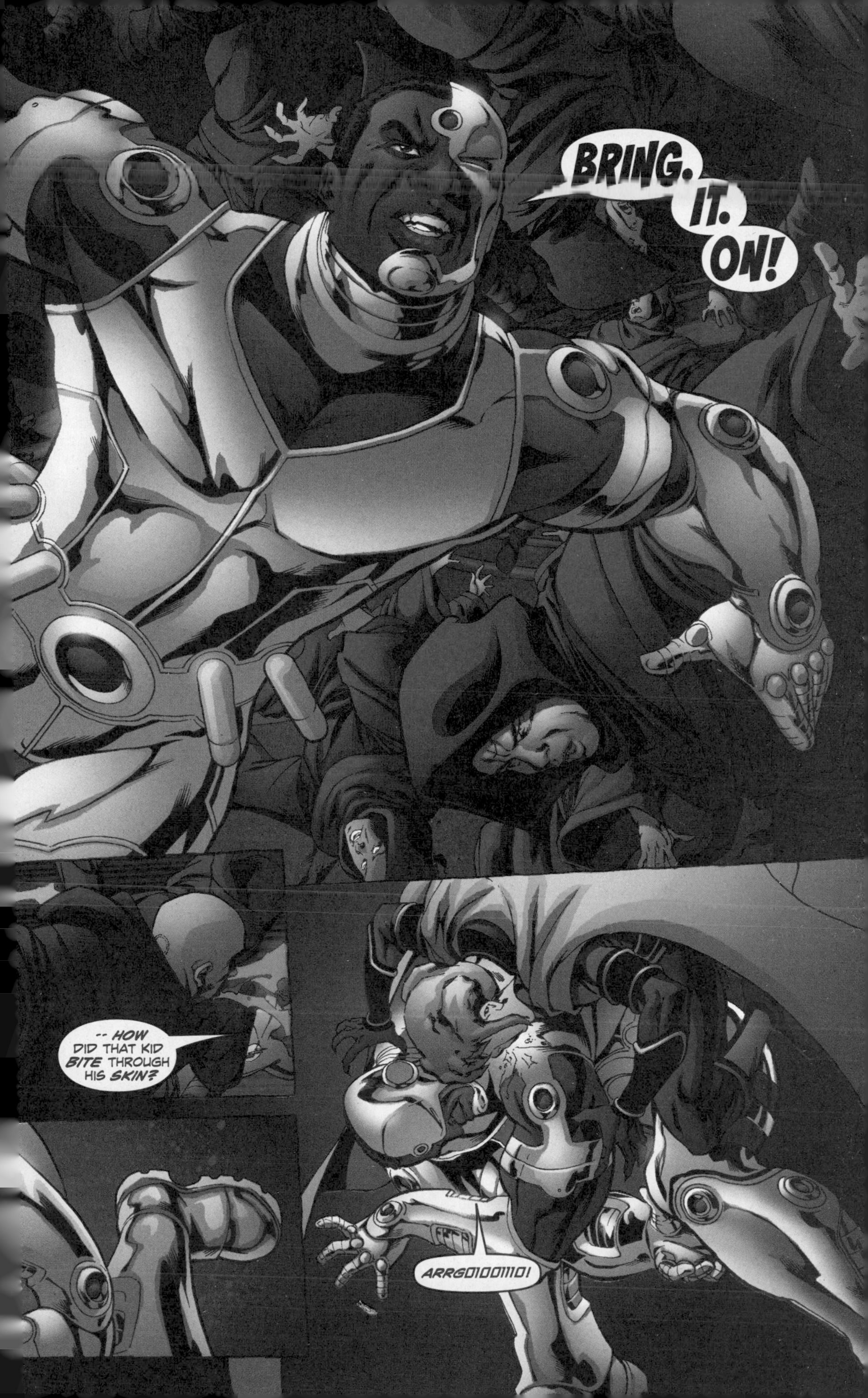
BRING. IT. ON!
-- HOW DID THAT KID BITE THROUGH HIS SKIN?
ARRG01001101

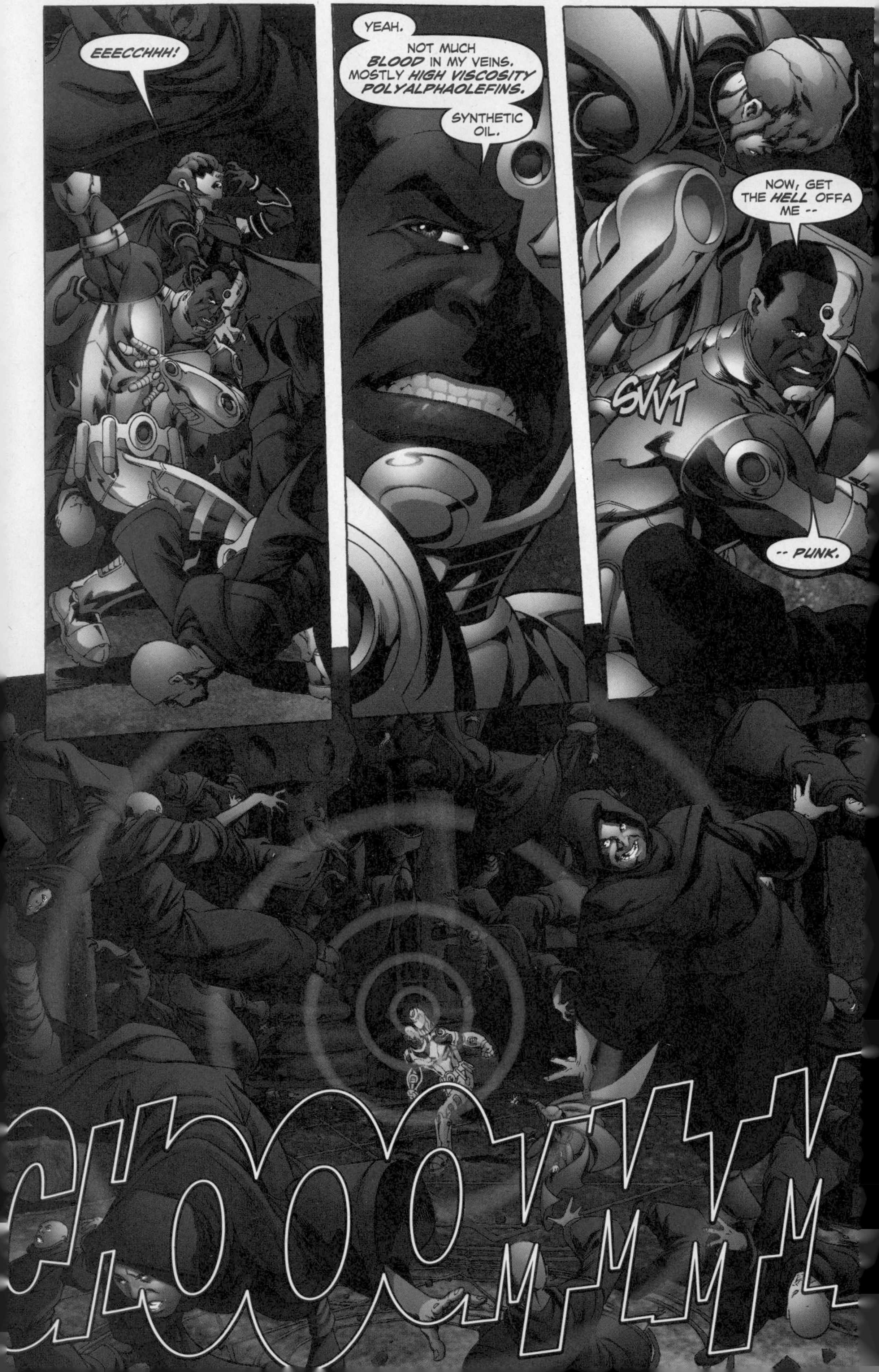
EEECCHHH!
YEAH.
NOT MUCH BLOOD IN MY VEINS. MOSTLY HIGH VISCOSITY POLYALPHAOLEFINS.
SYNTHETIC OIL.
NOW, GET THE HELL OFFA ME --
SVVT
-- PUNK.
CHOOOVVVMMMM

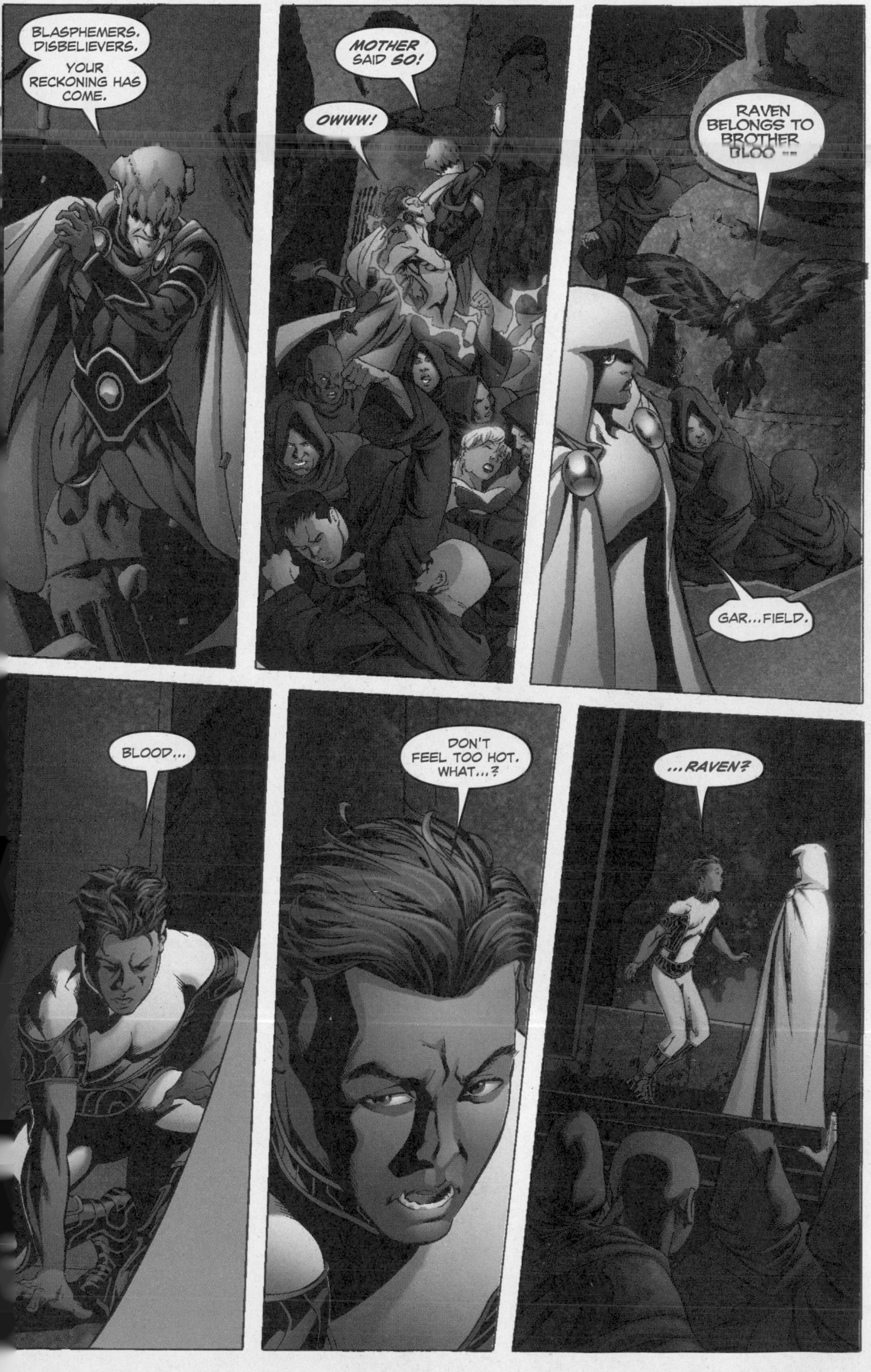
BLASPHEMERS. DISBELIEVERS.
YOUR RECKONING HAS COME.
MOTHER SAID SO!
OWWW!
RAVEN BELONGS TO BROTHER BLOO --
GAR...FIELD.
BLOOD...
DON'T FEEL TOO HOT. WHAT...?
...RAVEN?

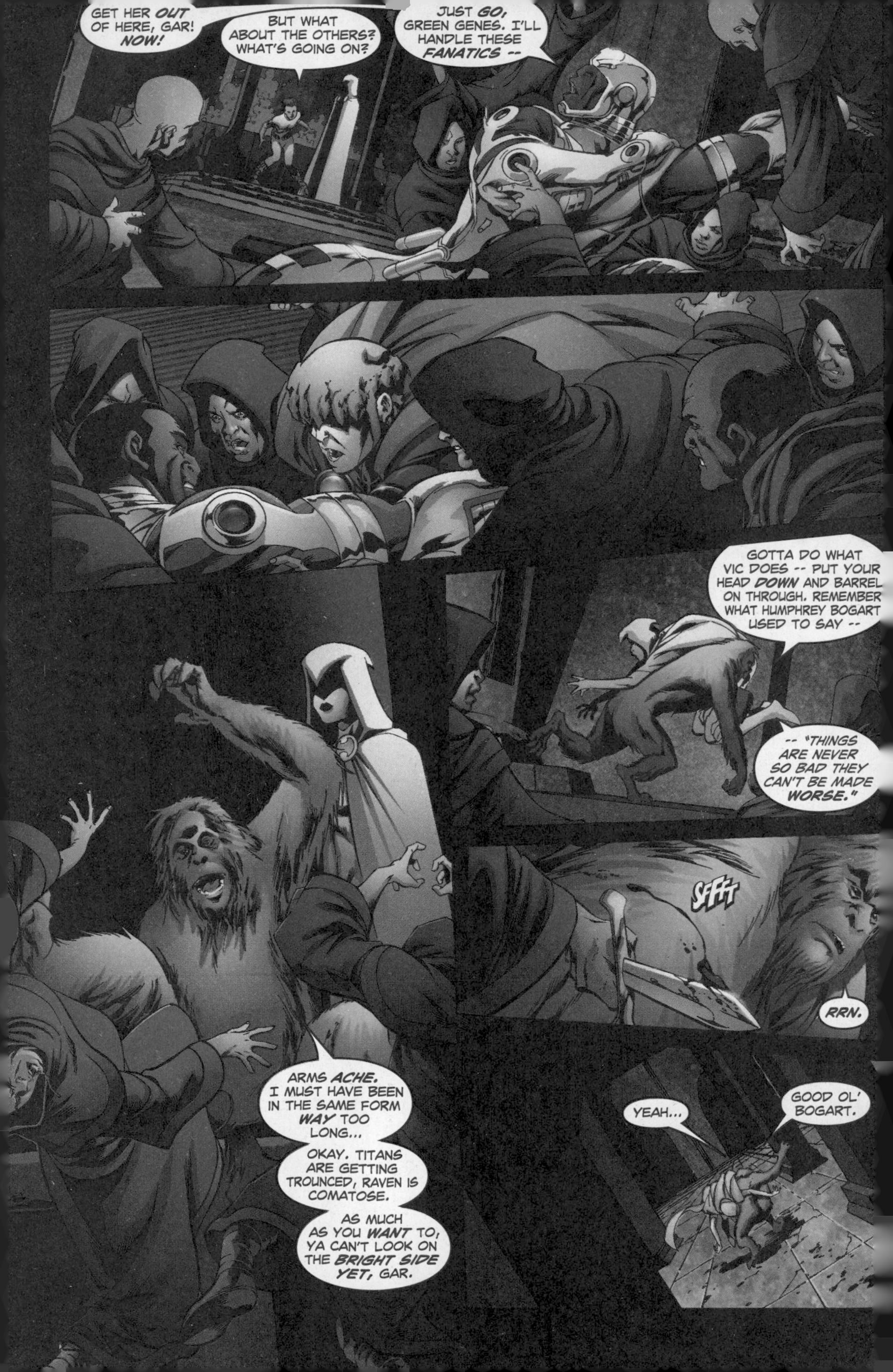
GET HER *OUT* OF HERE, GAR! ***NOW!***
BUT WHAT ABOUT THE OTHERS? WHAT'S GOING ON?
JUST *GO,* GREEN GENES. I'LL HANDLE THESE *FANATICS --*
GOTTA DO WHAT VIC DOES -- PUT YOUR HEAD *DOWN* AND BARREL ON THROUGH. REMEMBER WHAT HUMPHREY BOGART USED TO SAY --
-- "THINGS ARE NEVER SO BAD THEY CAN'T BE MADE *WORSE.*"
SFFFT
RRN.
ARMS *ACHE.* I MUST HAVE BEEN IN THE SAME FORM *WAY* TOO LONG...
OKAY. TITANS ARE GETTING TROUNCED, RAVEN IS COMATOSE.
AS MUCH AS YOU *WANT* TO, YA CAN'T LOOK ON THE *BRIGHT SIDE YET,* GAR.
YEAH...
GOOD OL' BOGART.

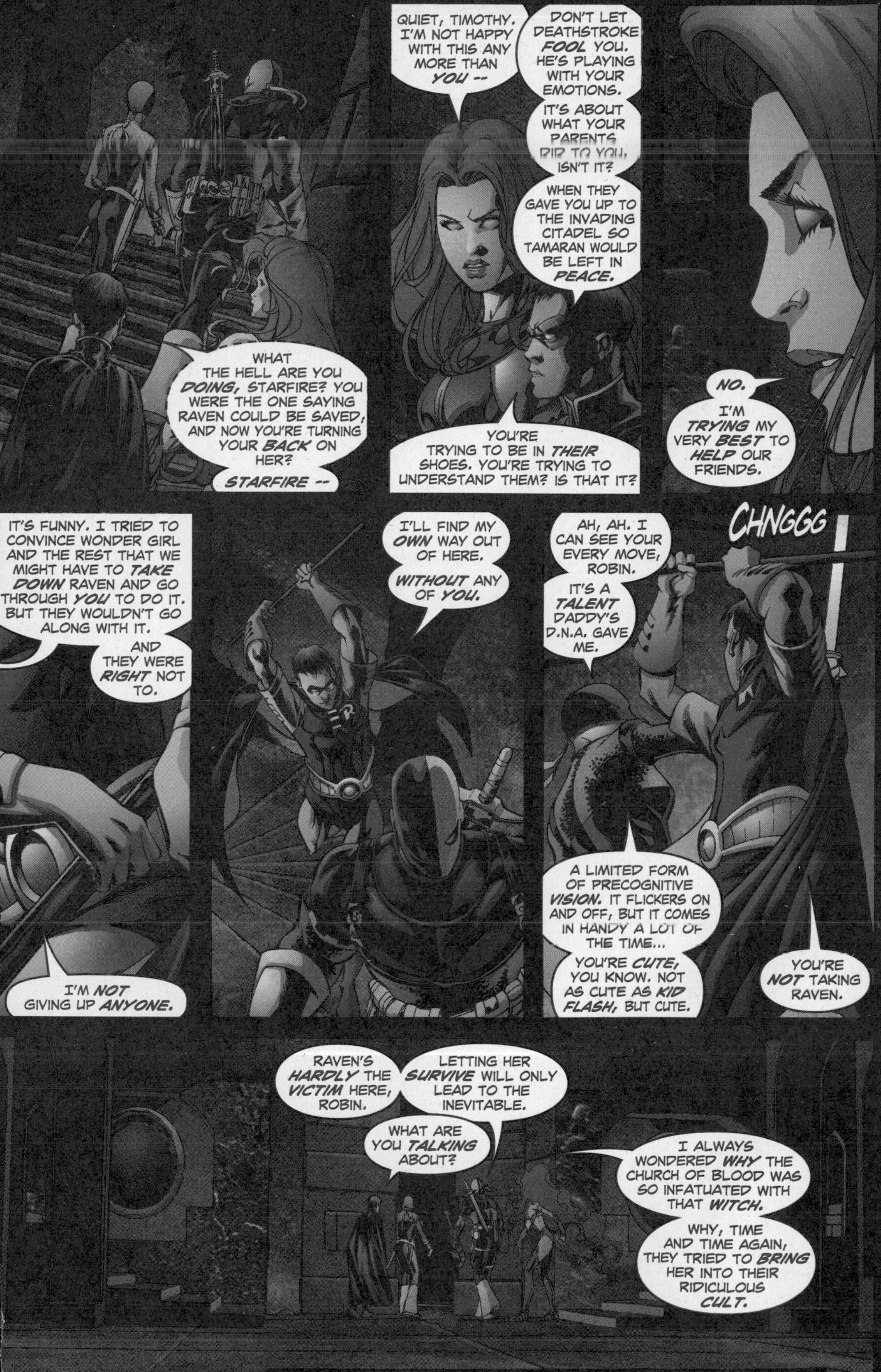
WHAT THE HELL ARE YOU DOING, STARFIRE? YOU WERE THE ONE SAYING RAVEN COULD BE SAVED, AND NOW YOU'RE TURNING YOUR BACK ON HER?
STARFIRE --
QUIET, TIMOTHY. I'M NOT HAPPY WITH THIS ANY MORE THAN YOU --
DON'T LET DEATHSTROKE FOOL YOU. HE'S PLAYING WITH YOUR EMOTIONS.
IT'S ABOUT WHAT YOUR PARENTS DID TO YOU, ISN'T IT?
WHEN THEY GAVE YOU UP TO THE INVADING CITADEL SO TAMARAN WOULD BE LEFT IN PEACE.
YOU'RE TRYING TO BE IN THEIR SHOES. YOU'RE TRYING TO UNDERSTAND THEM? IS THAT IT?
NO.
I'M TRYING MY VERY BEST TO HELP OUR FRIENDS.
IT'S FUNNY. I TRIED TO CONVINCE WONDER GIRL AND THE REST THAT WE MIGHT HAVE TO TAKE DOWN RAVEN AND GO THROUGH YOU TO DO IT. BUT THEY WOULDN'T GO ALONG WITH IT.
AND THEY WERE RIGHT NOT TO.
I'M NOT GIVING UP ANYONE.
I'LL FIND MY OWN WAY OUT OF HERE.
WITHOUT ANY OF YOU.
CHNGGG
AH, AH. I CAN SEE YOUR EVERY MOVE, ROBIN.
IT'S A TALENT DADDY'S D.N.A. GAVE ME.
A LIMITED FORM OF PRECOGNITIVE VISION. IT FLICKERS ON AND OFF, BUT IT COMES IN HANDY A LOT OF THE TIME...
YOU'RE CUTE, YOU KNOW. NOT AS CUTE AS KID FLASH, BUT CUTE.
YOU'RE NOT TAKING RAVEN.
RAVEN'S HARDLY THE VICTIM HERE, ROBIN.
LETTING HER SURVIVE WILL ONLY LEAD TO THE INEVITABLE.
WHAT ARE YOU TALKING ABOUT?
I ALWAYS WONDERED WHY THE CHURCH OF BLOOD WAS SO INFATUATED WITH THAT WITCH.
WHY, TIME AND TIME AGAIN, THEY TRIED TO BRING HER INTO THEIR RIDICULOUS CULT.

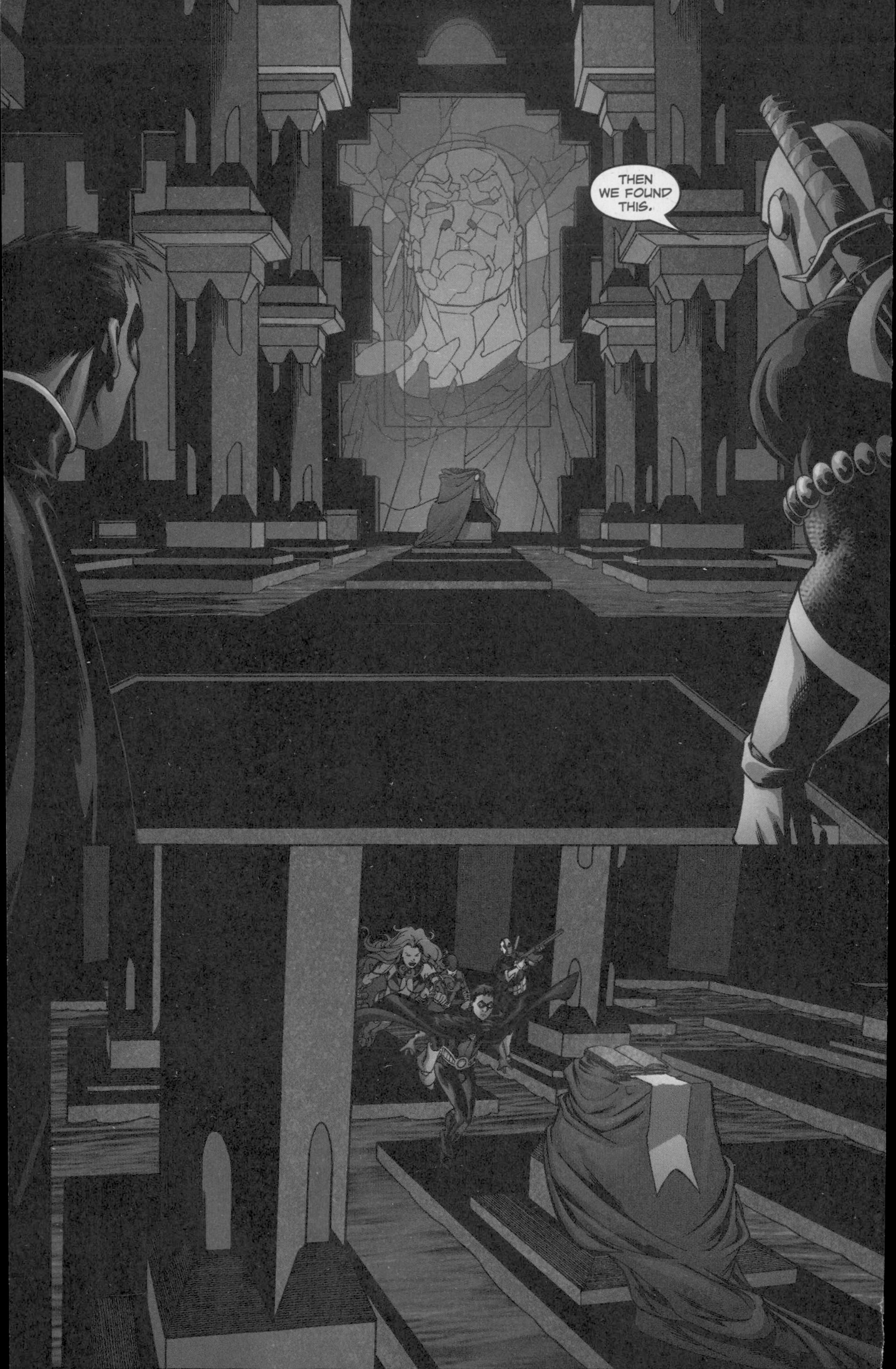
THEN WE FOUND THIS.

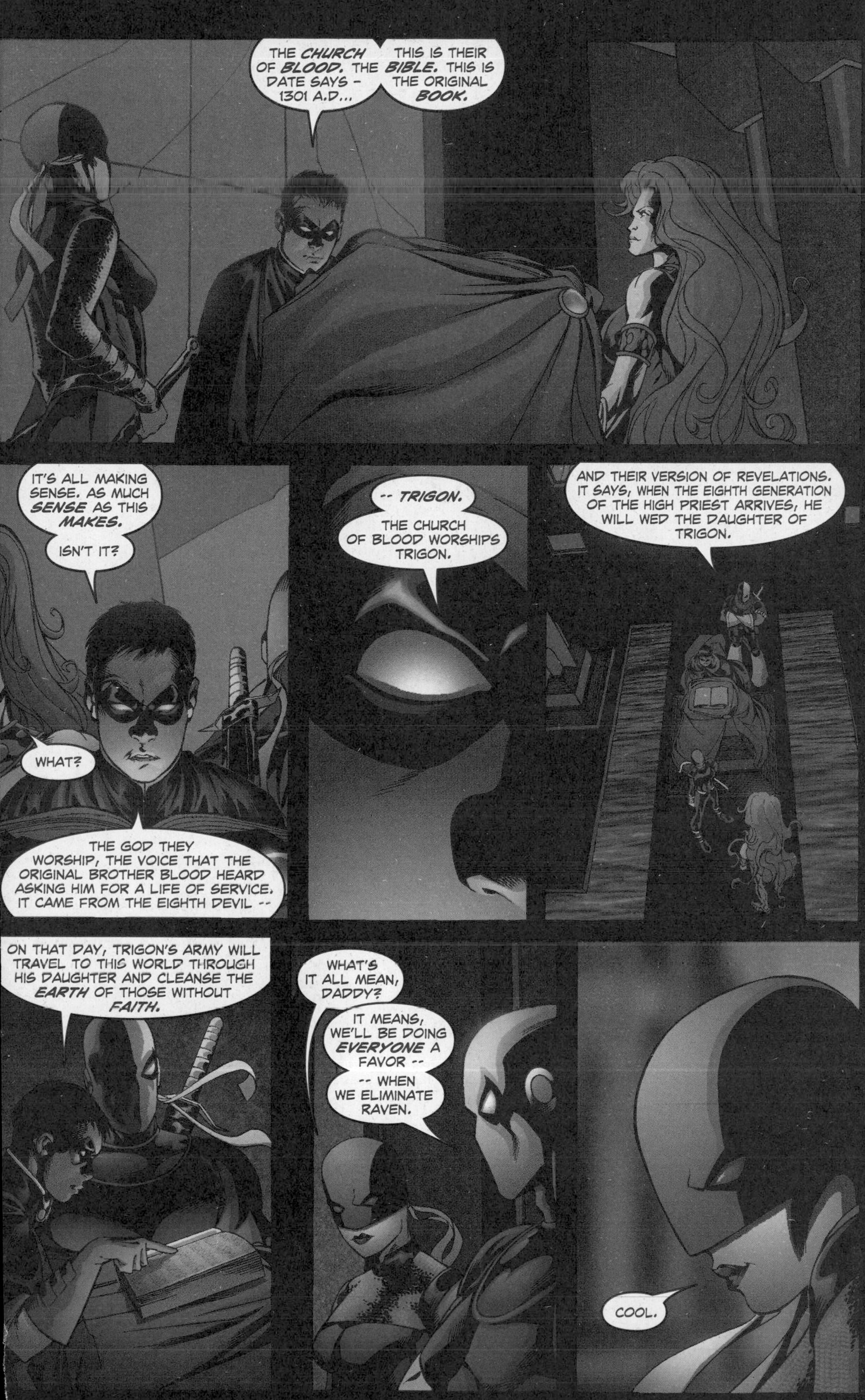
THE CHURCH OF BLOOD. THE DATE SAYS -- 1301 A.D...
THIS IS THEIR BIBLE. THIS IS THE ORIGINAL BOOK.
IT'S ALL MAKING SENSE. AS MUCH SENSE AS THIS MAKES.
ISN'T IT?
WHAT?
THE GOD THEY WORSHIP, THE VOICE THAT THE ORIGINAL BROTHER BLOOD HEARD ASKING HIM FOR A LIFE OF SERVICE. IT CAME FROM THE EIGHTH DEVIL --
-- TRIGON.
THE CHURCH OF BLOOD WORSHIPS TRIGON.
AND THEIR VERSION OF REVELATIONS. IT SAYS, WHEN THE EIGHTH GENERATION OF THE HIGH PRIEST ARRIVES, HE WILL WED THE DAUGHTER OF TRIGON.
ON THAT DAY, TRIGON'S ARMY WILL TRAVEL TO THIS WORLD THROUGH HIS DAUGHTER AND CLEANSE THE EARTH OF THOSE WITHOUT FAITH.
WHAT'S IT ALL MEAN, DADDY?
IT MEANS, WE'LL BE DOING EVERYONE A FAVOR --
-- WHEN WE ELIMINATE RAVEN.
COOL.

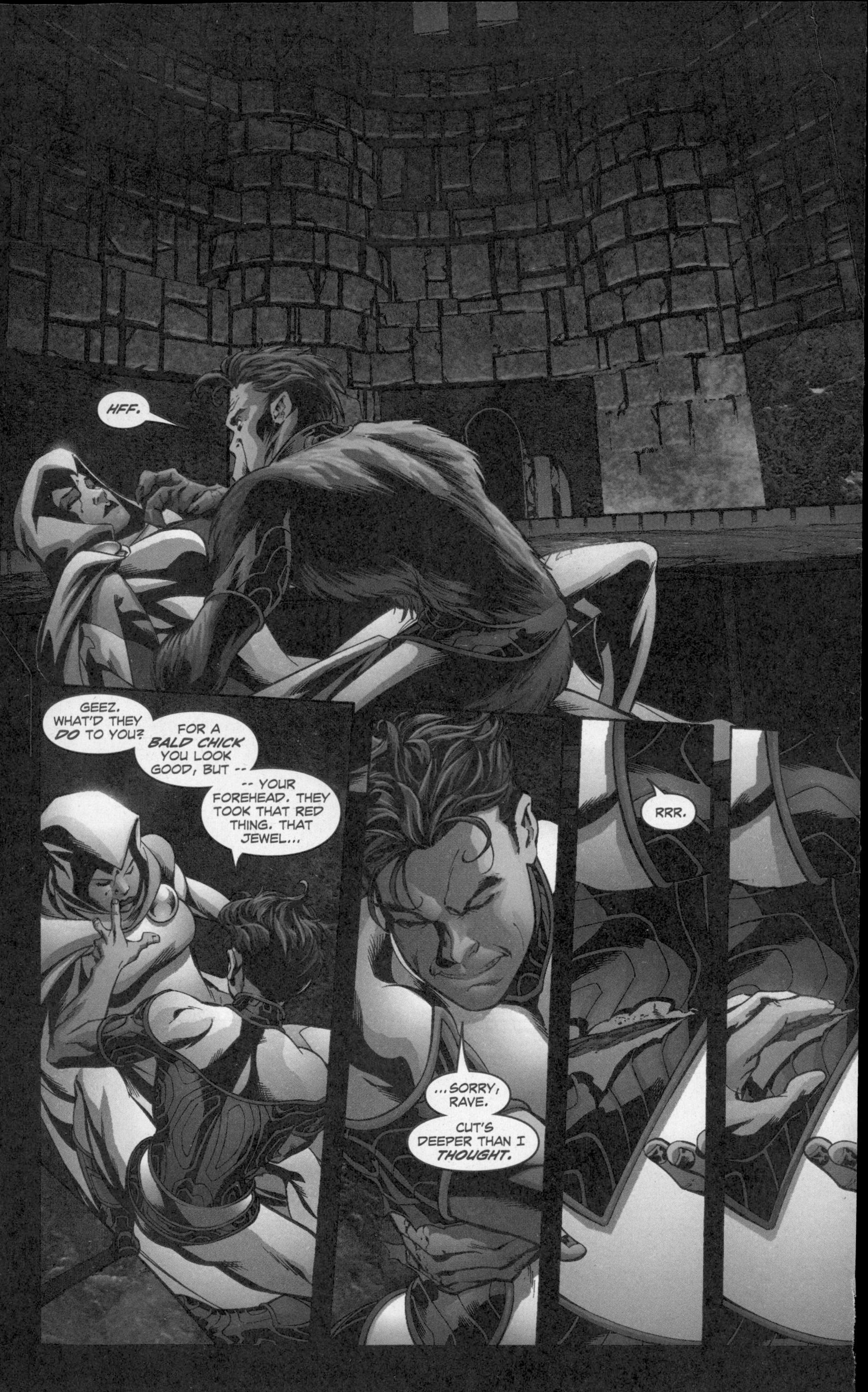
HFF.
GEEZ. WHAT'D THEY *DO* TO YOU?
FOR A *BALD CHICK* YOU LOOK GOOD, BUT --
-- YOUR FOREHEAD. THEY TOOK THAT RED THING. THAT JEWEL...
...SORRY, RAVE.
CUT'S DEEPER THAN I *THOUGHT*.
RRR.

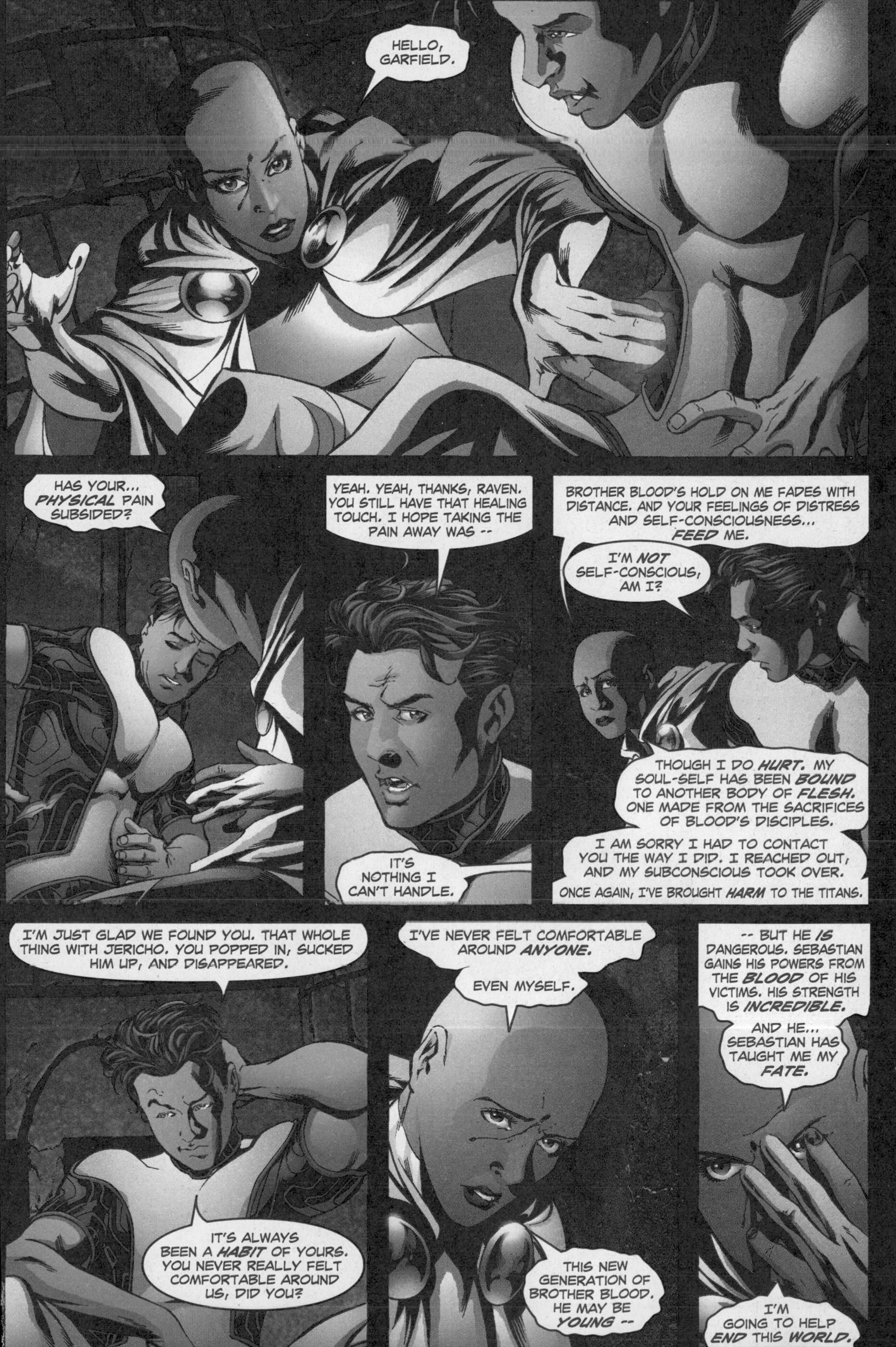
HELLO, GARFIELD.
HAS YOUR... PHYSICAL PAIN SUBSIDED?
YEAH. YEAH, THANKS, RAVEN. YOU STILL HAVE THAT HEALING TOUCH. I HOPE TAKING THE PAIN AWAY WAS --
IT'S NOTHING I CAN'T HANDLE.
BROTHER BLOOD'S HOLD ON ME FADES WITH DISTANCE. AND YOUR FEELINGS OF DISTRESS AND SELF-CONSCIOUSNESS... FEED ME.
I'M NOT SELF-CONSCIOUS, AM I?
THOUGH I DO HURT. MY SOUL-SELF HAS BEEN BOUND TO ANOTHER BODY OF FLESH. ONE MADE FROM THE SACRIFICES OF BLOOD'S DISCIPLES.
I AM SORRY I HAD TO CONTACT YOU THE WAY I DID. I REACHED OUT, AND MY SUBCONSCIOUS TOOK OVER.
ONCE AGAIN, I'VE BROUGHT HARM TO THE TITANS.
I'M JUST GLAD WE FOUND YOU. THAT WHOLE THING WITH JERICHO. YOU POPPED IN, SUCKED HIM UP, AND DISAPPEARED.
IT'S ALWAYS BEEN A HABIT OF YOURS. YOU NEVER REALLY FELT COMFORTABLE AROUND US, DID YOU?
I'VE NEVER FELT COMFORTABLE AROUND ANYONE.
EVEN MYSELF.
THIS NEW GENERATION OF BROTHER BLOOD. HE MAY BE YOUNG --
-- BUT HE IS DANGEROUS. SEBASTIAN GAINS HIS POWERS FROM THE BLOOD OF HIS VICTIMS. HIS STRENGTH IS INCREDIBLE.
AND HE... SEBASTIAN HAS TAUGHT ME MY FATE.
I'M GOING TO HELP END THIS WORLD.

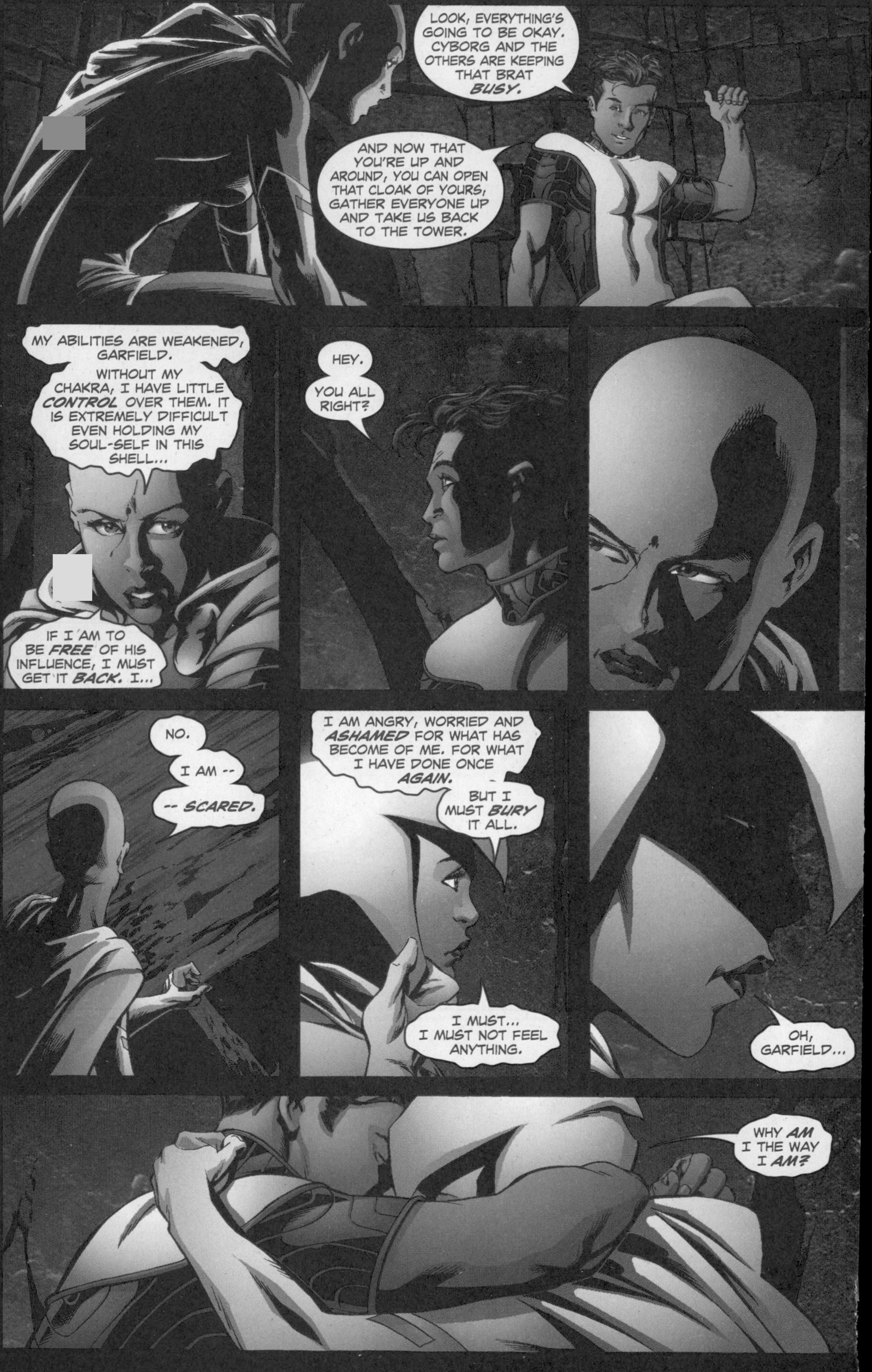
LOOK, EVERYTHING'S GOING TO BE OKAY. CYBORG AND THE OTHERS ARE KEEPING THAT BRAT BUSY.
AND NOW THAT YOU'RE UP AND AROUND, YOU CAN OPEN THAT CLOAK OF YOURS, GATHER EVERYONE UP AND TAKE US BACK TO THE TOWER.
MY ABILITIES ARE WEAKENED, GARFIELD.
WITHOUT MY CHAKRA, I HAVE LITTLE CONTROL OVER THEM. IT IS EXTREMELY DIFFICULT EVEN HOLDING MY SOUL-SELF IN THIS SHELL...
IF I AM TO BE FREE OF HIS INFLUENCE, I MUST GET IT BACK. I...
HEY.
YOU ALL RIGHT?
NO.
I AM --
-- SCARED.
I AM ANGRY, WORRIED AND ASHAMED FOR WHAT HAS BECOME OF ME. FOR WHAT I HAVE DONE ONCE AGAIN.
BUT I MUST BURY IT ALL.
I MUST... I MUST NOT FEEL ANYTHING.
OH, GARFIELD...
WHY AM I THE WAY I AM?

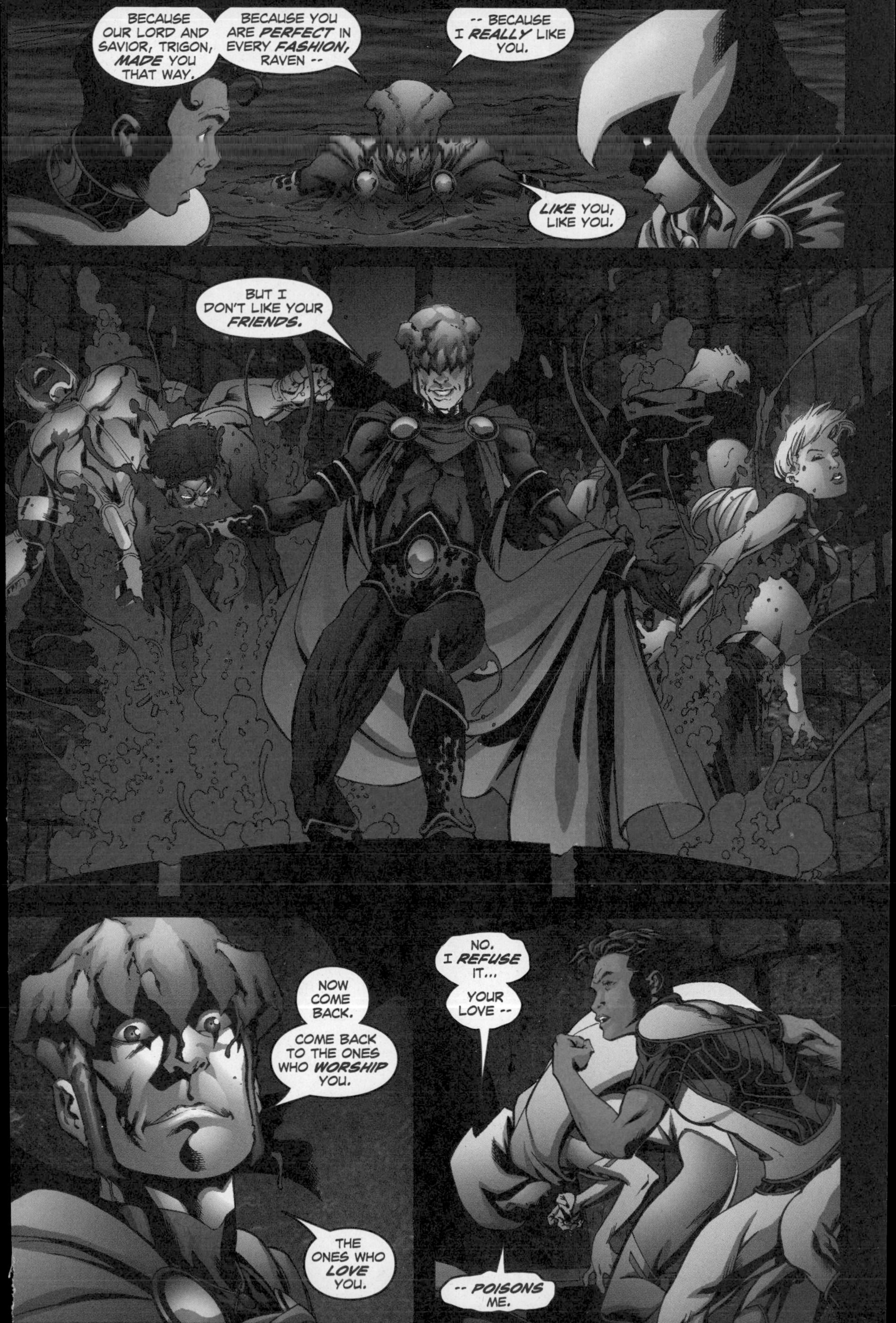
BECAUSE OUR LORD AND SAVIOR, TRIGON, MADE YOU THAT WAY.
BECAUSE YOU ARE PERFECT IN EVERY FASHION, RAVEN --
-- BECAUSE I REALLY LIKE YOU.
LIKE YOU, LIKE YOU.
BUT I DON'T LIKE YOUR FRIENDS.
NOW COME BACK.
COME BACK TO THE ONES WHO WORSHIP YOU.
THE ONES WHO LOVE YOU.
NO. I REFUSE IT...
YOUR LOVE --
-- POISONS ME.

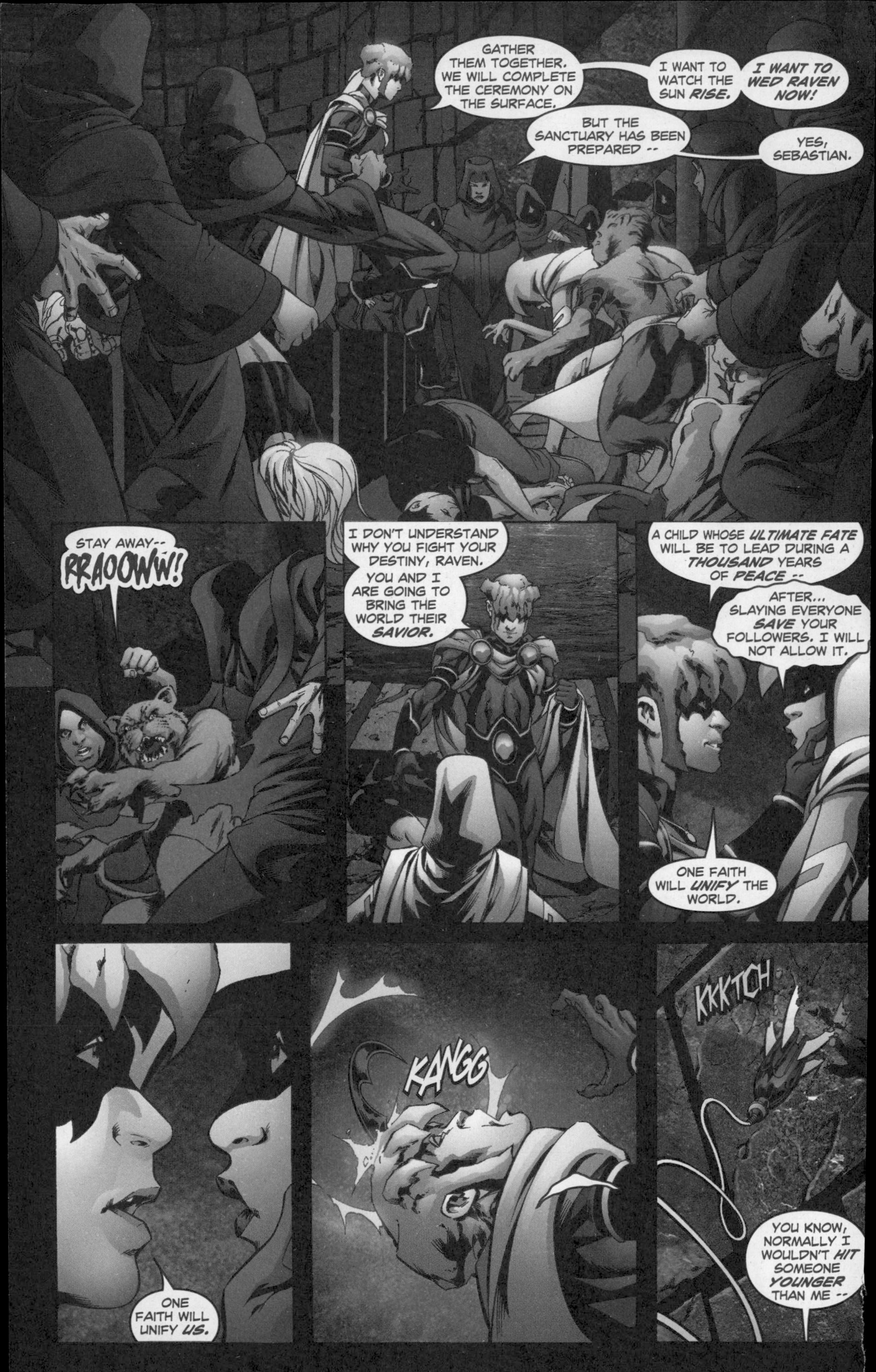
GATHER THEM TOGETHER. WE WILL COMPLETE THE CEREMONY ON THE SURFACE.
I WANT TO WATCH THE SUN RISE.
I WANT TO WED RAVEN NOW!
BUT THE SANCTUARY HAS BEEN PREPARED --
YES, SEBASTIAN.
STAY AWAY-- RRAOOWW!
I DON'T UNDERSTAND WHY YOU FIGHT YOUR DESTINY, RAVEN.
YOU AND I ARE GOING TO BRING THE WORLD THEIR SAVIOR.
A CHILD WHOSE ULTIMATE FATE WILL BE TO LEAD DURING A THOUSAND YEARS OF PEACE --
AFTER... SLAYING EVERYONE SAVE YOUR FOLLOWERS. I WILL NOT ALLOW IT.
ONE FAITH WILL UNIFY THE WORLD.
ONE FAITH WILL UNIFY US.
KANGG
KKKTCH
YOU KNOW, NORMALLY I WOULDN'T HIT SOMEONE YOUNGER THAN ME --

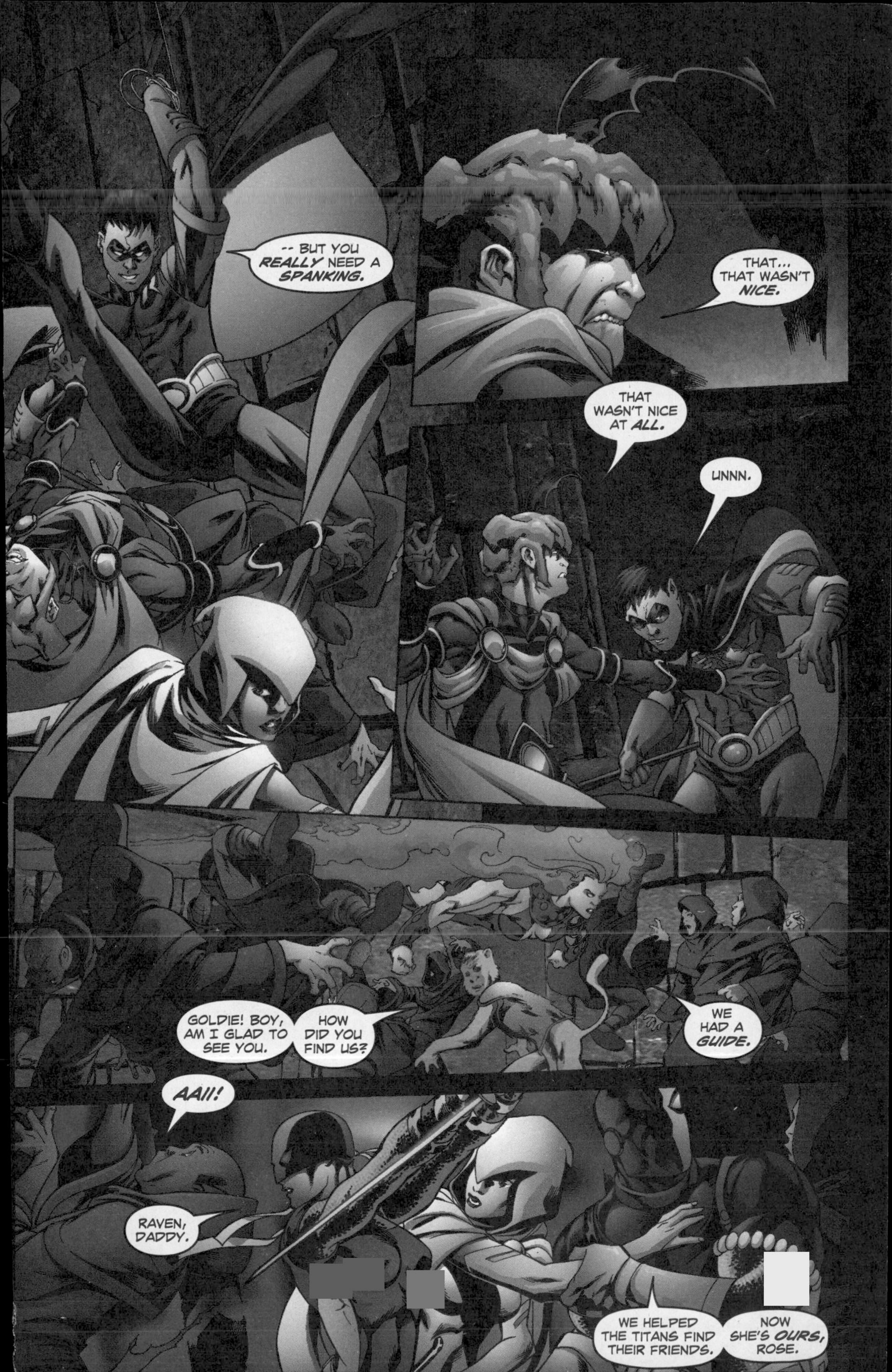
-- BUT YOU REALLY NEED A SPANKING.
THAT... THAT WASN'T NICE.
THAT WASN'T NICE AT ALL.
UNNN.
GOLDIE! BOY, AM I GLAD TO SEE YOU.
HOW DID YOU FIND US?
WE HAD A GUIDE.
AAII!
RAVEN, DADDY.
WE HELPED THE TITANS FIND THEIR FRIENDS.
NOW SHE'S OURS, ROSE.

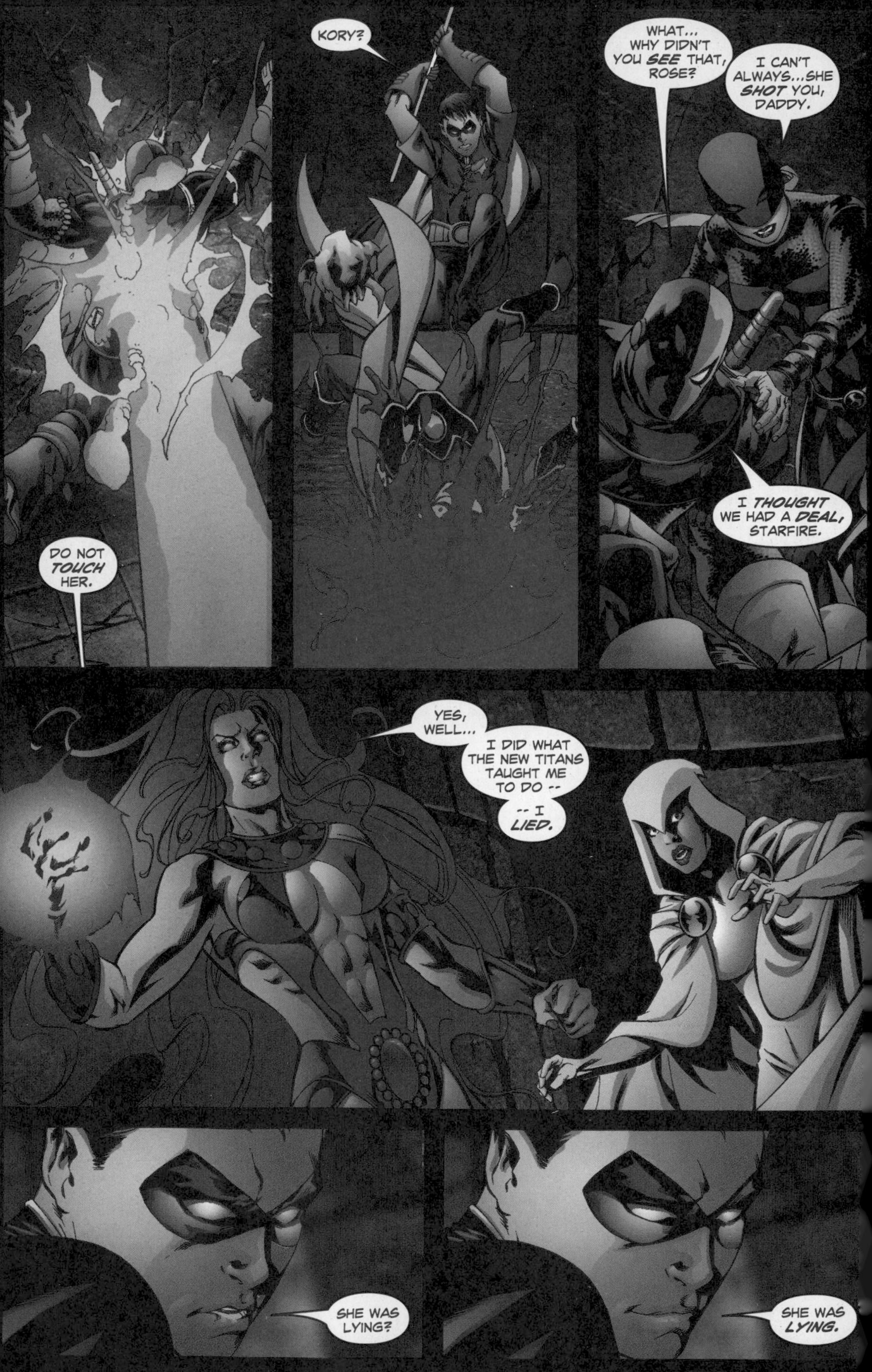
DO NOT *TOUCH* HER.
KORY?
WHAT... WHY DIDN'T YOU *SEE* THAT, ROSE?
I CAN'T ALWAYS...SHE *SHOT* YOU, DADDY.
I *THOUGHT* WE HAD A *DEAL,* STARFIRE.
YES, WELL...
I DID WHAT THE NEW TITANS TAUGHT ME TO DO --
-- I *LIED.*
SHE WAS LYING?
SHE WAS *LYING.*

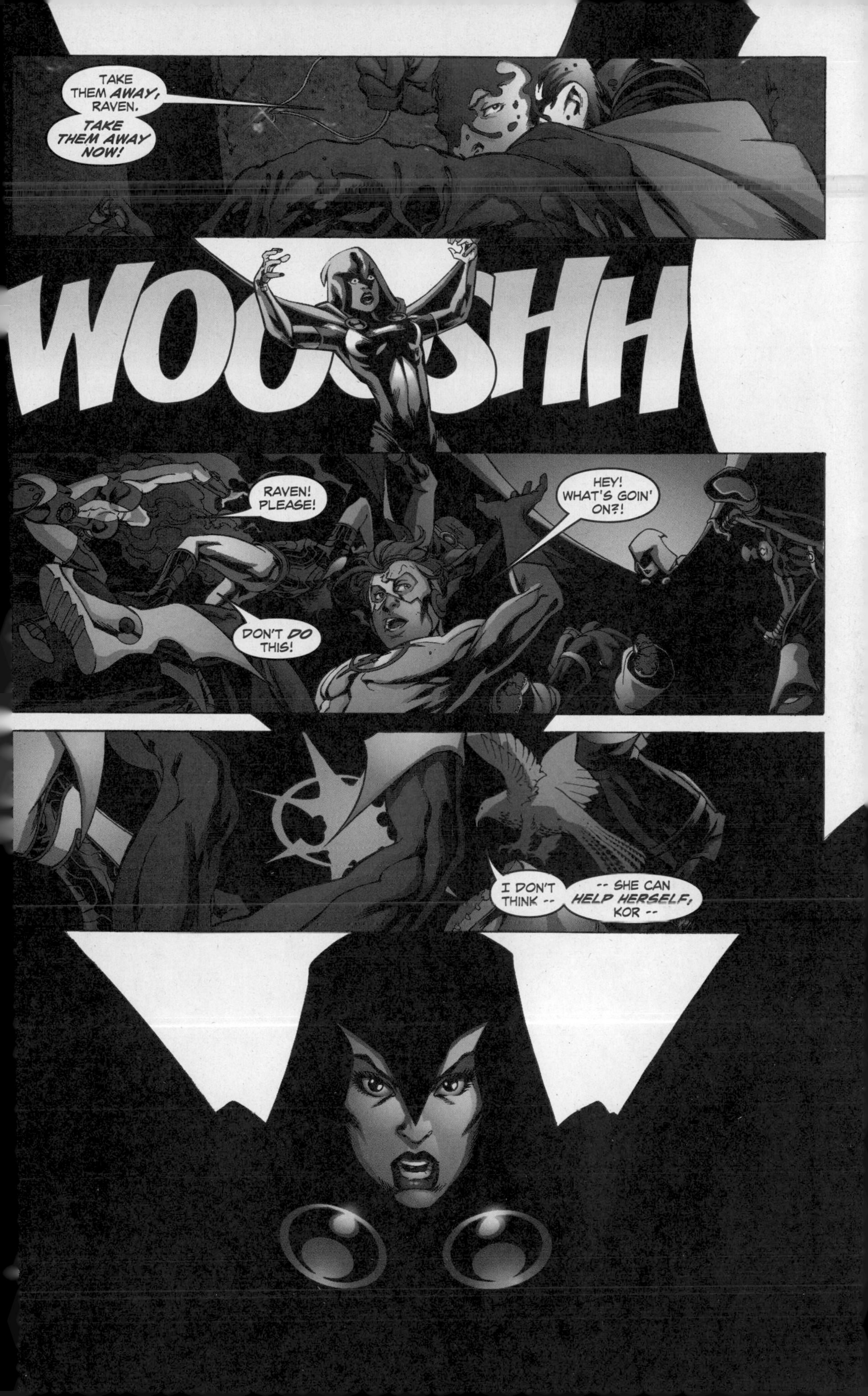
TAKE THEM AWAY, RAVEN. TAKE THEM AWAY NOW!
WOOSHH
RAVEN! PLEASE!
HEY! WHAT'S GOIN' ON?!
DON'T DO THIS!
I DON'T THINK --
-- SHE CAN HELP HERSELF, KOR --

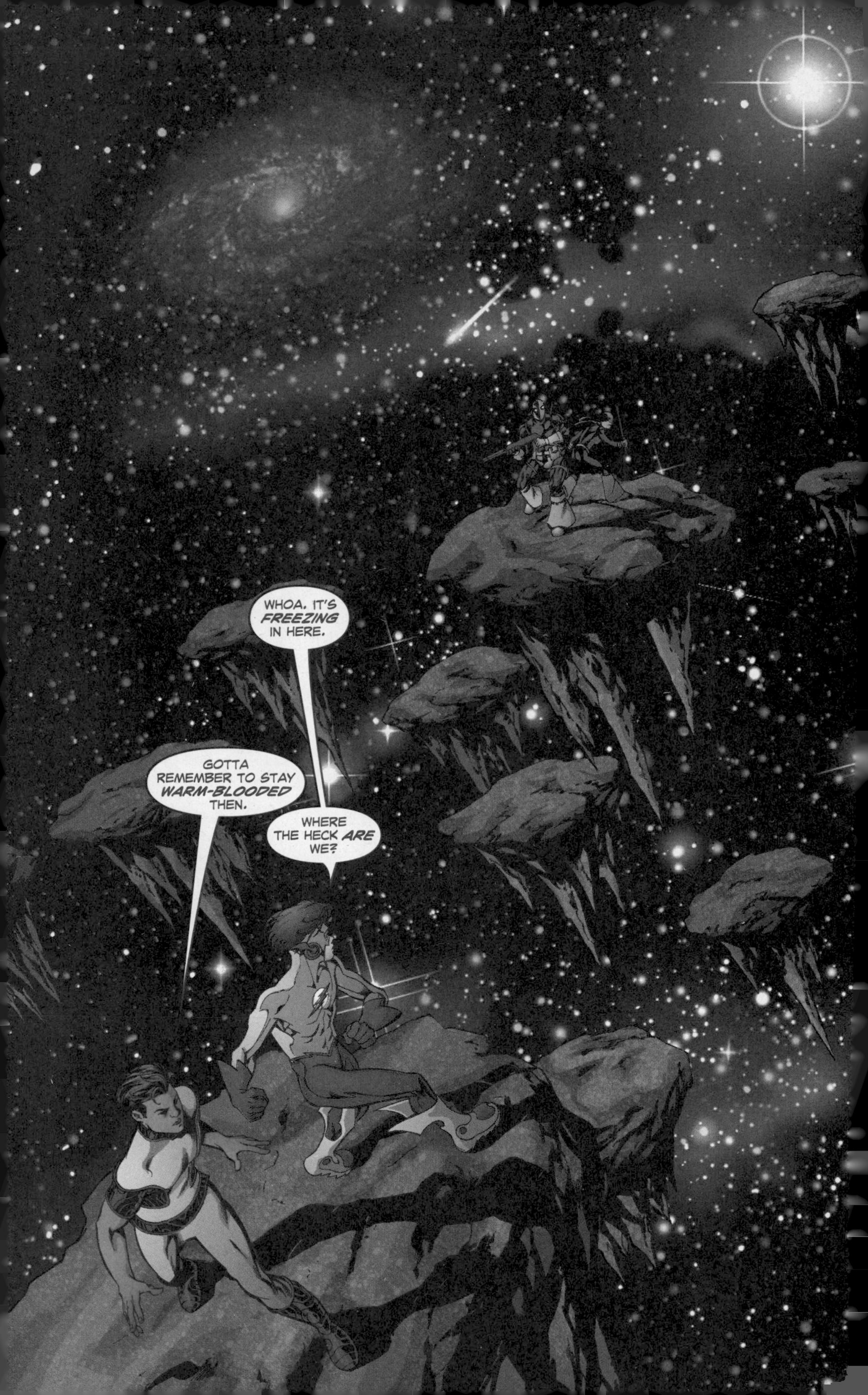
WHOA. IT'S *FREEZING* IN HERE.
GOTTA REMEMBER TO STAY *WARM-BLOODED* THEN.
WHERE THE HECK *ARE* WE?

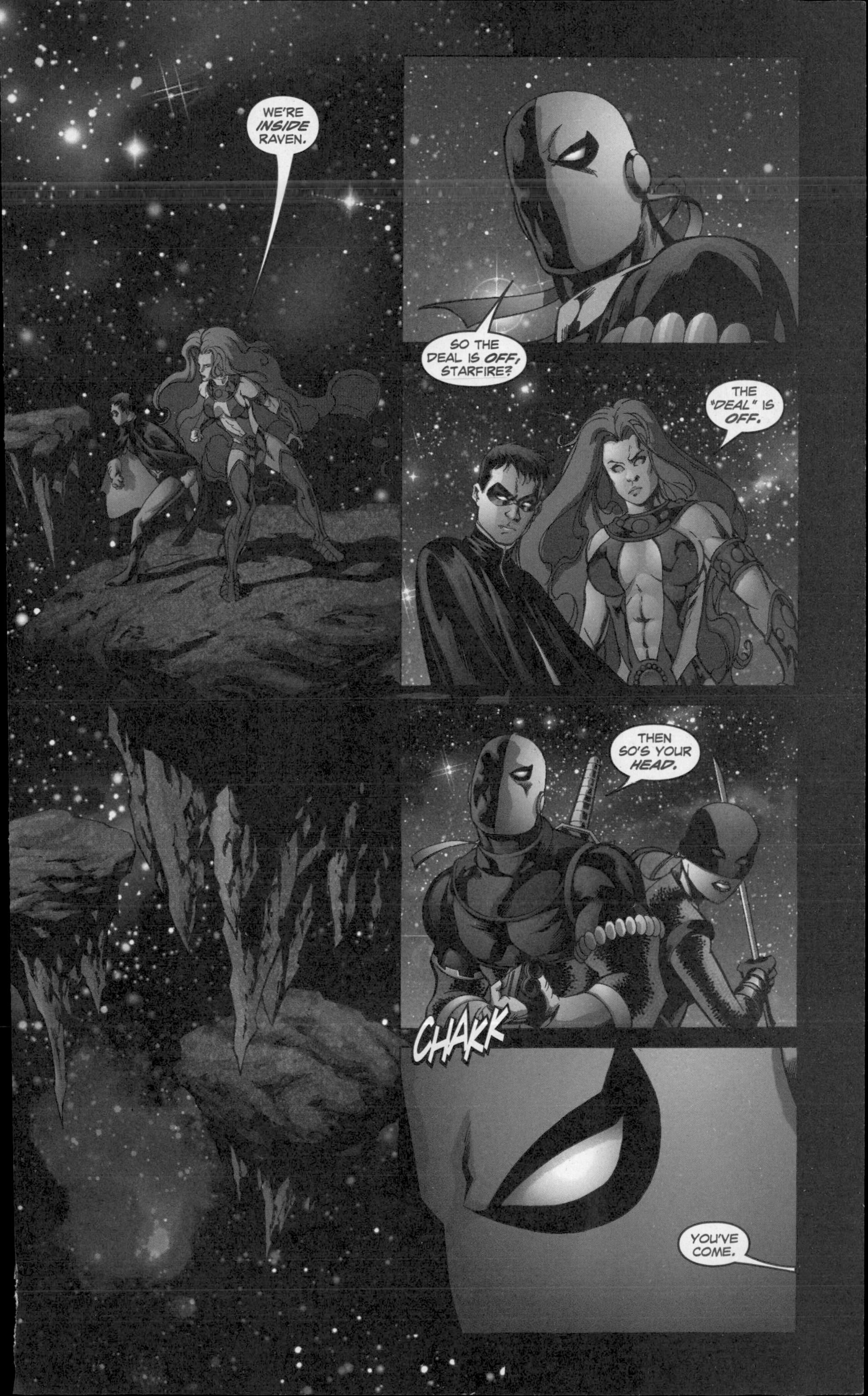

WE'RE *INSIDE* RAVEN.
SO THE DEAL IS *OFF*, STARFIRE?
THE "*DEAL*" IS *OFF*.
THEN SO'S YOUR *HEAD*.
CHAKK
YOU'VE COME.

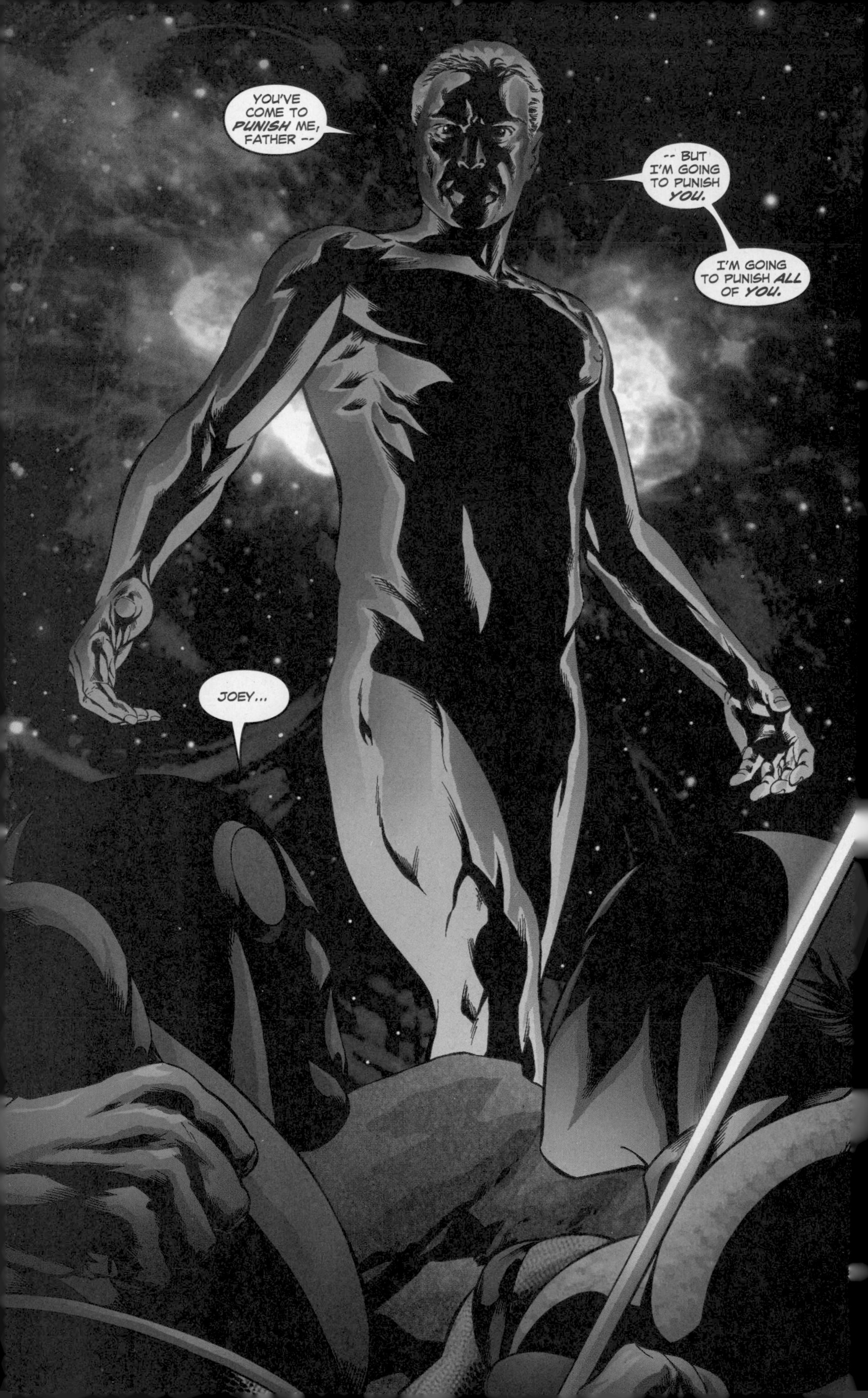
YOU'VE COME TO PUNISH ME, FATHER --
-- BUT I'M GOING TO PUNISH YOU.
I'M GOING TO PUNISH ALL OF YOU.
JOEY...

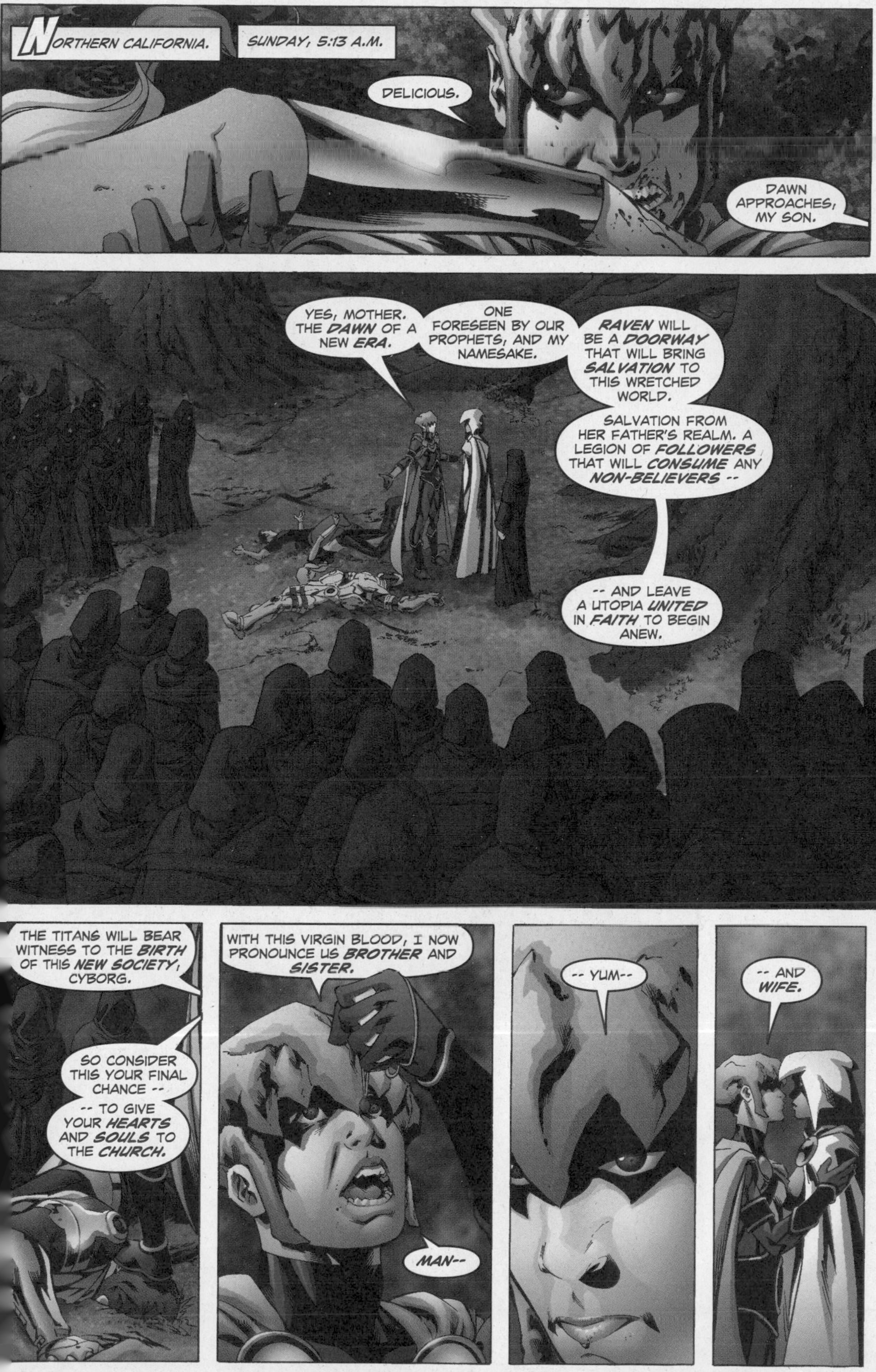
NORTHERN CALIFORNIA.
SUNDAY, 5:13 A.M.
DELICIOUS.
DAWN APPROACHES, MY SON.
YES, MOTHER. THE DAWN OF A NEW ERA.
ONE FORESEEN BY OUR PROPHETS, AND MY NAMESAKE.
RAVEN WILL BE A DOORWAY THAT WILL BRING SALVATION TO THIS WRETCHED WORLD.
SALVATION FROM HER FATHER'S REALM. A LEGION OF FOLLOWERS THAT WILL CONSUME ANY NON-BELIEVERS --
-- AND LEAVE A UTOPIA UNITED IN FAITH TO BEGIN ANEW.
THE TITANS WILL BEAR WITNESS TO THE BIRTH OF THIS NEW SOCIETY, CYBORG.
SO CONSIDER THIS YOUR FINAL CHANCE --
-- TO GIVE YOUR HEARTS AND SOULS TO THE CHURCH.
WITH THIS VIRGIN BLOOD, I NOW PRONOUNCE US BROTHER AND SISTER.
MAN--
-- YUM--
-- AND WIFE.

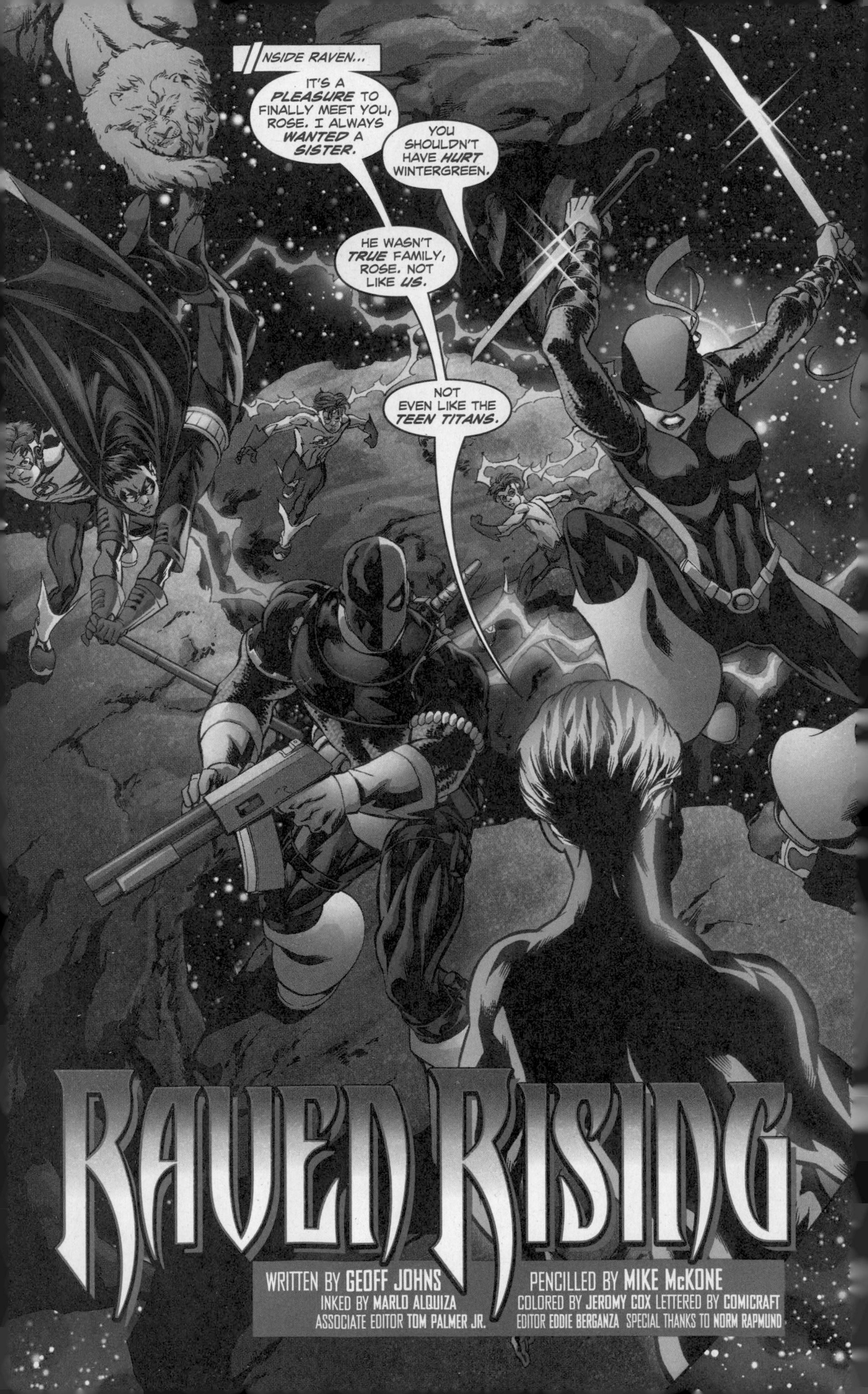
INSIDE RAVEN...
IT'S A PLEASURE TO FINALLY MEET YOU, ROSE. I ALWAYS WANTED A SISTER.
YOU SHOULDN'T HAVE HURT WINTERGREEN.
HE WASN'T TRUE FAMILY, ROSE. NOT LIKE US.
NOT EVEN LIKE THE TEEN TITANS.
RAVEN RISING
WRITTEN BY GEOFF JOHNS PENCILLED BY MIKE McKONE
INKED BY MARLO ALQUIZA COLORED BY JEROMY COX LETTERED BY COMICRAFT
ASSOCIATE EDITOR TOM PALMER JR. EDITOR EDDIE BERGANZA SPECIAL THANKS TO NORM RAPMUND

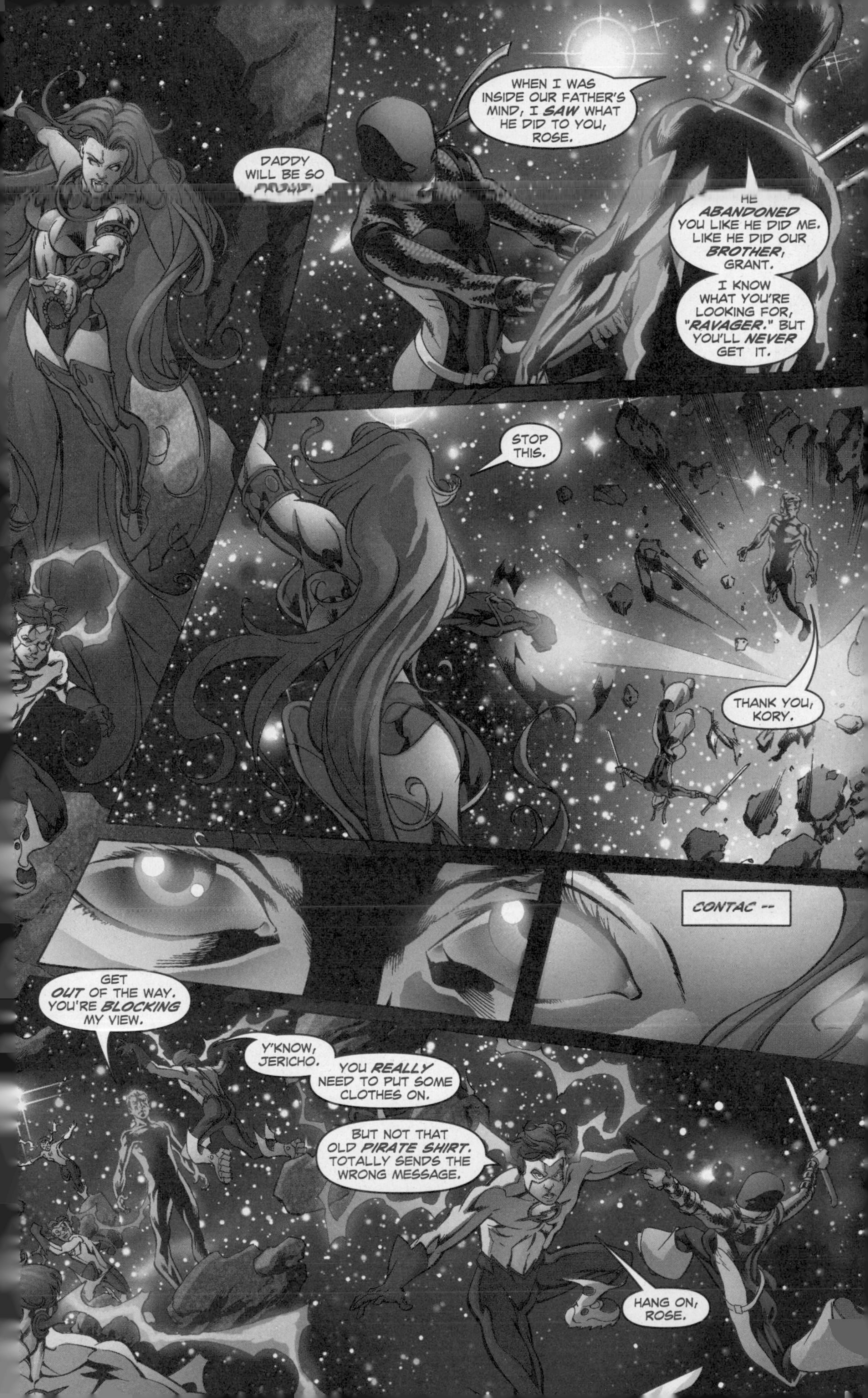

WHEN I WAS INSIDE OUR FATHER'S MIND, I *SAW* WHAT HE DID TO YOU, ROSE.
DADDY WILL BE SO
HE *ABANDONED* YOU LIKE HE DID ME. LIKE HE DID OUR *BROTHER*, GRANT.
I KNOW WHAT YOU'RE LOOKING FOR, "*RAVAGER*." BUT YOU'LL *NEVER* GET IT.
STOP THIS.
THANK YOU, KORY.
CONTAC --
GET *OUT* OF THE WAY. YOU'RE *BLOCKING* MY VIEW.
Y'KNOW, JERICHO.
YOU *REALLY* NEED TO PUT SOME CLOTHES ON.
BUT NOT THAT OLD *PIRATE SHIRT*. TOTALLY SENDS THE WRONG MESSAGE.
HANG ON, ROSE.

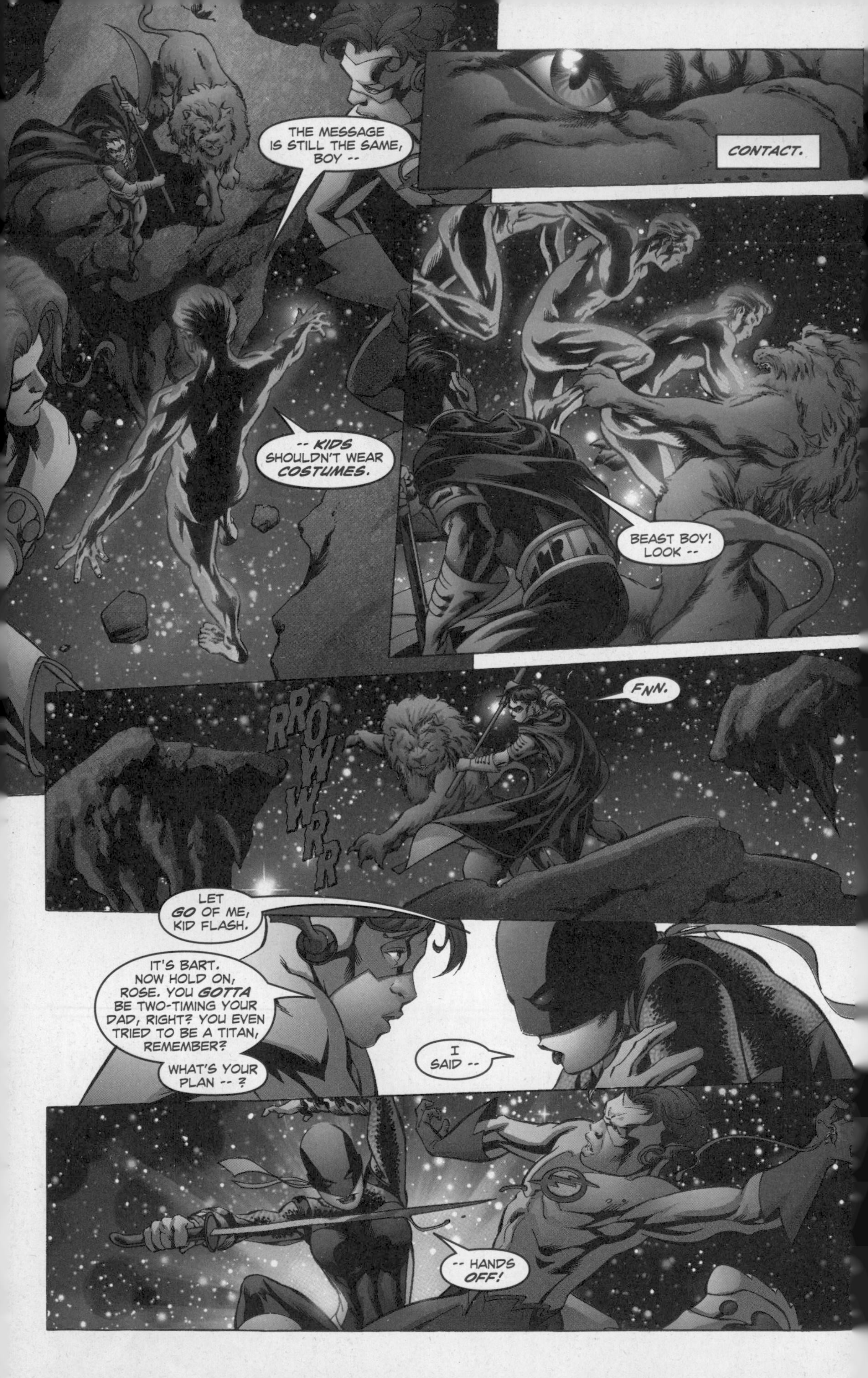
CONTACT.
THE MESSAGE IS STILL THE SAME, BOY --
-- KIDS SHOULDN'T WEAR COSTUMES.
BEAST BOY! LOOK --
RROWWRR
FNN.
LET GO OF ME, KID FLASH.
IT'S BART. NOW HOLD ON, ROSE. YOU GOTTA BE TWO-TIMING YOUR DAD, RIGHT? YOU EVEN TRIED TO BE A TITAN, REMEMBER?
WHAT'S YOUR PLAN -- ?
I SAID --
-- HANDS OFF!

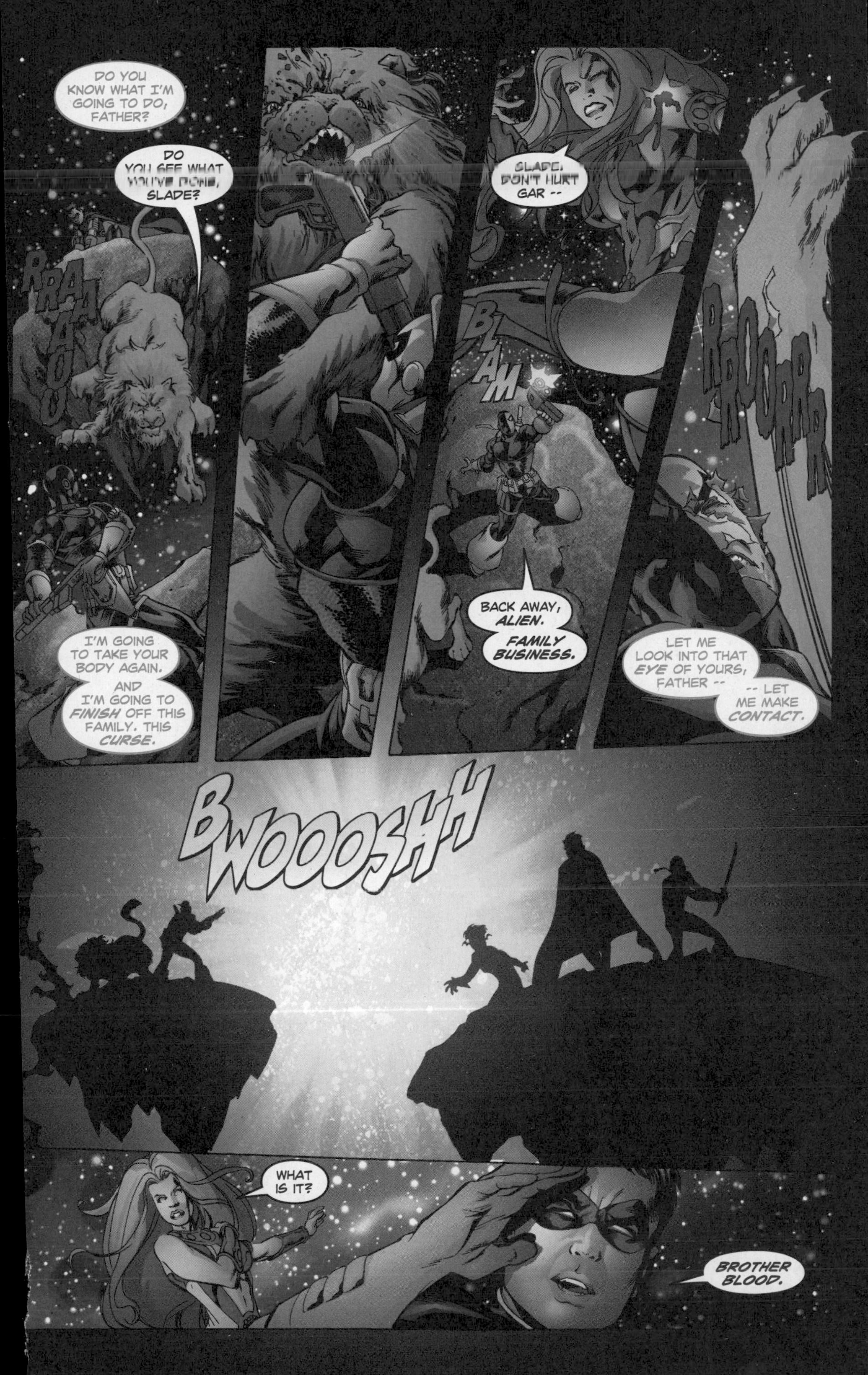
DO YOU KNOW WHAT I'M GOING TO DO, FATHER?
DO YOU SEE WHAT YOU'VE DONE, SLADE?
RRAAAOO
I'M GOING TO TAKE YOUR BODY AGAIN.
AND I'M GOING TO FINISH OFF THIS FAMILY. THIS CURSE.
SLADE! DON'T HURT GAR --
BLAM
BACK AWAY, ALIEN. FAMILY BUSINESS.
RROORRR
LET ME LOOK INTO THAT EYE OF YOURS, FATHER --
-- LET ME MAKE CONTACT.
BWOOOSHH
WHAT IS IT?
BROTHER BLOOD.

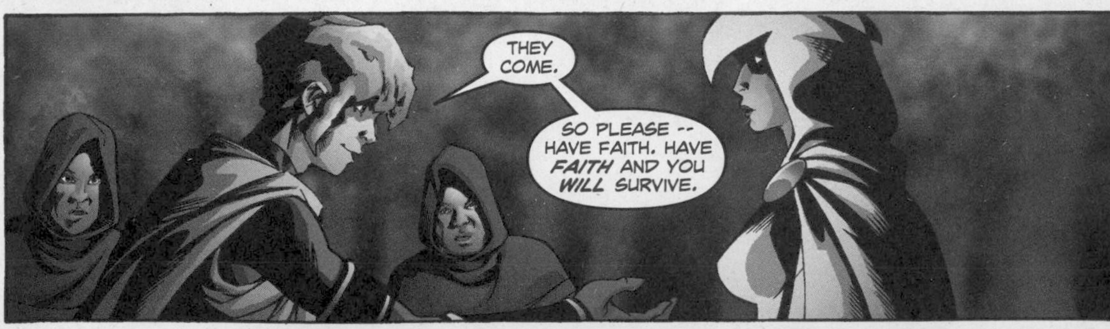
THEY COME.
SO PLEASE -- HAVE FAITH. HAVE *FAITH* AND YOU *WILL* SURVIVE.

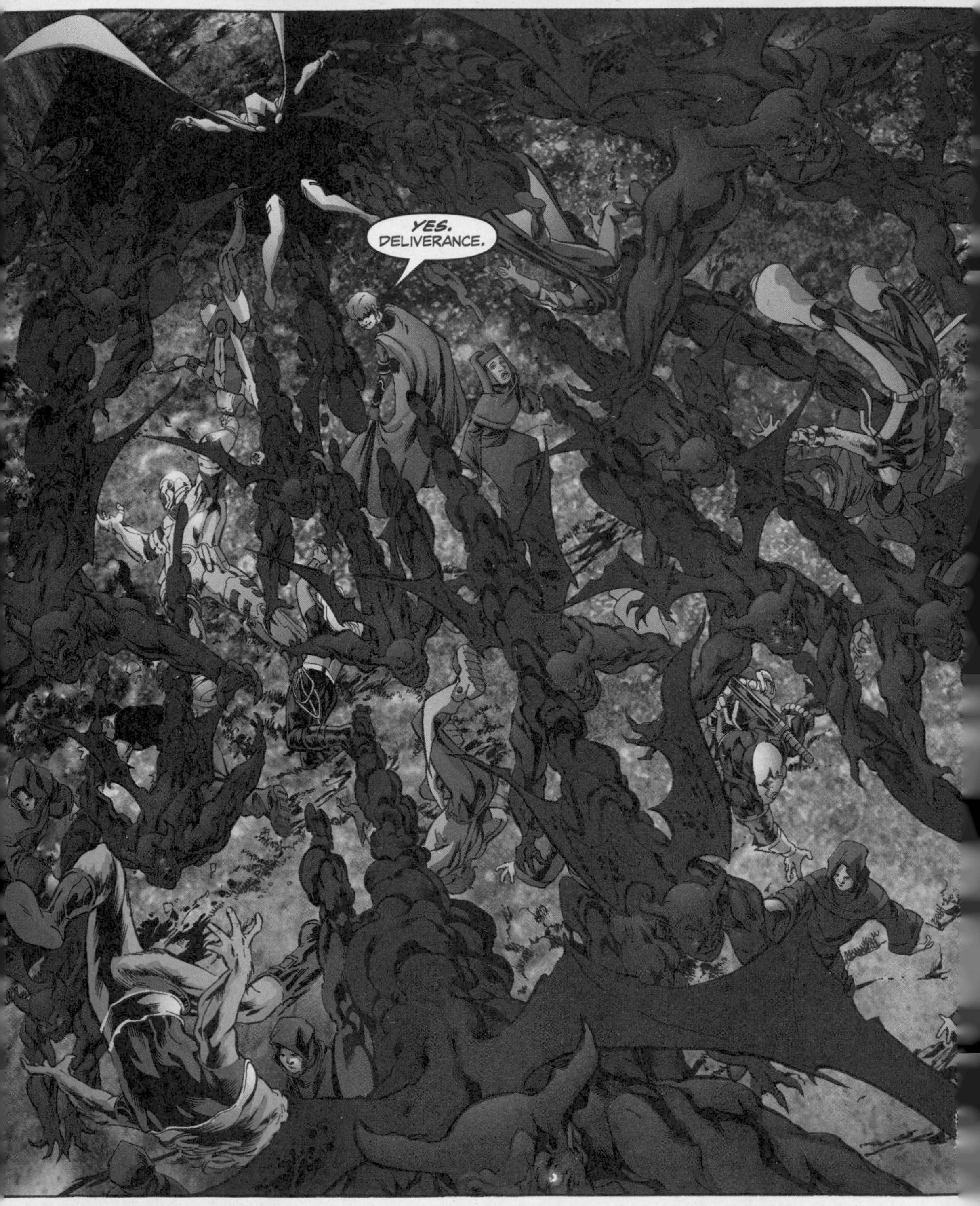
YES. DELIVERANCE.

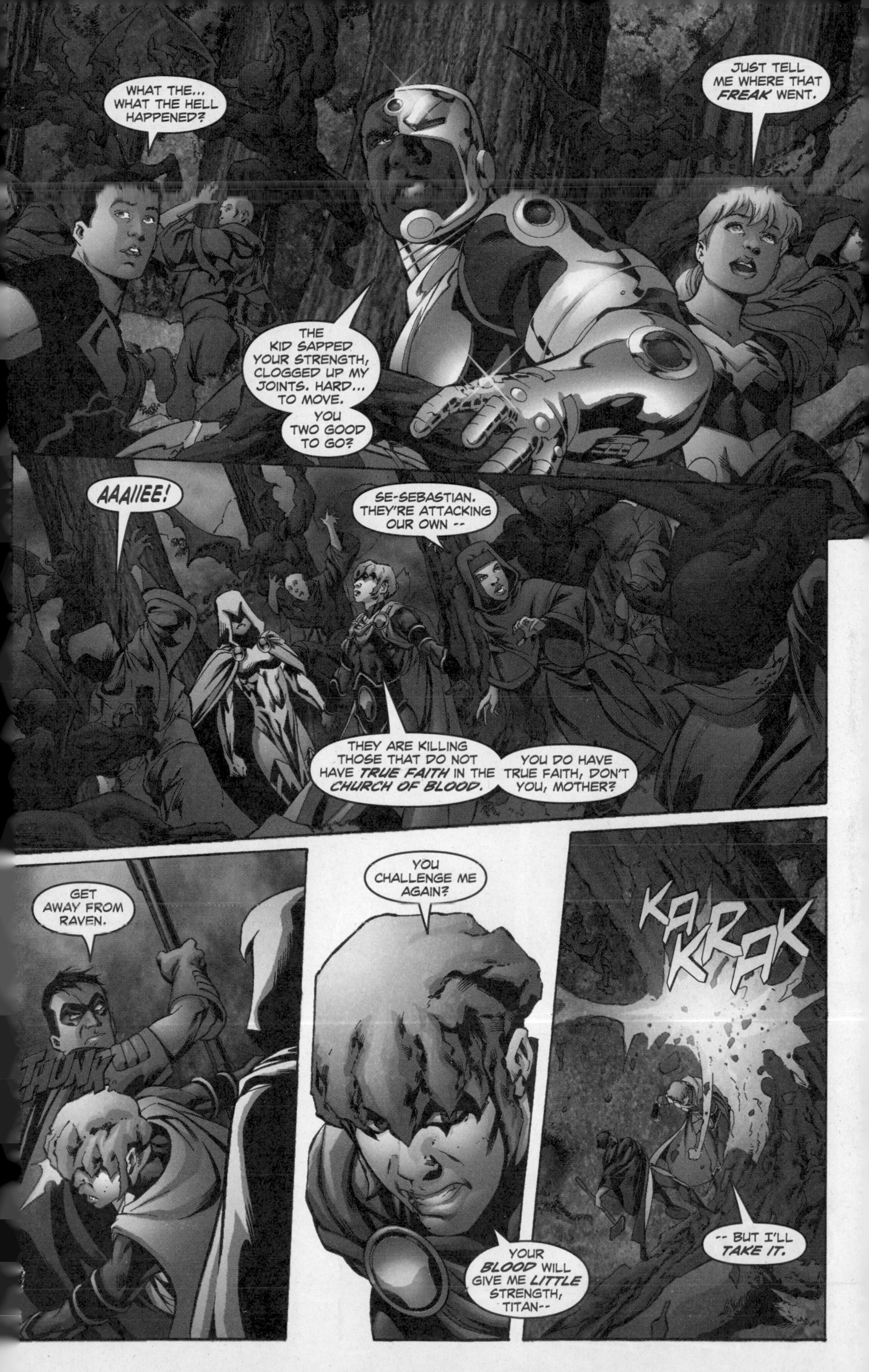
WHAT THE... WHAT THE HELL HAPPENED?
JUST TELL ME WHERE THAT *FREAK* WENT.
THE KID SAPPED YOUR STRENGTH, CLOGGED UP MY JOINTS. HARD... TO MOVE.
YOU TWO GOOD TO GO?
AAAIIEE!
SE-SEBASTIAN. THEY'RE ATTACKING OUR OWN --
THEY ARE KILLING THOSE THAT DO NOT HAVE *TRUE FAITH* IN THE *CHURCH OF BLOOD*.
YOU DO HAVE TRUE FAITH, DON'T YOU, MOTHER?
GET AWAY FROM RAVEN.
THUNK
YOU CHALLENGE ME AGAIN?
YOUR *BLOOD* WILL GIVE ME *LITTLE* STRENGTH, TITAN--
KA KRAK
-- BUT I'LL *TAKE IT.*

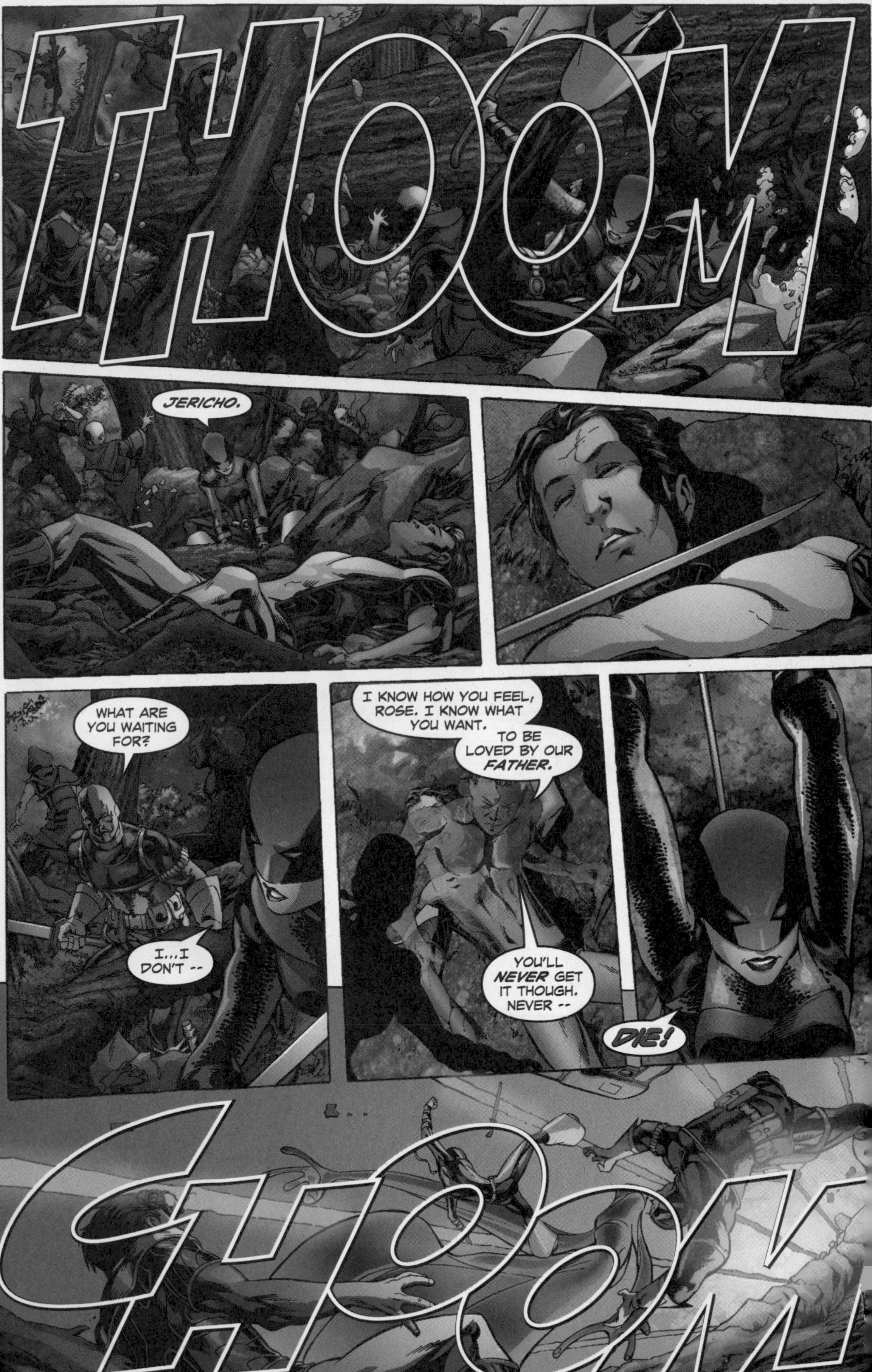
THOOM
JERICHO.
WHAT ARE YOU WAITING FOR?
I...I DON'T --
I KNOW HOW YOU FEEL, ROSE. I KNOW WHAT YOU WANT.
TO BE LOVED BY OUR FATHER.
YOU'LL NEVER GET IT THOUGH. NEVER --
DIE!
CHOOOM

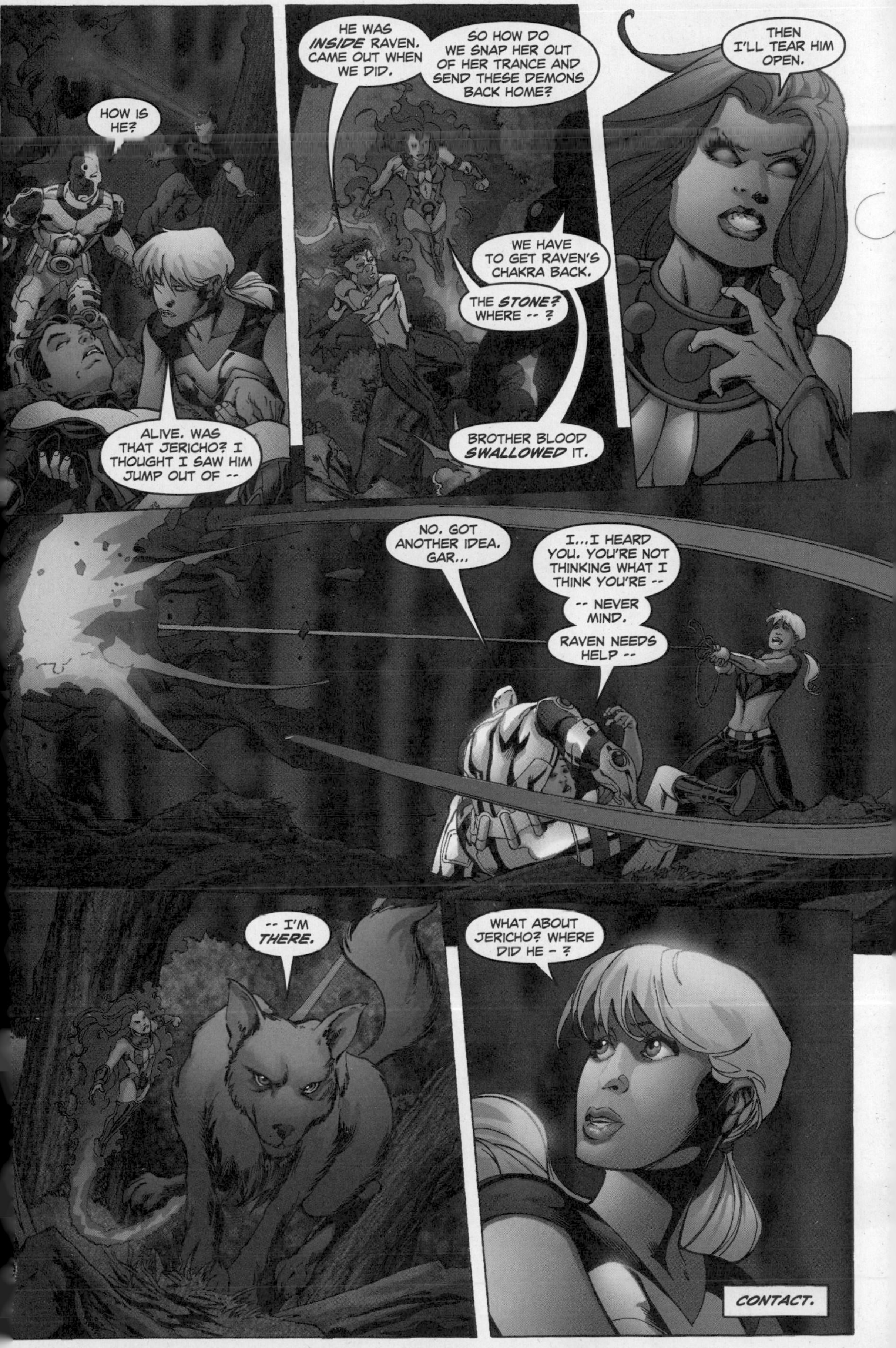
HOW IS HE?
ALIVE. WAS THAT JERICHO? I THOUGHT I SAW HIM JUMP OUT OF --
HE WAS INSIDE RAVEN. CAME OUT WHEN WE DID.
SO HOW DO WE SNAP HER OUT OF HER TRANCE AND SEND THESE DEMONS BACK HOME?
WE HAVE TO GET RAVEN'S CHAKRA BACK.
THE STONE? WHERE -- ?
BROTHER BLOOD SWALLOWED IT.
THEN I'LL TEAR HIM OPEN.
NO. GOT ANOTHER IDEA. GAR...
I...I HEARD YOU. YOU'RE NOT THINKING WHAT I THINK YOU'RE --
-- NEVER MIND.
RAVEN NEEDS HELP --
-- I'M THERE.
WHAT ABOUT JERICHO? WHERE DID HE - ?
CONTACT.

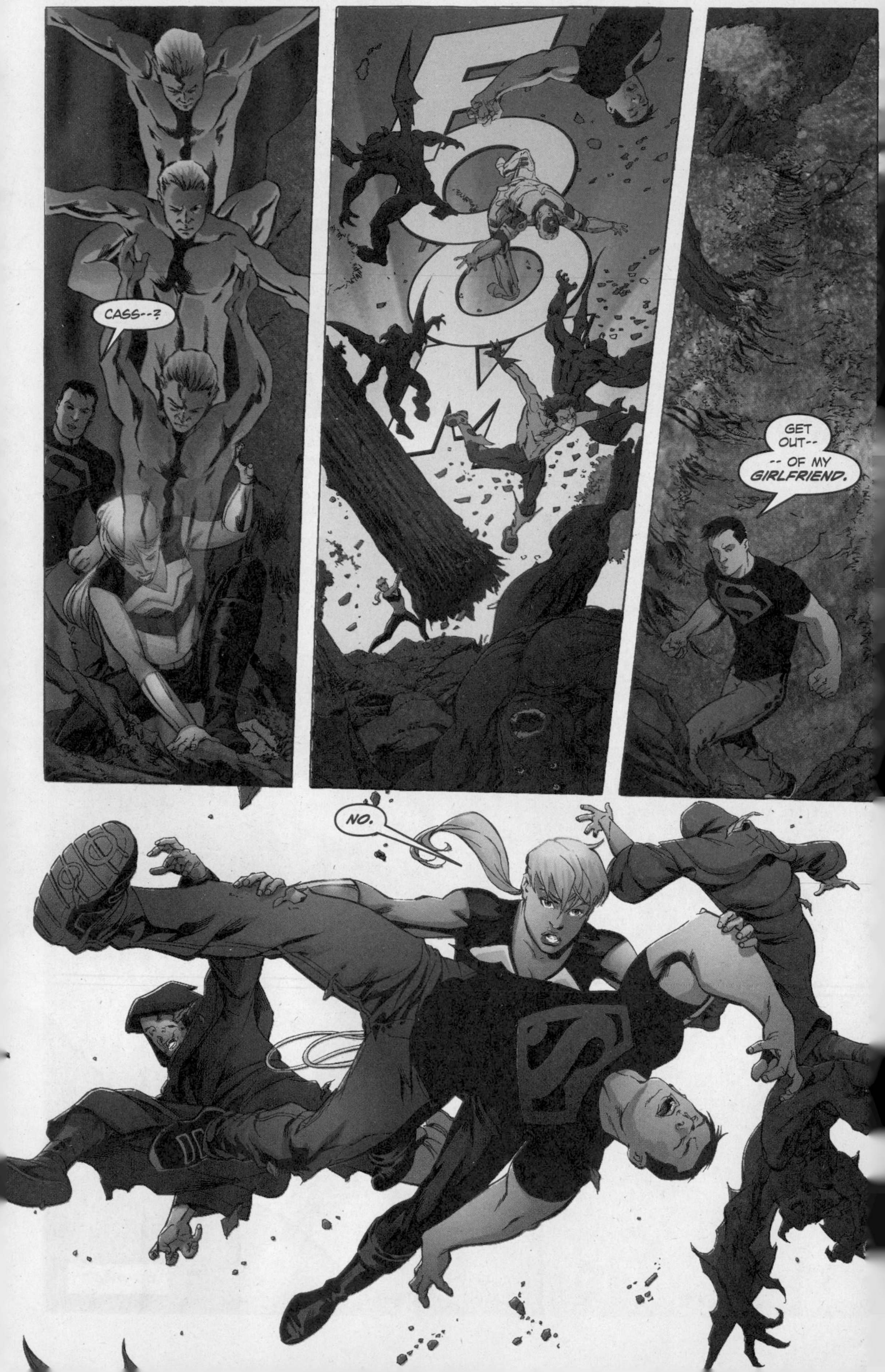
CASS--?
GET OUT--
-- OF MY GIRLFRIEND.
NO.

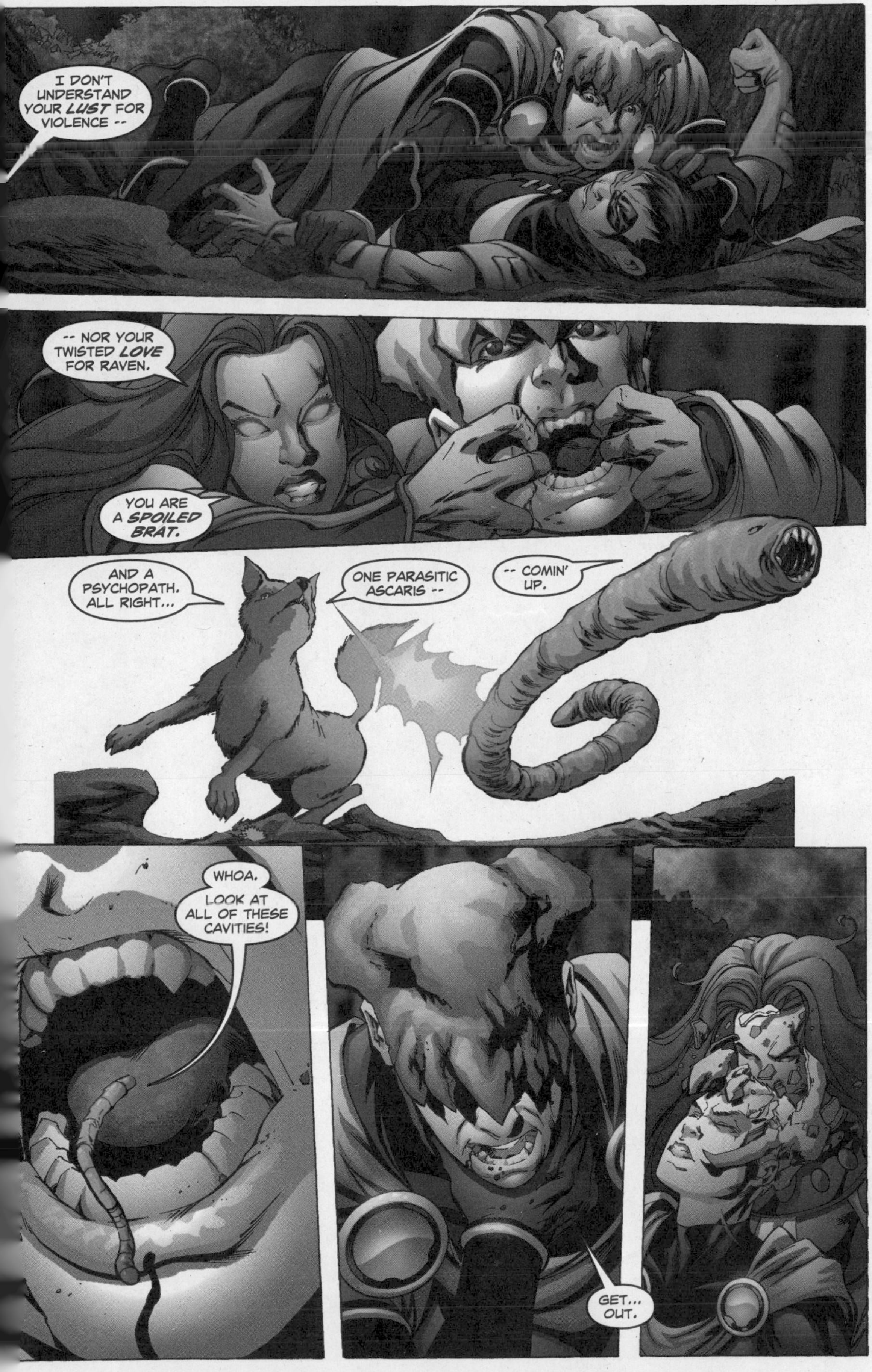
I DON'T UNDERSTAND YOUR LUST FOR VIOLENCE --
-- NOR YOUR TWISTED LOVE FOR RAVEN.
YOU ARE A SPOILED BRAT.
AND A PSYCHOPATH. ALL RIGHT...
ONE PARASITIC ASCARIS --
-- COMIN' UP.
WHOA. LOOK AT ALL OF THESE CAVITIES!
GET... OUT.

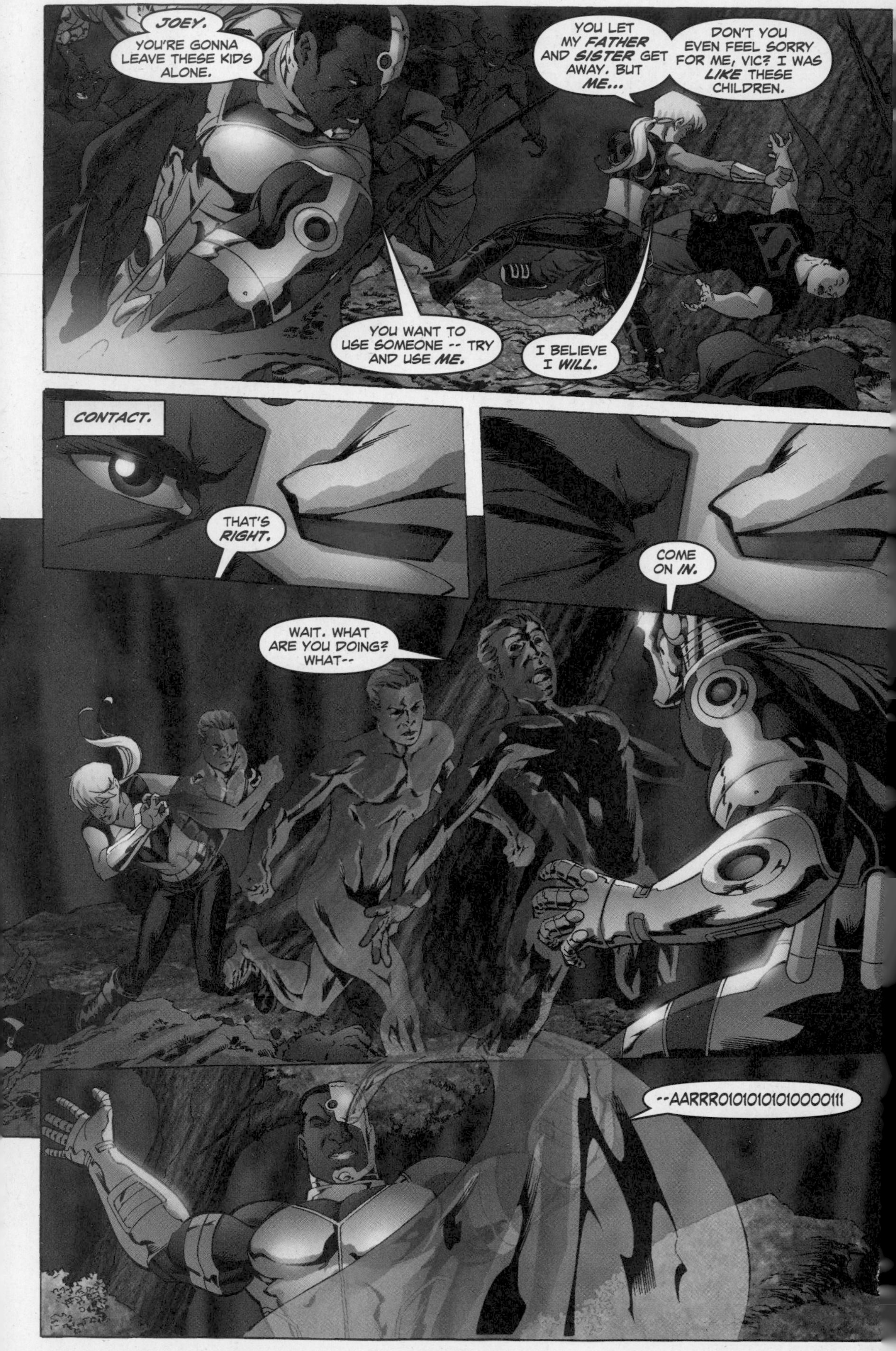
JOEY. YOU'RE GONNA LEAVE THESE KIDS ALONE.
YOU LET MY FATHER AND SISTER GET AWAY. BUT ME...
DON'T YOU EVEN FEEL SORRY FOR ME, VIC? I WAS LIKE THESE CHILDREN.
YOU WANT TO USE SOMEONE -- TRY AND USE ME.
I BELIEVE I WILL.
CONTACT.
THAT'S RIGHT.
COME ON IN.
WAIT. WHAT ARE YOU DOING? WHAT--
--AARRR010101010101000111

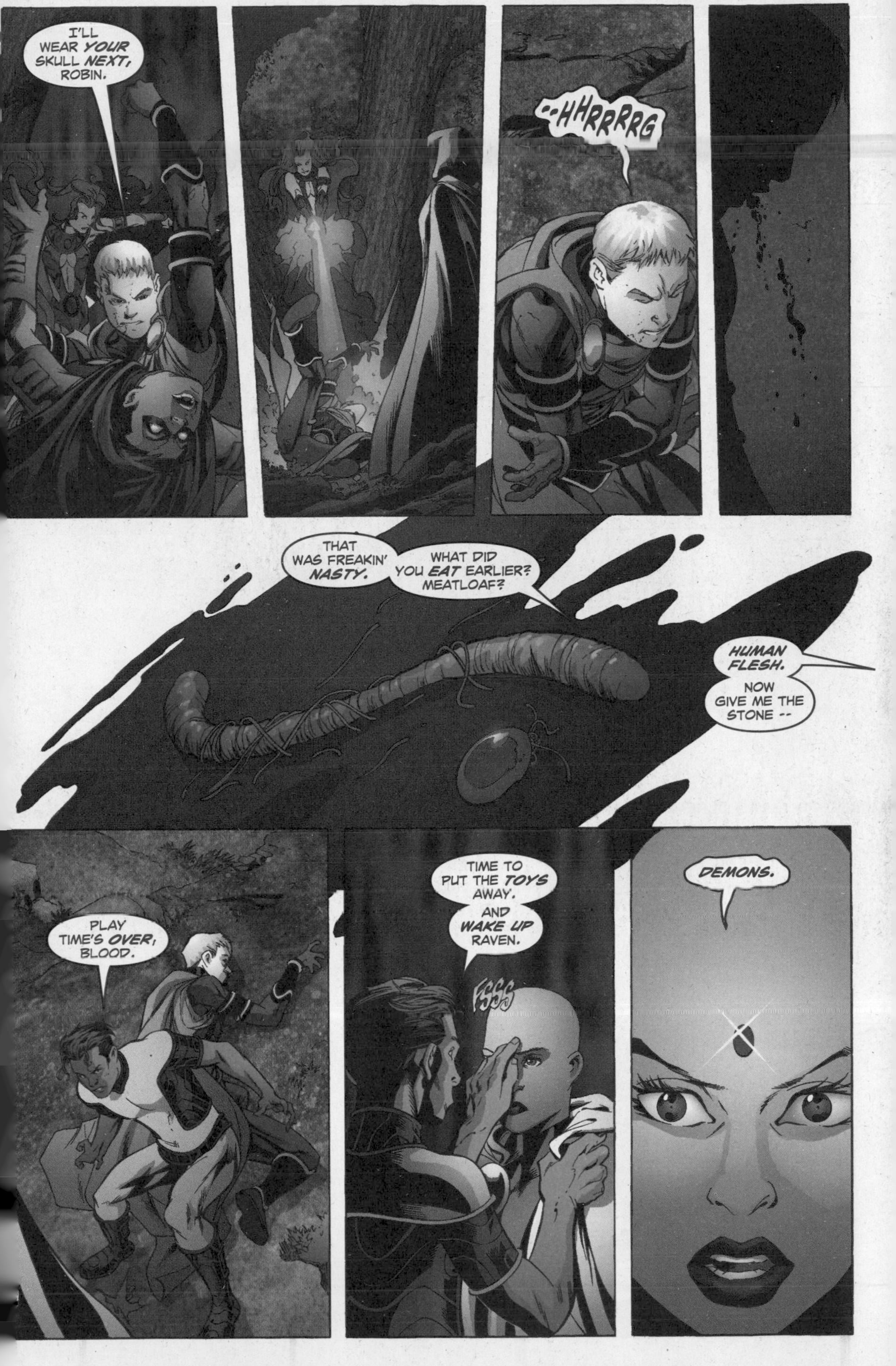
I'LL WEAR YOUR SKULL NEXT, ROBIN.
--HHRRRRG
THAT WAS FREAKIN' NASTY.
WHAT DID YOU EAT EARLIER? MEATLOAF?
HUMAN FLESH.
NOW GIVE ME THE STONE --
PLAY TIME'S OVER, BLOOD.
TIME TO PUT THE TOYS AWAY.
AND WAKE UP RAVEN.
FSSS
DEMONS.

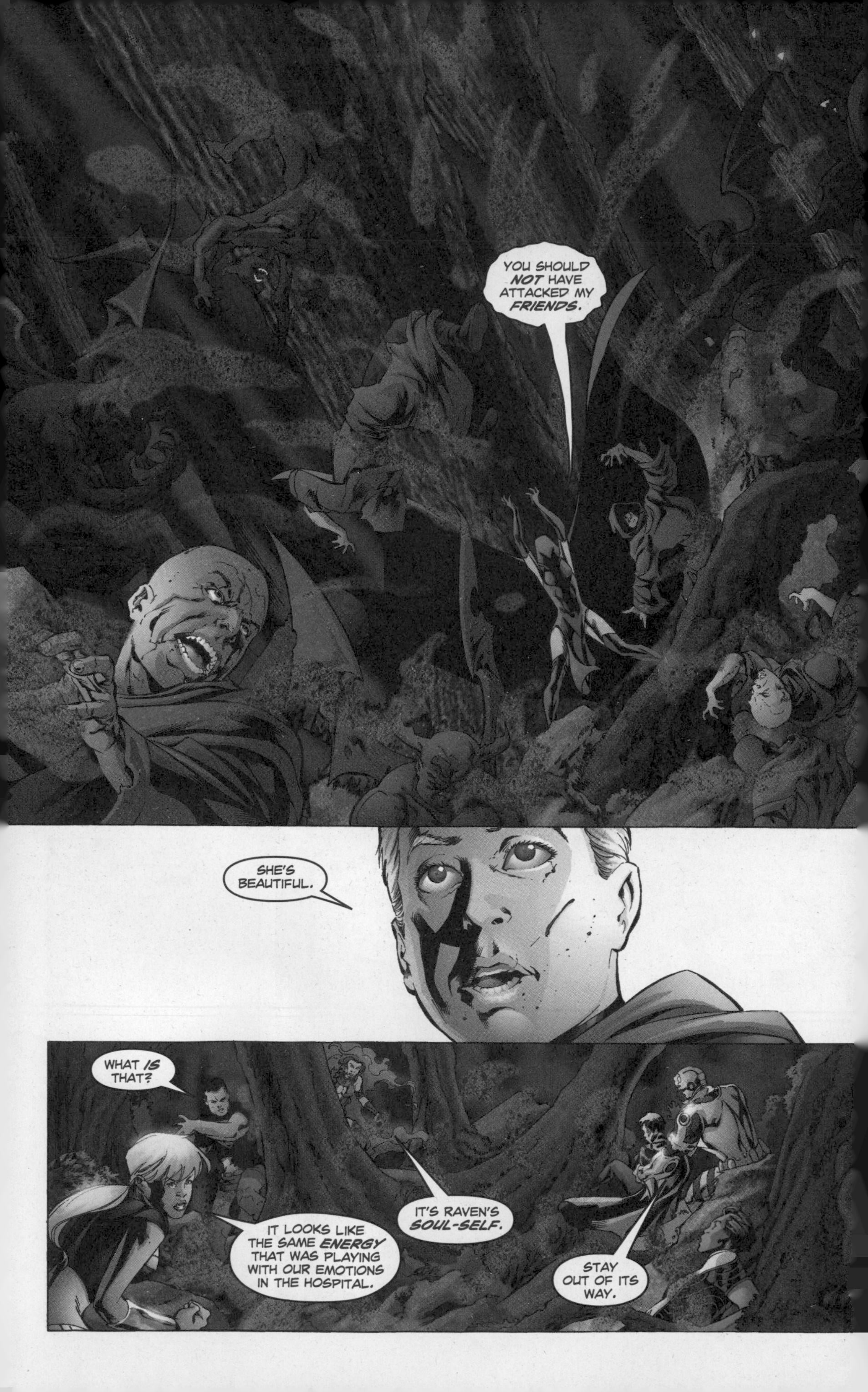

YOU SHOULD *NOT* HAVE ATTACKED MY *FRIENDS*.
SHE'S BEAUTIFUL.
WHAT *IS* THAT?
IT LOOKS LIKE THE SAME *ENERGY* THAT WAS PLAYING WITH OUR EMOTIONS IN THE HOSPITAL.
IT'S RAVEN'S *SOUL-SELF*.
STAY OUT OF ITS WAY.

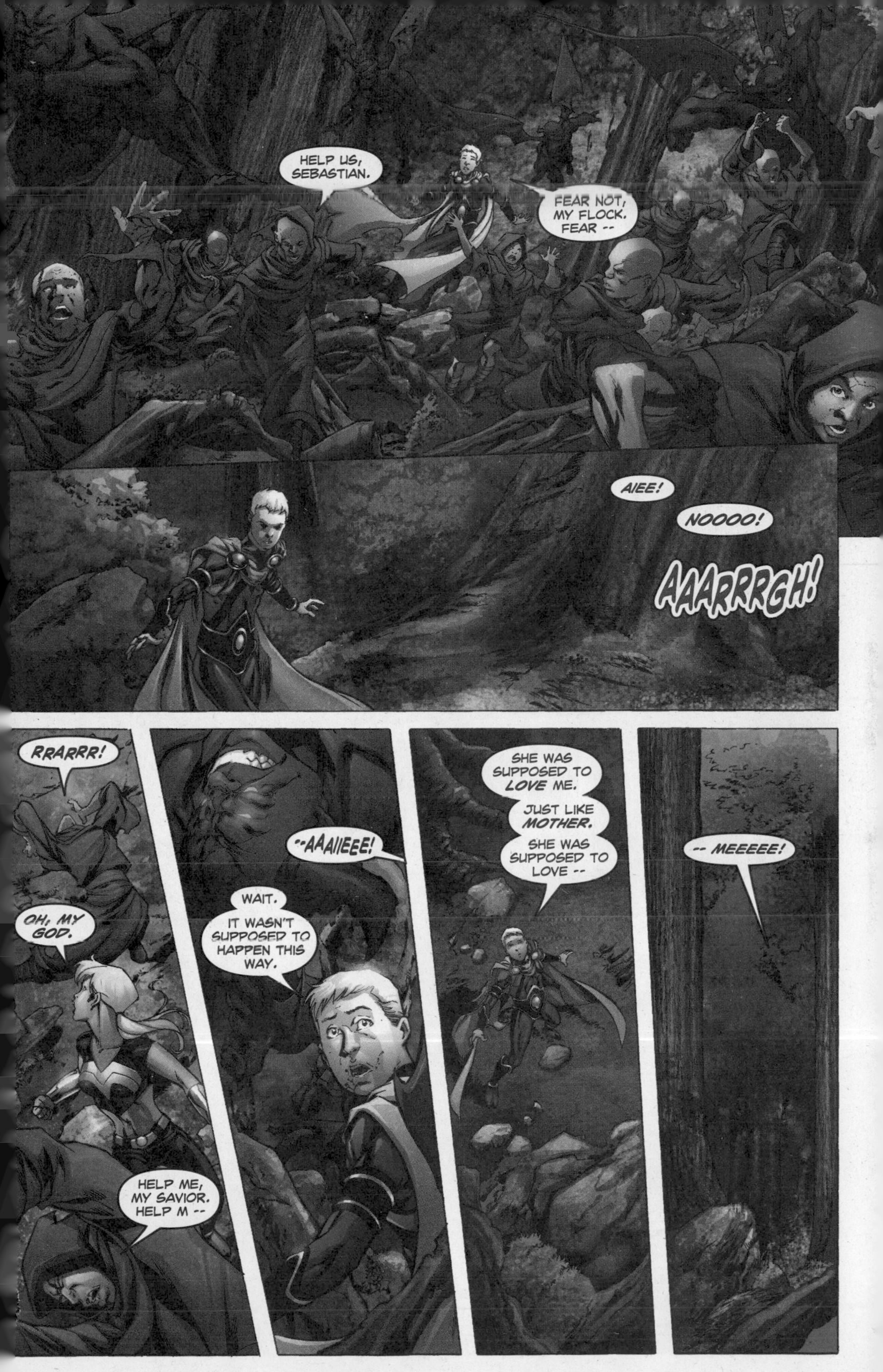
HELP US, SEBASTIAN.
FEAR NOT, MY FLOCK. FEAR --
AIEE!
NOOOO!
AAARRRGH!
RRARRR!
OH, MY GOD.
HELP ME, MY SAVIOR. HELP M --
--AAAIIEEE!
WAIT. IT WASN'T SUPPOSED TO HAPPEN THIS WAY.
SHE WAS SUPPOSED TO LOVE ME.
JUST LIKE MOTHER.
SHE WAS SUPPOSED TO LOVE --
-- MEEEEE!

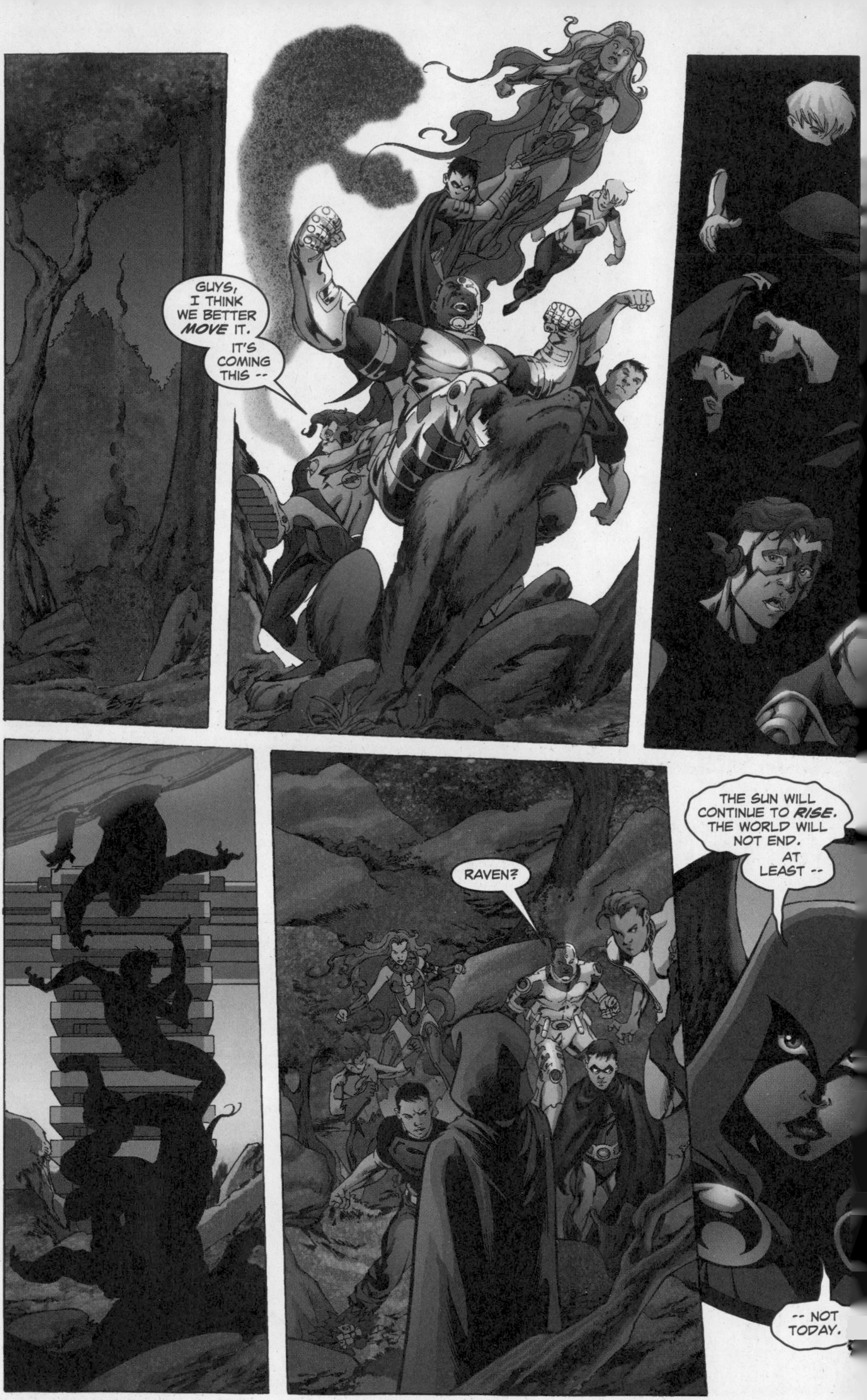
GUYS, I THINK WE BETTER MOVE IT.
IT'S COMING THIS --
RAVEN?
THE SUN WILL CONTINUE TO RISE. THE WORLD WILL NOT END.
AT LEAST --
-- NOT TODAY.

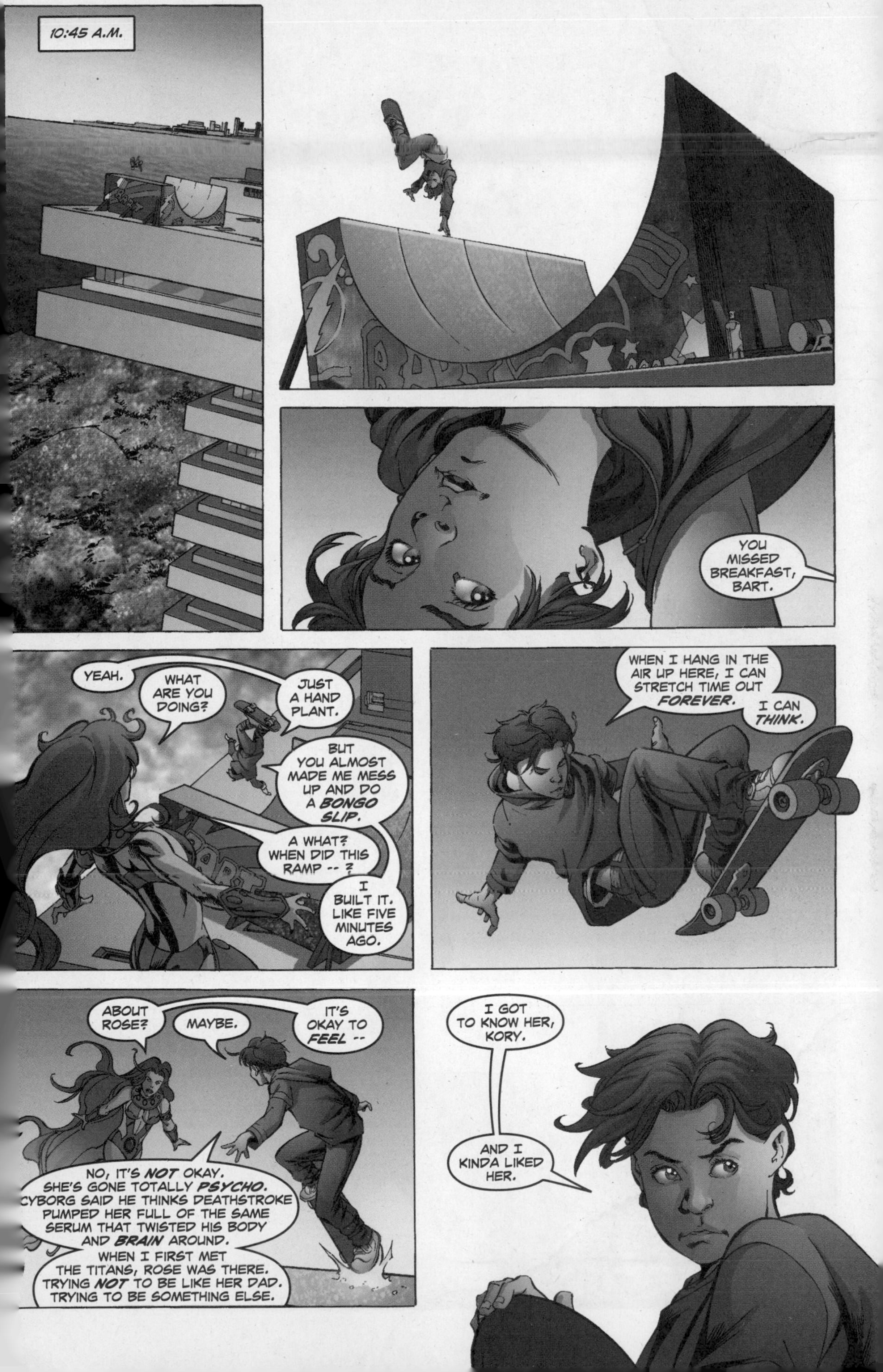

10:45 A.M.
YOU MISSED BREAKFAST, BART.
YEAH.
WHAT ARE YOU DOING?
JUST A HAND PLANT.
BUT YOU ALMOST MADE ME MESS UP AND DO A BONGO SLIP.
A WHAT? WHEN DID THIS RAMP -- ?
I BUILT IT. LIKE FIVE MINUTES AGO.
WHEN I HANG IN THE AIR UP HERE, I CAN STRETCH TIME OUT FOREVER.
I CAN THINK.
ABOUT ROSE?
MAYBE.
IT'S OKAY TO FEEL --
NO, IT'S NOT OKAY. SHE'S GONE TOTALLY PSYCHO. CYBORG SAID HE THINKS DEATHSTROKE PUMPED HER FULL OF THE SAME SERUM THAT TWISTED HIS BODY AND BRAIN AROUND.
WHEN I FIRST MET THE TITANS, ROSE WAS THERE. TRYING NOT TO BE LIKE HER DAD. TRYING TO BE SOMETHING ELSE.
I GOT TO KNOW HER, KORY.
AND I KINDA LIKED HER.

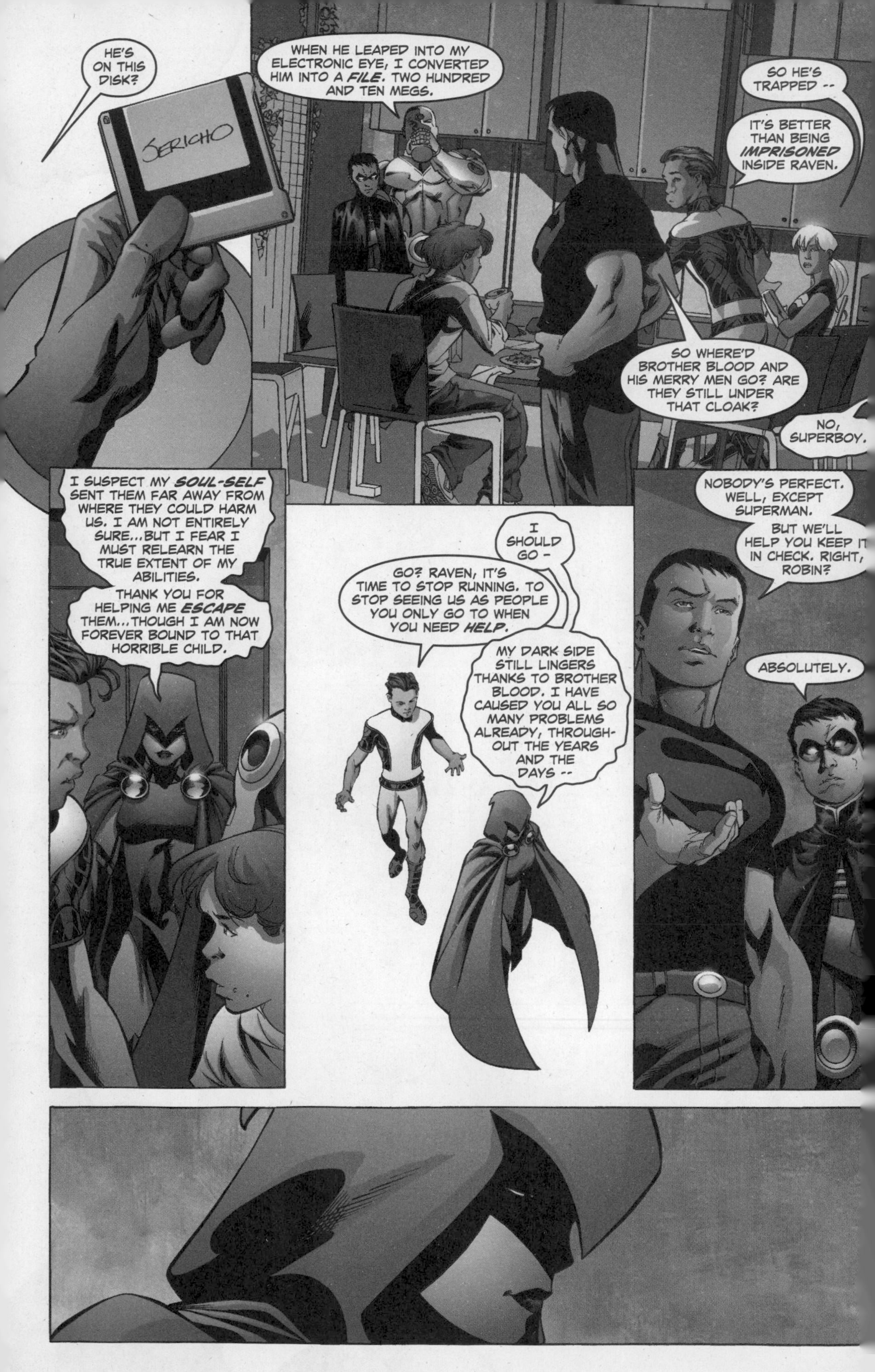
HE'S ON THIS DISK?
WHEN HE LEAPED INTO MY ELECTRONIC EYE, I CONVERTED HIM INTO A *FILE*. TWO HUNDRED AND TEN MEGS.
SO HE'S TRAPPED --
IT'S BETTER THAN BEING *IMPRISONED* INSIDE RAVEN.
SERICHO
SO WHERE'D BROTHER BLOOD AND HIS MERRY MEN GO? ARE THEY STILL UNDER THAT CLOAK?
NO, SUPERBOY.
I SUSPECT MY *SOUL-SELF* SENT THEM FAR AWAY FROM WHERE THEY COULD HARM US. I AM NOT ENTIRELY SURE...BUT I FEAR I MUST RELEARN THE TRUE EXTENT OF MY ABILITIES.
THANK YOU FOR HELPING ME *ESCAPE* THEM...THOUGH I AM NOW FOREVER BOUND TO THAT HORRIBLE CHILD.
I SHOULD GO --
GO? RAVEN, IT'S TIME TO STOP RUNNING. TO STOP SEEING US AS PEOPLE YOU ONLY GO TO WHEN YOU NEED *HELP*.
MY DARK SIDE STILL LINGERS THANKS TO BROTHER BLOOD. I HAVE CAUSED YOU ALL SO MANY PROBLEMS ALREADY, THROUGH-OUT THE YEARS AND THE DAYS --
NOBODY'S PERFECT. WELL, EXCEPT SUPERMAN.
BUT WE'LL HELP YOU KEEP IT IN CHECK. RIGHT, ROBIN?
ABSOLUTELY.

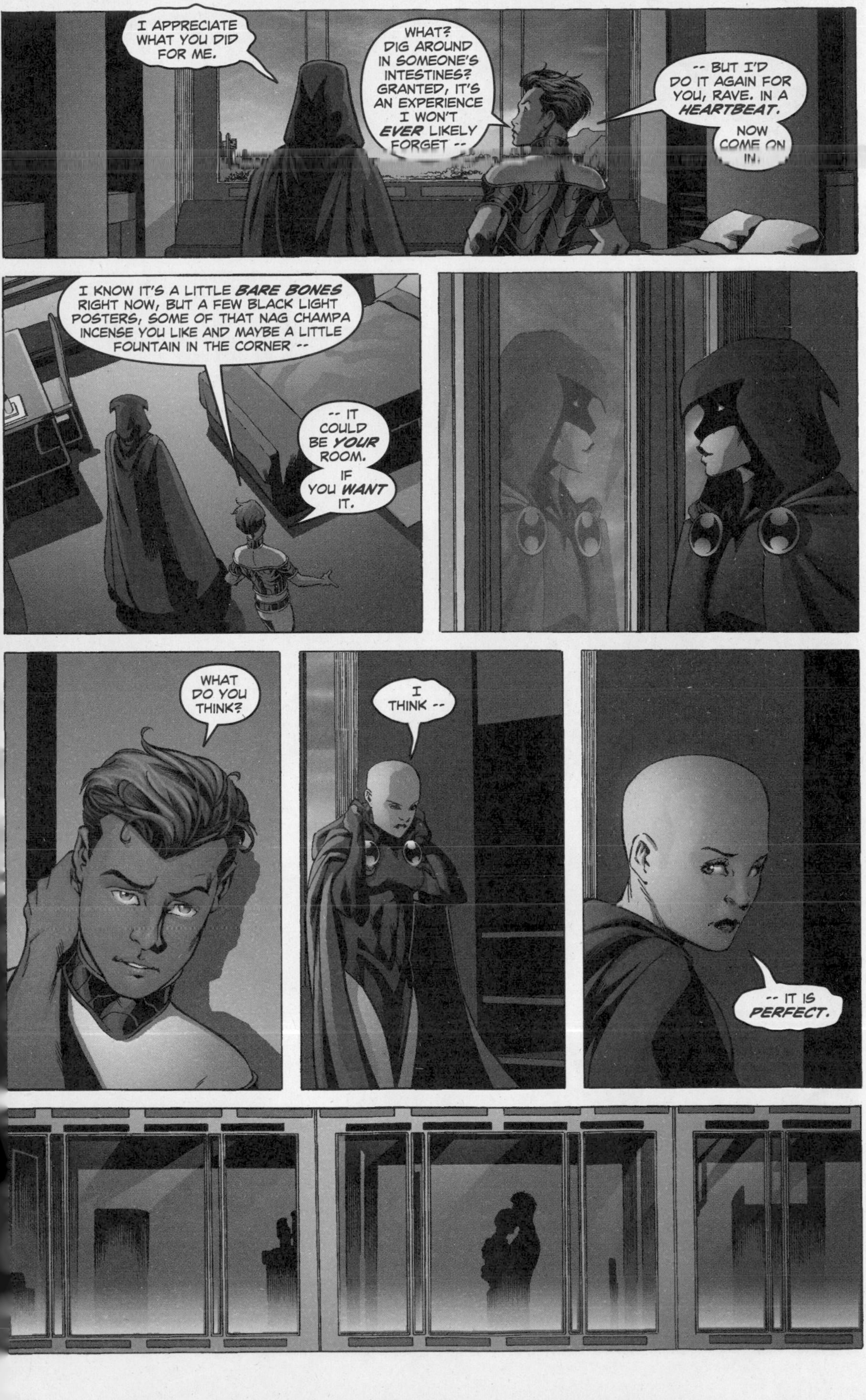
I APPRECIATE WHAT YOU DID FOR ME.
WHAT? DIG AROUND IN SOMEONE'S INTESTINES? GRANTED, IT'S AN EXPERIENCE I WON'T EVER LIKELY FORGET --
-- BUT I'D DO IT AGAIN FOR YOU, RAVE. IN A HEARTBEAT.
NOW COME ON IN.
I KNOW IT'S A LITTLE BARE BONES RIGHT NOW, BUT A FEW BLACK LIGHT POSTERS, SOME OF THAT NAG CHAMPA INCENSE YOU LIKE AND MAYBE A LITTLE FOUNTAIN IN THE CORNER --
-- IT COULD BE YOUR ROOM.
IF YOU WANT IT.
WHAT DO YOU THINK?
I THINK --
-- IT IS PERFECT.

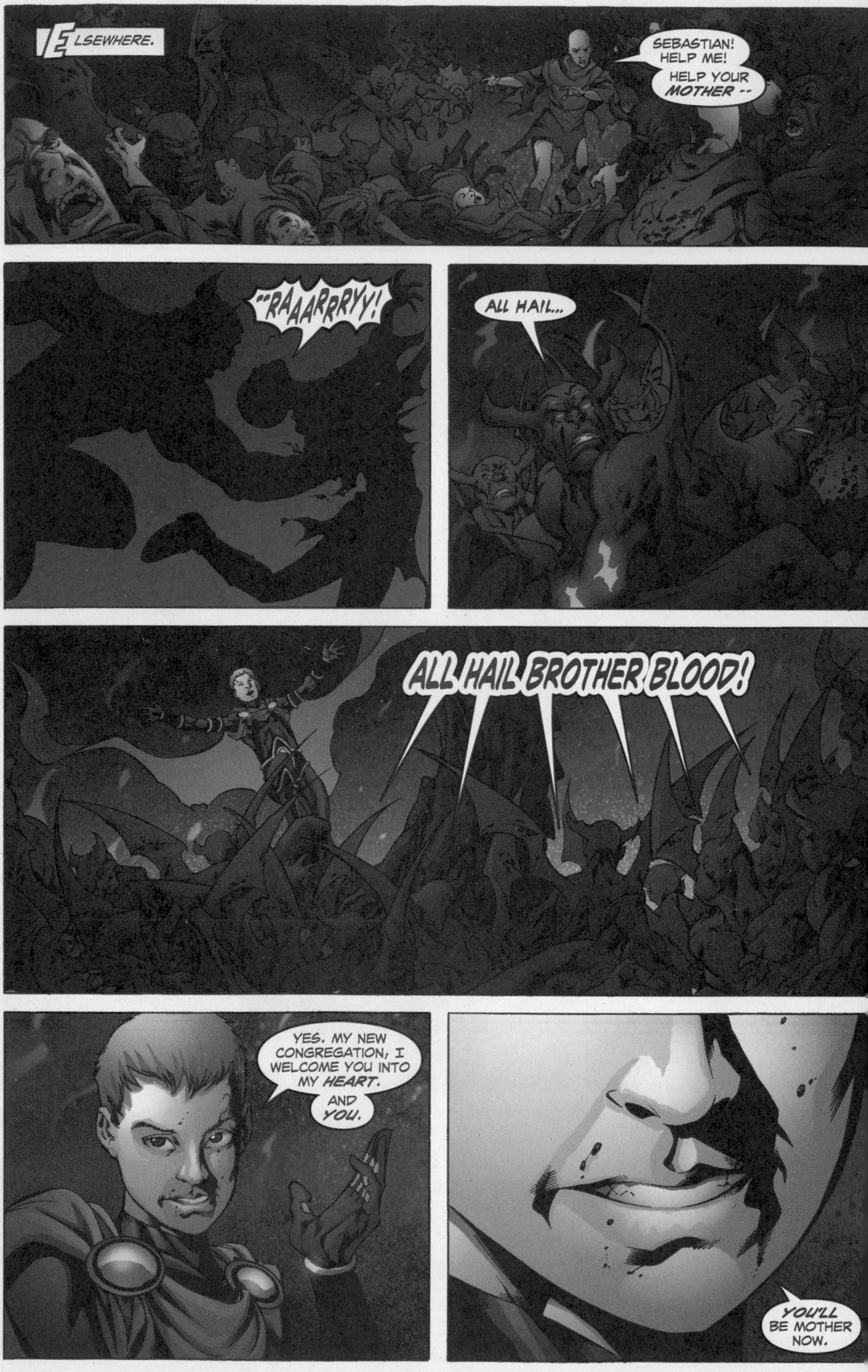
ELSEWHERE.
SEBASTIAN! HELP ME! HELP YOUR MOTHER --
"RAAARRRYY!
ALL HAIL...
ALL HAIL BROTHER BLOOD!
YES. MY NEW CONGREGATION, I WELCOME YOU INTO MY HEART.
AND YOU.
YOU'LL BE MOTHER NOW.

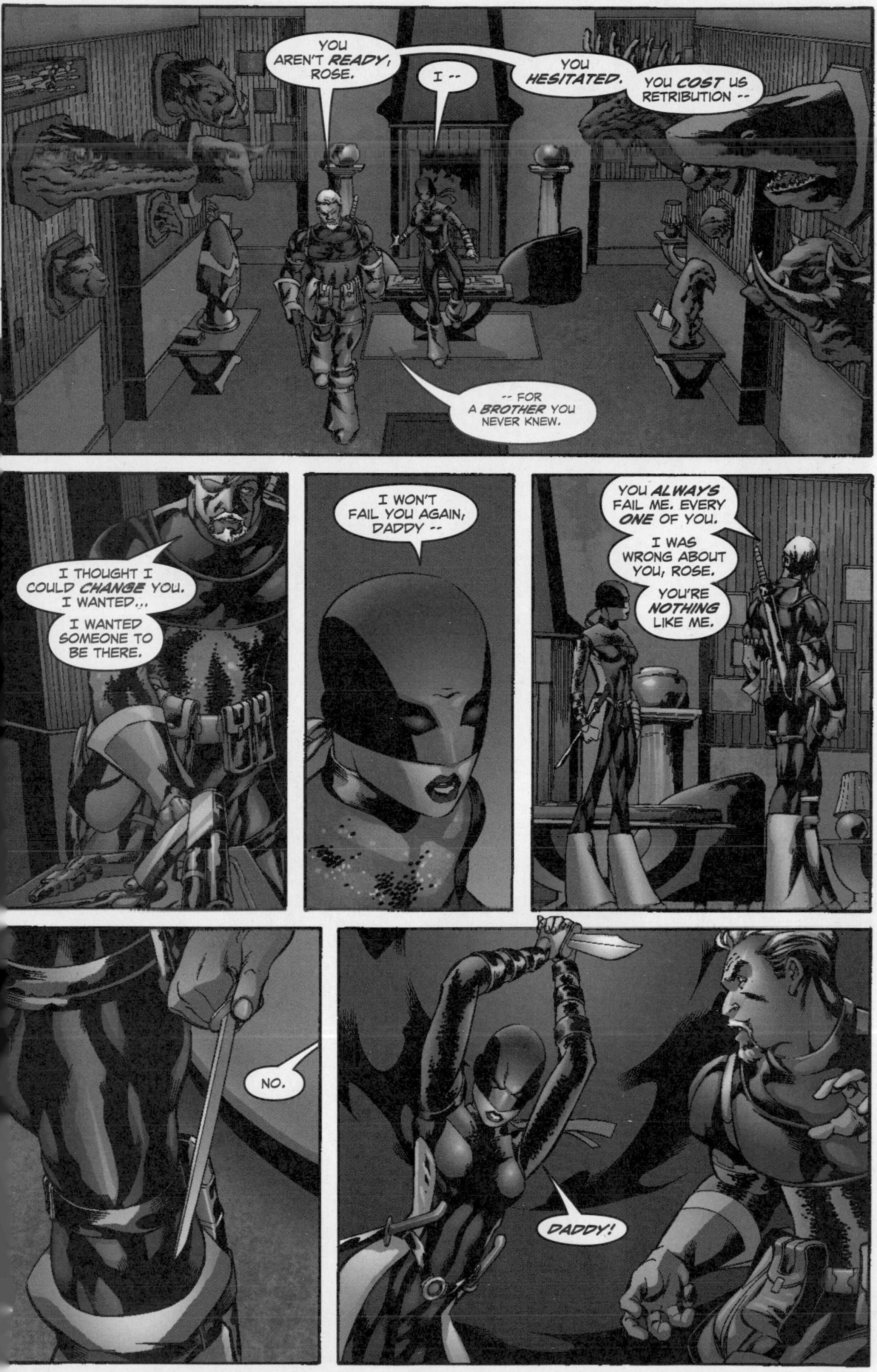
YOU AREN'T *READY*, ROSE.
I --
YOU *HESITATED*.
YOU *COST* US RETRIBUTION --
-- FOR A *BROTHER* YOU NEVER KNEW.
I THOUGHT I COULD *CHANGE* YOU. I WANTED...
I WANTED SOMEONE TO BE THERE.
I WON'T FAIL YOU AGAIN, DADDY --
YOU *ALWAYS* FAIL ME. EVERY *ONE* OF YOU.
I WAS WRONG ABOUT YOU, ROSE.
YOU'RE *NOTHING* LIKE ME.
NO.
DADDY!

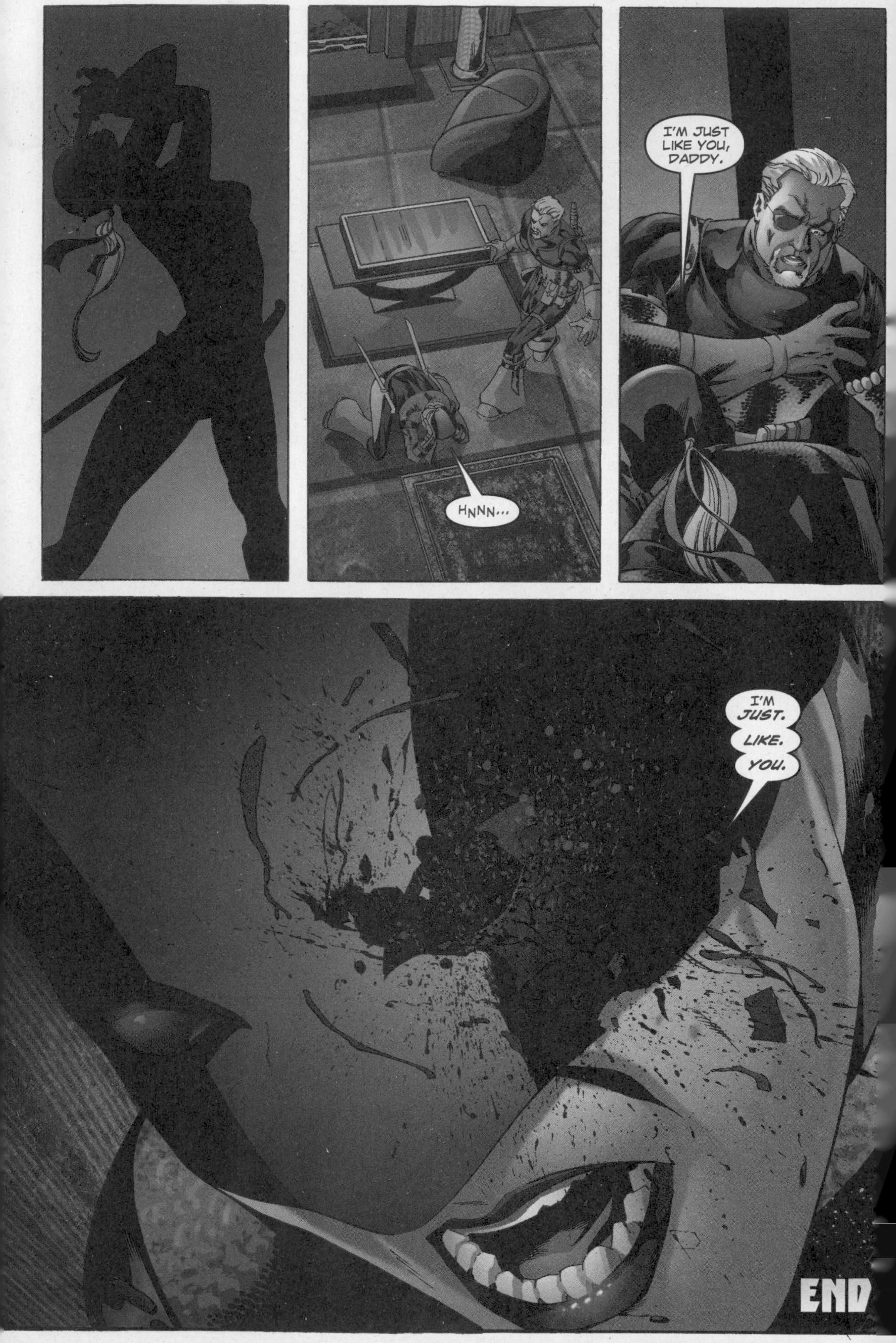
HNNN...
I'M JUST LIKE YOU, DADDY.
I'M JUST. LIKE. YOU.
END

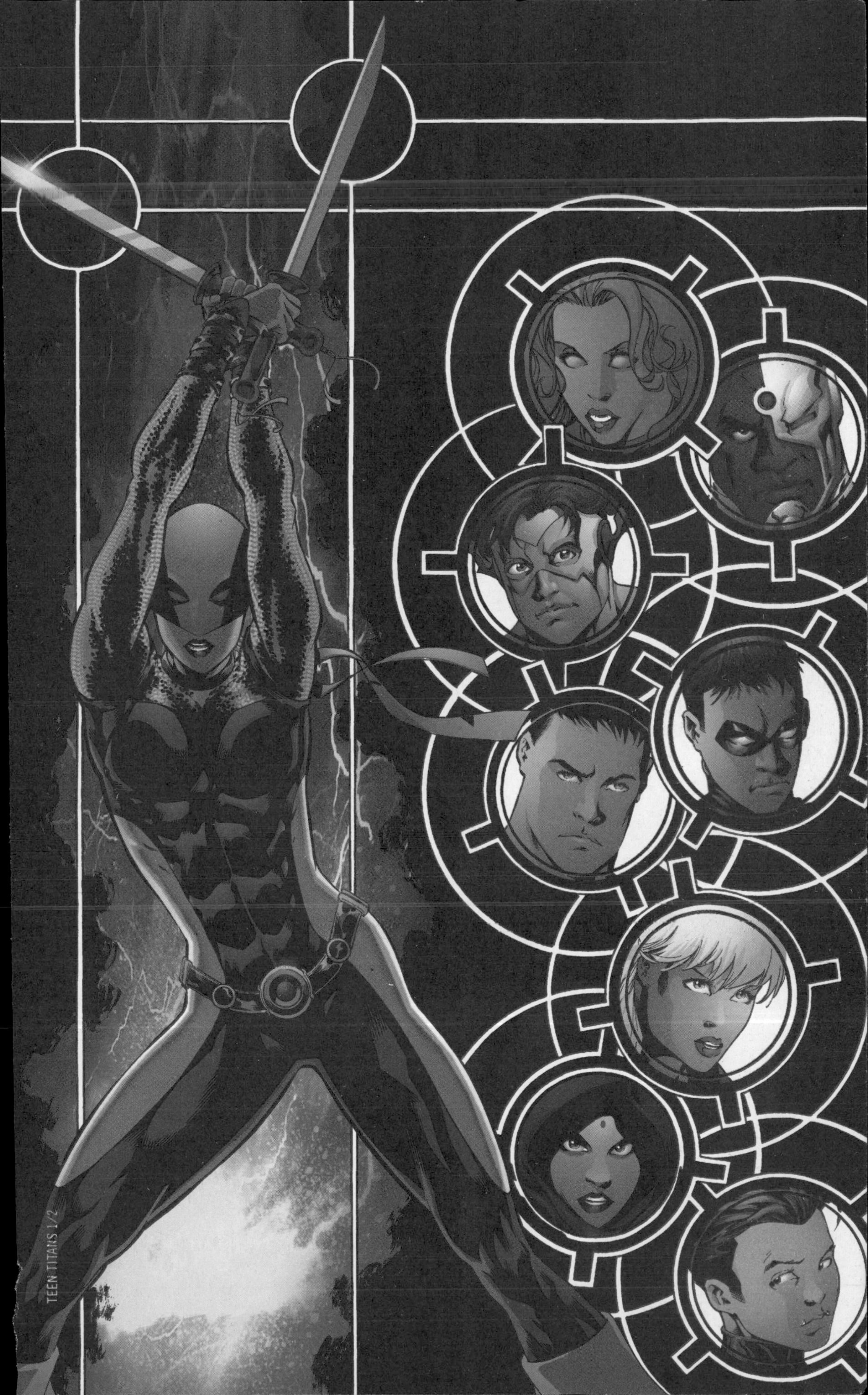
TEEN TITANS 1/2

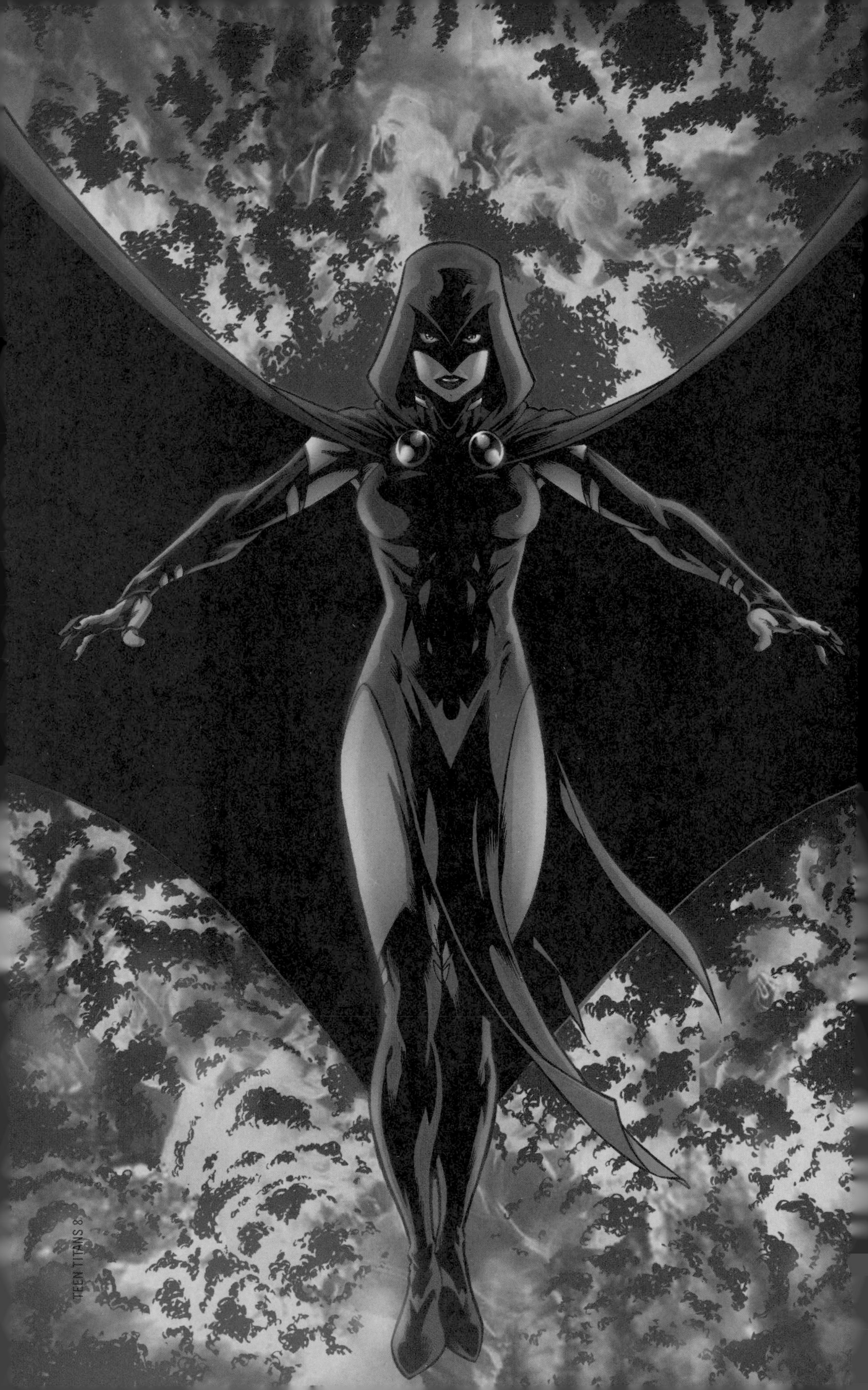
TEEN TITANS 8

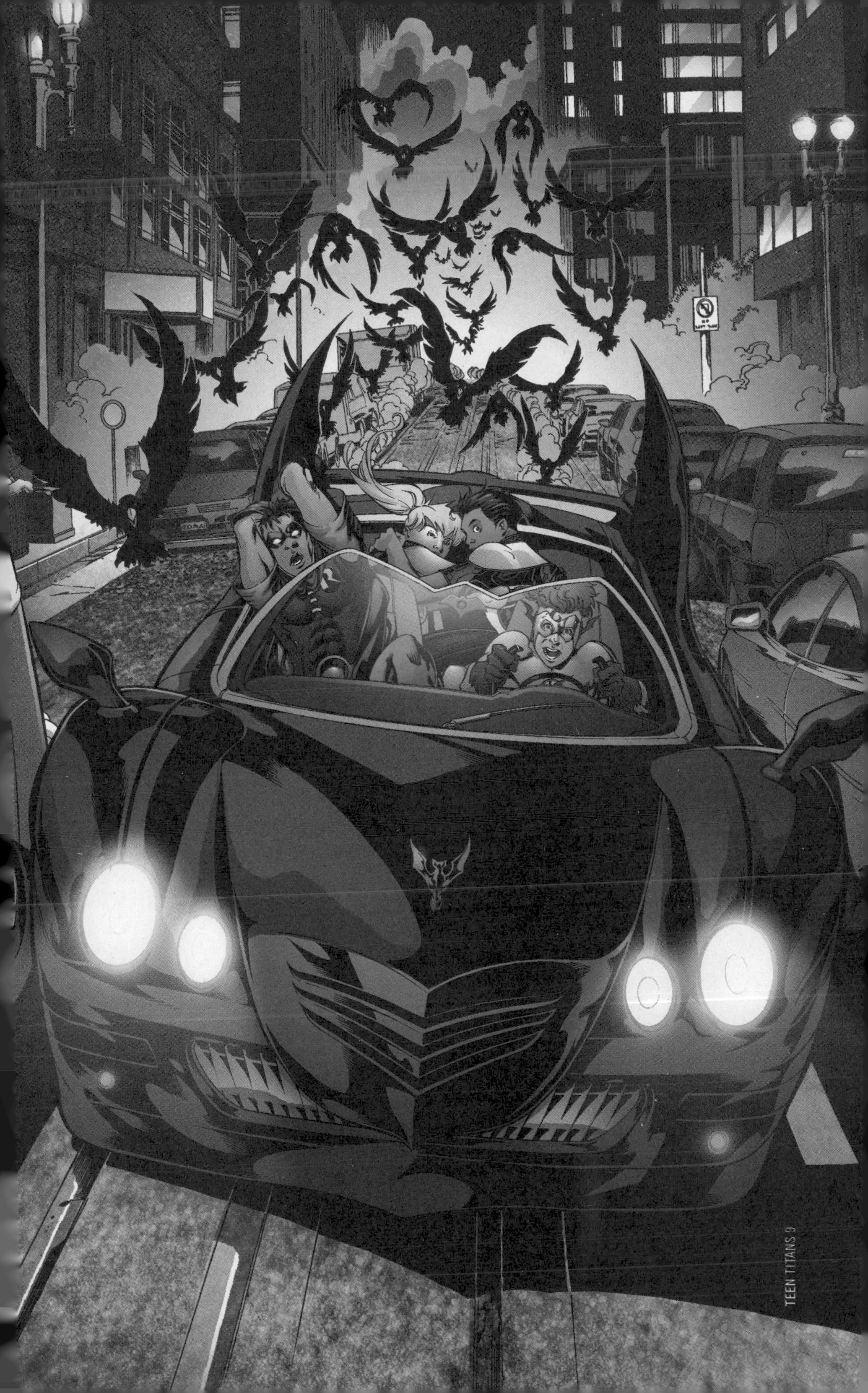
TEEN TITANS 9

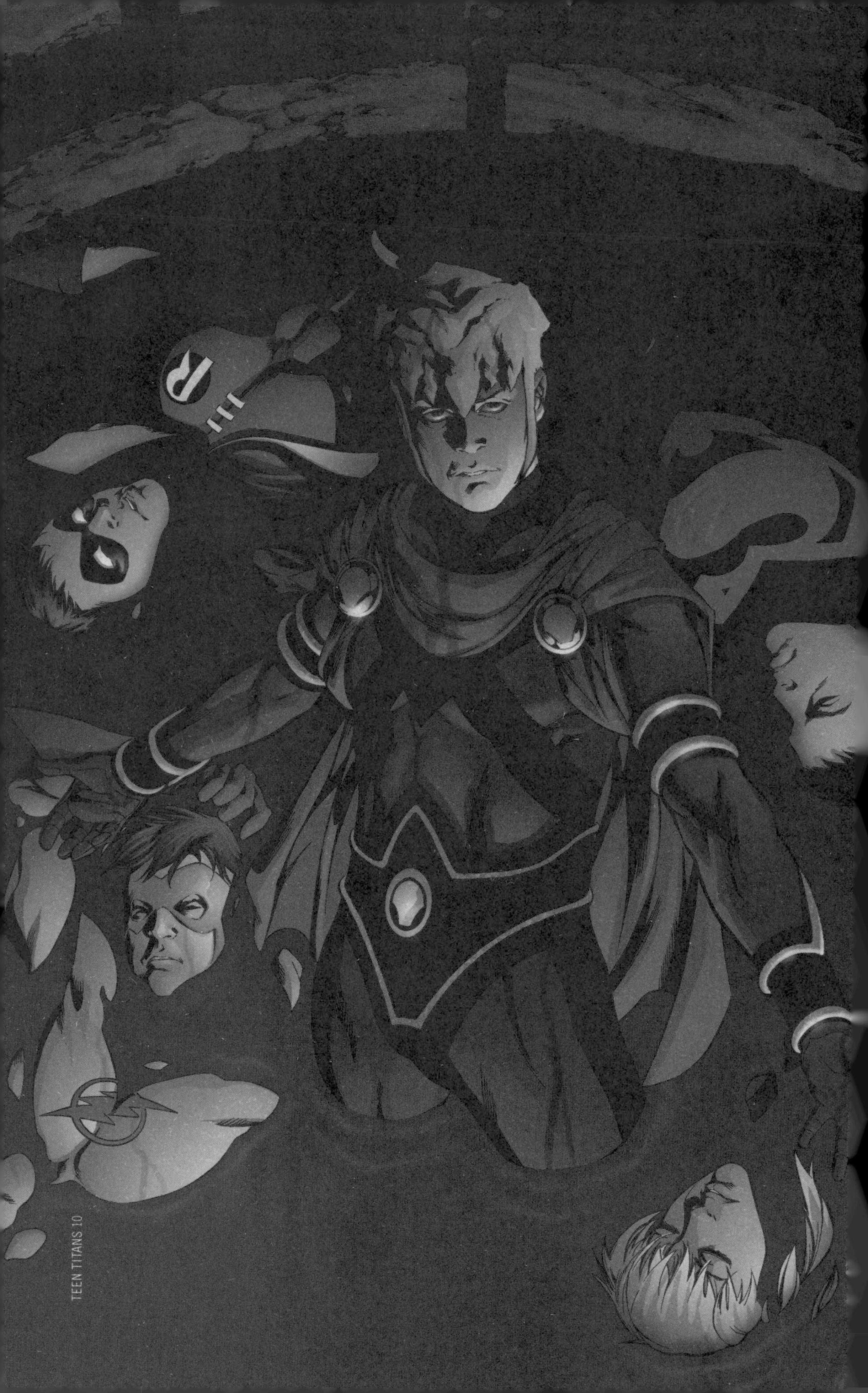
TEEN TITANS 10

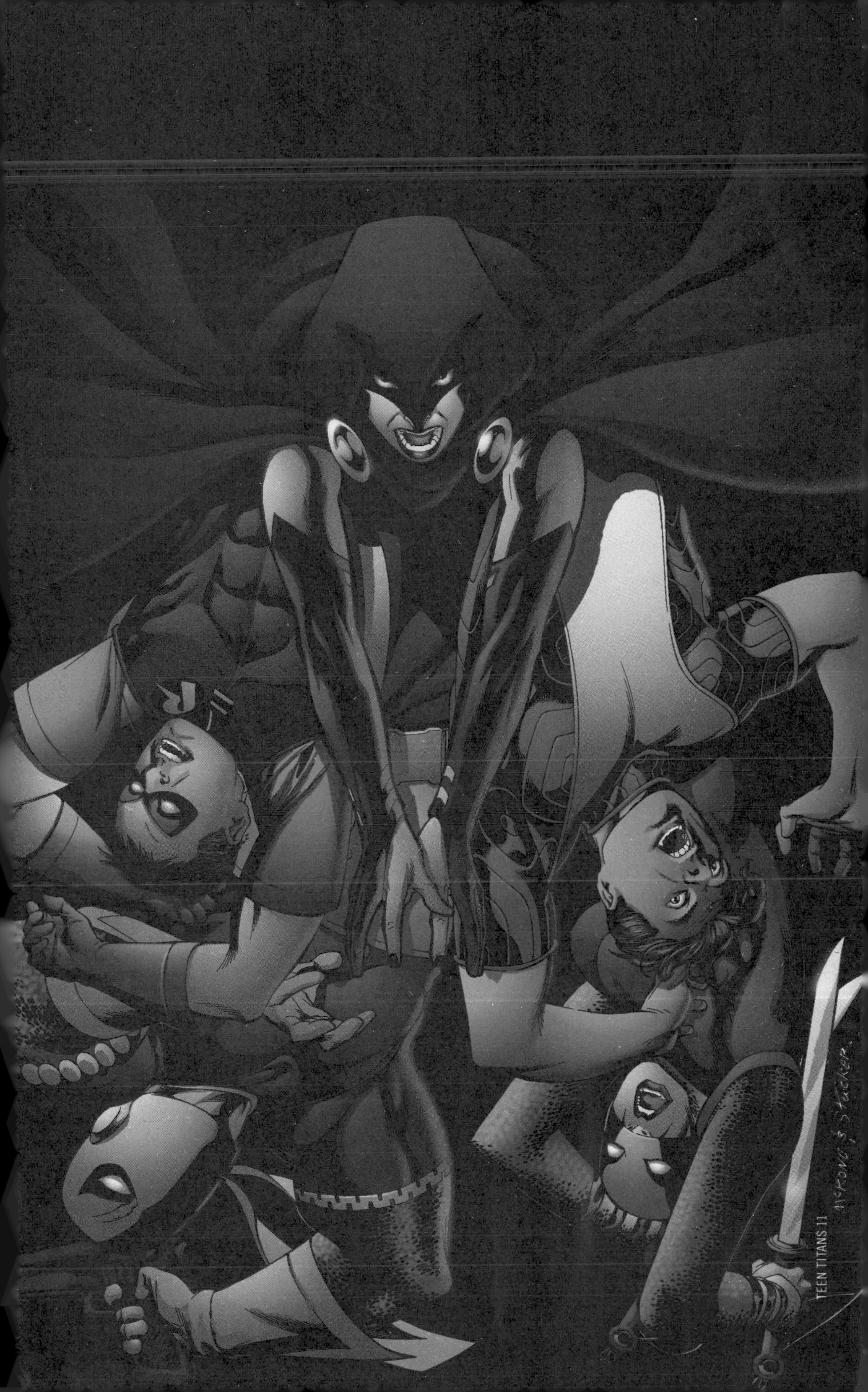
TEEN TITANS 11

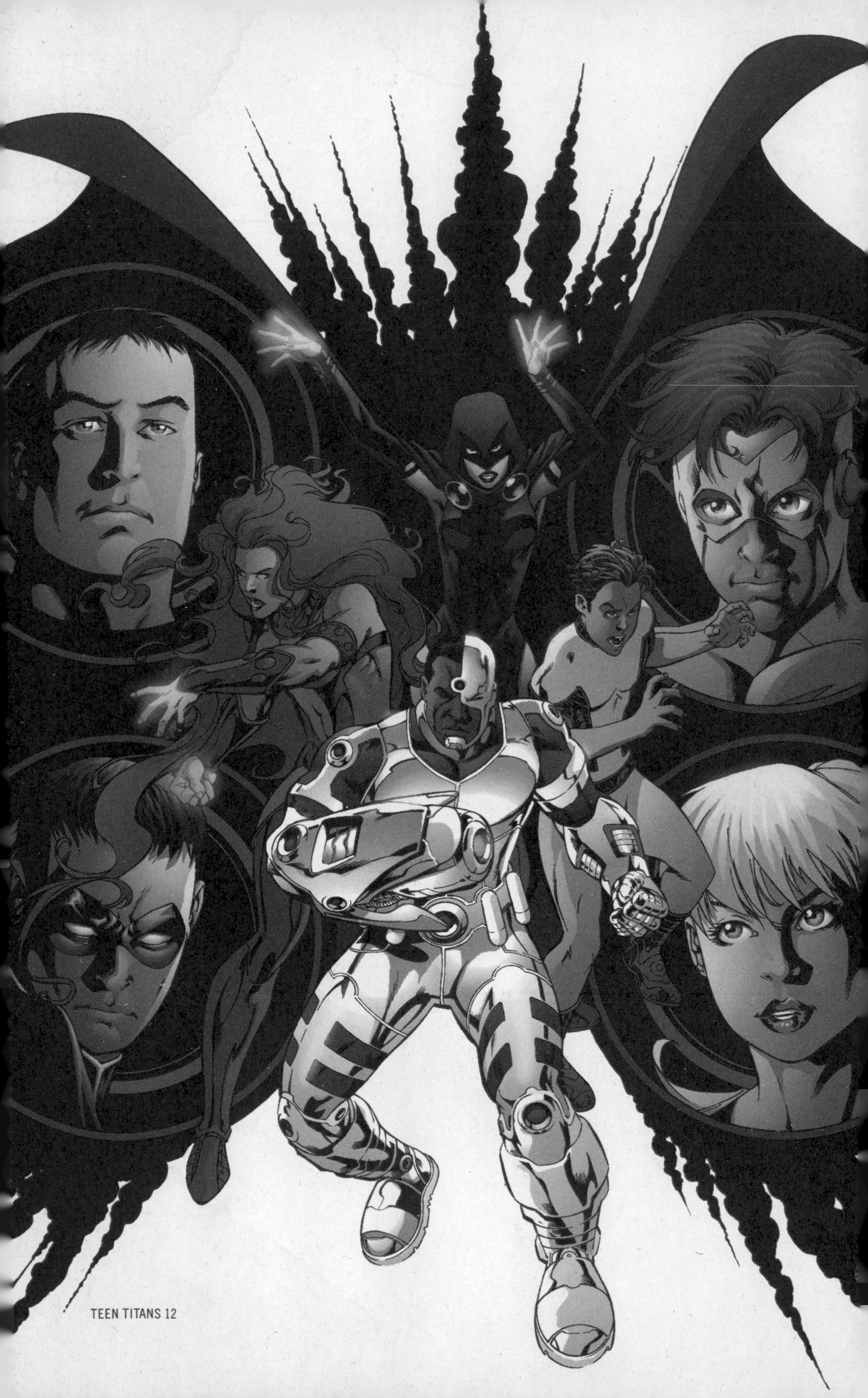

TEEN TITANS 12